Now That I'm Saved.... What in the World are They Talking About!

Kristina Eby Bean

Now That I'm Saved....
What in the World are
They Talking About!

A Complete Nuts-and-Bolts, No-Nonsense Study to Help You Gain Valuable Knowledge and Wisdom in Laying Your Foundation for a Life in Christ

Kristina Eby Bean

United in Christ Ministries, LLC
Nampa, ID

Unless otherwise indicated, all Scripture quotations are taken from HOLY BIBLE, NEW KING JAMES VERSION.

Published by United In Christ Ministries, LLC

Cover photo by Kristina Bean. All rights reserved.
Edited by JoEllen Claypool
Logo designed by Shon Watkins. www.shontoons.com

For more information or to order additional copies of this book, please contact:
Kristina Bean
united.n.christ.outreach@gmail.com

First printing 2019

ISBN – 978-1-7333468-0-1
Library of Congress Number - 2019916464

CONTENTS

Introduction 1

Chapter 1 5

Now That I'm Saved… What in the World are They Talking About! 6

- **Sin, The Fall - What is it and How Did it Happen?** 7
- **It Begins With the Garden** 8
- **Why did God put such care into preparing this garden?** 8
- **The Human in the Garden** 9
- **The Two Trees in the Garden** 10
- **Companions for Adam** 11
- **Sin, The Fall** 12
- **What are the results of sin?** 14
- **Is there anything that I can do to save myself from sin and the results?** 15
- **What did God do about our condition?** 15
- **What is grace?** 15
- **How do I receive the salvation God has provided in Jesus Christ?** 16
- **What happens when I put my faith in Jesus Christ?** 18
- **For what purpose am I saved?** 19

Chapter 2 21

The Body, Soul and Spirit 22

- **Our Body** 22
- **Our Soul** 23
- **Our Spirit** 25
- **Material and spiritual natures of man are clearly distinguished in Scripture:** 26
- **The Intermediate State** 27
- **The Structure of a Person** 28
- **The Salvation of a Person** 29

Chapter 3 31

Father God 32

- **How does God reveal Himself?** 34
- **Who are the members of the Trinity?** 36
- **What is God like?** 37
- **The Natural Attributes** 38
- **The Moral Attributes** 39

Chapter 4 43
Powerful Names of God 44

Chapter 5 51
The Ten Commandments and You 52
Personal Application 52
Chart: The Modern Version of the Ten Commandments and You 53
Respect for God 53
Respect for People 54
The Ten Commandments (NKJV) 55
The Beatitudes 57
What do the Beatitudes mean? 57

Chapter 6 61
My Savior Is Jesus 62
Who is Jesus Christ? 62
Jesus Christ is God 65
Jesus Christ is the Savior 66
Jesus Christ Is the Lamb of God, the Lion and King 67

Chapter 7 71
Jesus Is 72

Chapter 8 75
Who is the Holy Spirit, and why is He my helper? 76
Who is the Holy Spirit? 76
What does the Holy Spirit do? 77
Do not grieve the Holy Spirit. What does that mean? 80

Chapter 9 85
How do I strive for holiness? 86
Can I live a holy life? 86
Why do we need to be sanctified? 88
What did God do about the problem of our sin nature? 88
What must I do in order to experience deliverance from sin? 89
Is sanctification a one-time experience or a long process? 90
What happens if I sin? 90

What is the simplest way to understand sanctification? 91
For a Deeper Study 92

Chapter 10 97
What is baptism in the Holy Spirit? 98
How to Receive the Baptism in the Holy Spirit. 101

Chapter 11 105
The Four Types of Tongues 106
There is a twofold function of the gift of tongues. 106
One: Personal Edification 106
You may be asking, "What am I supposes to do?" 107
Two: Tongues for Intercession 107
Clarification About Private Tongues 108
Here are the following reasons for speaking with tongues. 109
Three: Public Demonstration as a Sign 110
Four: Tongues for Interpretation 111
The Difference Between the Two Public Tongues 111
The function of tongues for public exhortation, the church, is a valuable part of worship. 113

Chapter 12 117
The Three Baptisms 118
Baptism *of* the Holy Spirit 118
Water Baptism 118
Baptism *in* the Holy Spirit 120
What shall we do? 121

Chapter 13 123
Embrace The Gifts of the Trinity 124
The Gifts of the Godhead 125
Gifts of the Father 127
Gifts of the Holy Spirit 128
Gifts of the Son 132
Special Graces 134
What are the Fruits of the Spirit? 136

What is good fruit? 136
What is bad fruit? 137
Let's take a look at "The 9-fold Fruit of the Spirit" 137
Bearing Fruit 138

Chapter 14 141
The Word of God for Me - The Bible 142
A Tribute to the Bible 143
What are the other names of the Bible? 143
How was the Bible given? 143
Nine Ways the Bible was Given — Through: 144
What are the languages of the Bible? 144
How do we know the Bible is the Word of God? 145
How did we come to have the English Bible we use today? 145
What are the parts of the Bible? 146
Bible Chronology 147
What is the message of the Bible? 148
Why should I study the interpretation of the Bible? 148
What are the basic principles of Bible Study? How do I start? 149
How to Start 151
What is a Rhema and Logos word? 152
What does the word 'Selah' mean? 153
What does 'Anointed' mean? 154
Anointing For Healing 154
What does: "There was a real anointing present" mean? 155
Anointed 155
What does it mean to Bind and Loose in Matthew 18:18? 155

Chapter 15 159
I can talk to God — Prayer 160
What is prayer? 160
Different Kinds of Prayer 161
How should I pray? 163
When should I pray? 163
Why should I pray? 164
How can I pray effectively? 164
Helps to Prayer 165

Hindrances to Prayer 165
The Lord's Prayer 165
The Lord's Prayer is a prayer outline. 167

Chapter 16 169
My Family, The Church 170
What is the church? 170
The Church is God's Family and My Family 171
The Church is the Body of Christ 171
The Church is the Bride of Christ 172
What does the church do? 172
Why should I belong to a local church? 174
The local church needs you. 175

Chapter 17 177
I Will Worship 178
Who should worship God? 178
When should we worship God? 178
Where should we worship God? 179
Corporate Worship 179
Why should we worship God? 180
How should we worship God? 181
What is worship? 183

Chapter 18 185
I will praise the Lord! 186
What is the difference between praise and worship? 186
The Pathway of Praise 187
Praise Cures "Dry Times" 187
Power in Unity of Praise 187
Powerful Praise Births Victory 188
Praise Stops the Advancement of Wickedness 188
Praise Spotlights God 189
Praise, the Pathway to God's Presence 189
Sing Praises With Understanding 189
Praise, the Road to Success 189
Praise Releases Blessings and Satisfaction 189

Creative Praise Stays Lively 190
Teach Your Children Praise 190
A Mighty Appeal to Praise 190
The Glorious Garment of Praise 191
Perfected Praise Produces Power 191
Praise Springs Open Prison Doors 191
Encouraging One Another in Praise 191
Praise Releases the Spirit of Prophecy 192
The Sacrifice of Praise 192
Worshipful Walk With God 192

Chapter 19 195
Stewardship 196
What is stewardship? 196
Time is Short – Use it Well 196
Take Time to Be Holy 197
Redeem the Time 197
Tithing: Managing Material Wealth 198
Good Stewards of God's Gifts 199
Our Lifestyle and Body 200
Our Bodies Belong to God 200
The Temple of the Holy Ghost 201
Judgment on Poor Stewardship of the Body 201

Chapter 20 207
The Great Commission "GO" 208
What is a Disciple? 208
Who is supposed to carry out the Great Commission? 209
His Field—A Promise of Harvest 210
The Gospel and "The End" 210
What is the scope of our responsibility? 210
Our responsibility includes three levels: 210

Chapter 21 215
Jesus said, "I will be back for you!" 216
Confirmed: Jesus Will Return 216
The second coming of Christ will be different from the first in several ways: 216

The Threefold Announcement of the Lord's Coming 217
Only the Father Knows When Christ Will Return 218
What will happen when Jesus Christ returns? 218
Who will be in the Bride of Christ? 219
Make yourself ready! 220
The Marriage of the Lamb 223

Chapter 22 227
Sacraments Are for Me 228
Water Baptism 228
Why do we celebrate the Lord's Supper? 228
Biblical Teachings on Holy Communion 229
Examine Yourself 230
How should we receive the Lord's Supper? 230

Chapter 23 235
Jesus Descended into Hell 236
The Bible does say, "He descended." 236
These are things Jesus didn't do in hell, according to the Word of God. 237

Chapter 24 239
Why do Christians worship on Sunday instead of the Sabbath? 240
10 Reasons Why Christians Keep Sunday 240

Chapter 25 243
Put On… the Whole Armor of God For Spiritual Warfare 244
Dressed For Spiritual Warfare 244
Three Illustrations of a Christian 244
Seven Observations About Spiritual Warfare 245
Redemption— The Reason Why We Can Walk in Authority 246
Dressed For Warfare— The Whole Armor of God 247
Four Observations Concerning Our Loins Girt With Truth 251
Five Truths Concerning Righteousness 254
Five Truths for Effective Spiritual Warfare 257
Important Truths About the Words You Speak 260
The Whole Armor of God—The Metaphor 263
How do I put on the whole armor of God? 267

Chapter 26 **269**
Satan—The Devil—Lucifer—Demons **270**
What he is not **271**
What he is **271**
Personal names and titles are given to him. **272**
The Origin of Satan **272**
Was Satan here before Adam? **272**
The Fall of Satan **274**
The Work of Satan **275**
The Purpose of Satan in Producing Giants **277**
Note the following regarding Satan and his activities. **278**
26 Branches of Satan's Work **278**
War on the Saints **279**
Reminder: Six Earmarks of Holy Spirit Manifestation **280**
The Character of Satan **281**
The Doom of Satan **282**

Chapter 27 **285**
Magic— Sorcery—Witchcraft—Divination— Occult **286**
Witchcraft —Sorcery—Mediums **287**
Conjuring Spells **289**
Spiritism **289**
Wicca—Witchcraft **290**
Familiar Spirits **290**
Occult Bondage **291**
Curses **291**
12 Forbidden Heathen Practices **291**
The good news is that you can deliver yourself! **293**
What does it mean to Bind and Loose in Matthew 18:18 **293**

Chapter 28 **295**
Forgiveness **296**
Why should I have to forgive? **296**
To understand forgiveness, what I must do? **297**
What are the results of forgiveness? **298**
There are three areas to be realized: **298**
What is your attitude? **298**

Unforgiveness and Bitterness **299**
What if you can't forgive yourself? **299**
Holy Spirit Conviction or Demonic Condemnation? **300**
Let the Past Be the Past **301**
My Testimony **303**

DEDICATION

This is a legacy of my life. My heritage of Faith I give to my children, grandchildren and great grandchildren in the future.

To my first son, Casey Spencer, daughter-in-law Kim, grandchildren, Cameron and Alexis.

To my second son, Christopher Spencer, daughter-in-law Annie, grandchildren, Conner and Faith.

To my stepson, Jeff Bean, and grandchild, Rylan.

To my older sister, Vicki Eby, and my deceased brother, Stanley Murray Eby.

Stanley Murray Eby

July 7, 1950 — November 30, 1992

And to those who were raised in an alcoholic, abusive, dysfunctional environment. There is hope. Never give up, never!

"Take a lesson from the dead!"

Quote from the movie, *Remember the Titans* [a sport/drama] released in 2000

ACKNOWLEDGMENTS

The main person I would like to thank is my Lord Jesus Christ for looking out for me as a child during those dreadful years and showing me that He knew me while I was in my mother's womb. He knew my name and has shown me that I am not a mistake. I thank Him for His forgiveness, for raising me up. I am thankful that I can be and do .... all things in Christ Jesus Who strengthens me.

House of Praise in Victor, Montana – Pastor Jim Andrusky

August 1996 Camp Tent meeting with Evangelist Larry Rovack from Colorado.

First Things First author, Russell Board

Karl and Brenda Williams

Abundant Life Fellowship Roseville, California

Pastor Doug Bird, Pastor Chris Dunton, Pastor John Devlin, Pastor Roy Davis

Abundant Life School of Ministry (Rhema), Roseville, California

Sacramento Law Enforcement Chaplaincy; Frank and Mendy Russell

Sacramento Regional Criminal Justice Training Center Community Chaplains Academy

Basic Critical Incident Stress Management Course

I thank all the above for the years of speaking into my life and teaching and training me.

Public Safety Academy Meridian, Idaho

My friend, author Becca Howell, for her steadfast encouragement.

My editor, author JoEllen Claypool, for her patience, having excitement for me, and giving me encouragement.

My hubby, Jim Bean, for his wisdom and knowledge, for his encouragement and the many evenings he ate cereal for dinner. He cheered and waved me on with his pom poms. He is my soulmate. We have laughed, cried, prayed, got dirty together and drove each other nuts a time or two. I thank him for the wonderful adventure in the years of ministry and love. He is such a wonderful blessing in my life.

I thank my best girlfriend from the 6th grade on, Debbie Pine Whitehurst, who "knows all my dirt" and still loves me. She has spoken into my life millions of times and was always ready to go into battle for me and with me. I thank her mother, Sharon, who fed me when I was starving. I spent the night many times, and she cooked pancakes until I was stuffed. She drove miles out of her way to take me to softball practice and to our games. She never said a word to me about my situation until I was in my 50s. However … she knew.

NOTE: In order to have a better understanding, it is important to read all the scriptures listed in each chapter, which are in the parentheses.

Bible devotionals are a very important part of your everyday life. You can either purchase a daily devotional at a Christian book store or you can download Bible reading plans of your choice for free at www.biblereadingproject.com. Print it out and keep it in your Bible.

To purchase, go to www.liferesources.cc and look under "Life Journal".

This is a list of the abbreviations used for the books of the Bible:

Genesis – Gen.
Exodus – Exod.
Leviticus – Lev.
Numbers – Num.
Deuteronomy – Deut.
Joshua – Jos.
Judges – Judg.
Ruth – Ruth
1 Samuel – 1 Sam.
2 Samuel – 2 Sam.
1 Kings – 1 Kings.
2 Kings – 2 Kings.
1 Chronicles – 1 Chron.
2 Chronicles – 2 Chron.
Ezra – Ezra
Nehemiah – Neh.
Esther – Esth.
Job – Job
Psalms – Psa.

Proverbs – Prov.
Ecclesiastes – Eccl.
Song of Songs – Song
Isaiah – Isa.
Jeremiah – Jer.
Lamentations – Lam.
Ezekiel – Ezek.
Daniel – Dan.
Hosea – Hos.
Joel – Joel
Amos – Amos
Obadiah – Obad.
Jonah – Jonah
Micah – Mic.
Nahum – Nah.
Habbakuk – Hab.
Zephaniah – Zeph.
Haggai – Hag.
Zechariah –Zech.

Malachi – Mal.
Matthew – Matt.
Mark – Mk.
Luke – Lk.
John – Jn.
Acts – Acts
Romans – Rom.
1 Corinthians – 1 Cor.
2 Corinthians – 2 Cor.
Galatians – Gal..
Ephesians – Eph.
Philippians – Phil.
Colossians – Col.
1 Thesssalonians – 1 Thess.
2 Thessalonians – 2 Thess.
1 Timothy – 1 Tim.
2 Timothy – 2 Tim.
Titus – Titus
Philemon – Philem.

Hebrews – Heb.
James – James
1 Peter – 1 Pet.
2 Peter – 2 Pet.
1 John – 1 Jn.
2 John – 2 Jn.
3 John – 3 Jn.
Jude – Jude
Revelation – Rev.

INTRODUCTION

Through the years, the one thing that I do know is how important it is to have a strong, solid foundation with anything that we build upon. Usually, you will have building inspectors to check out your foundation before you can build upon it to make sure the structure will not collapse. There are necessary steps for building any structure and inspectors to inspect and pass it so that you can proceed to the next step.

The reason I wrote *Now That I'm Saved ... What in the World Are They Talking About!* is because of the questions that I have asked over the years and ended up doing my own research for the answers. The things that I have found, I wrote down for you in order to help with your walk with the Lord. There is always hope. Never give up. You can start a new life today. Never give up!

If you call yourself a child of God, but you don't experience peace and rest and your life is surrounded by a lot of strife and confusion, there's something wrong. You need to be made aware of who you are in Christ, the authority He has given you, and the arsenal of weapons He has equipped you with to fight and win back your life, your peace. You can have a good life. We need to start with a good solid foundation.

When it comes to being a Christian, it is very important to build your foundation on solid ground and have a strong structure with a balanced knowledge. The lessons in this book will cover basic truths and much more that every Christian needs to know in order to have a balanced and solid foundation that will bring Christian growth and discipleship. What took me years to figure out – "What in the world are they talking about!" – I am sharing with you. The Bible says, *"My people are destroyed for lack of knowledge,"(New King James Version, Hos. 4:6).*

This book is a jumpstart to "NO MORE LACK OF KNOWLEDGE" along with your Bible. This will lead you to bigger and deeper things of God. Sometimes, we just don't know where to start. It will help you begin growing and building yourself up and will start the healing process with this Bible-based truth so you can avoid any confusion along the way; this is also true spiritually. You naturally want to know your Heavenly Father, Jesus Christ, and who the Holy Spirit is. This is what this book is about. You will study and learn who you are in Christ and how to have the power to resist the devil. No matter what commentary you read, always make sure it lines up with the Word of God. Make your Bible the book you read daily. Make "no way" and don't "leave any door open" for the enemy to sneak in and steal your joy, steal your health, or your identity in Christ.

Anyone who believes in their heart that God raised Jesus from the dead and confesses with their mouth that Jesus is Lord shall be saved (see Romans 10:9). Saved from what? Saved from sin, the devil, death, sickness, fear, rejection and strongholds—anything that has to do with mankind's bondage to the devil and his lying kingdom.

Many adults who are struggling today were children only yesterday. Many who battle addictions and bondages first encountered the snares of the enemy as children. Many began their addictions in their teenage years, never knowing where their addictions would eventually lead. When children are left alone to tend to themselves day in and day out, not having the love or guidance from a parent, it messes with their minds, their identities. They develop wrongful thinking about themselves and others, making it very hard to trust anyone. They are in survivor mode. They start to look for love in all the wrong places; they want to belong somewhere. The choices they make aren't good ones and before they know it, they are in trouble.

The lying devil attempts to choose his victims while they are very young. Cruel words, sexual abuse, anger, and the other physical and emotional weapons create a hole in the emotions of a person. As the neglect, abuse, and sexual sins continue and the previous holes become bigger and bigger, eventually a person feels so unclean inside, so unworthy, and rejected. Rejection alone messes with your identity, making a person believe so wrongfully about themselves. Sometimes, but not all the time, alcohol or drugs are used to dull the pain.

The holes in our souls must be sealed off before wholeness can begin. Prayer and seeking God is what it takes to seal up those leaky emotions. The good news is that repenting of our sins, getting real with ourselves, coughing up those ugly hairballs of sin, and placing our faith in Christ will bring not only deliverance from our bondages but also wholeness in our inner souls, having a sound mind! When we repent, our slate is clean, our past is a thing of the past. God will not bring it up again. And our past doesn't determine our future. We are a new creature in Christ Jesus.

I live by faith in God now instead of my physical senses, and so can you. In the spiritual realm, we are now the conquerors because of what Jesus has done for us, provided we truly believe God's version of what happened at the cross. I have total confidence in God and His Word more than that defeated, lying snake of a devil who tries to drag me back into my past with a physical type of warfare in which I depended on my physical strength, senses, or feelings to live my life. When God says it doesn't pay to sin, I believe Him instead of the devil who tells us it won't hurt us or that we can get away with it if we want. Just because it may look good or delicious doesn't mean that it is good for you.

When we are saved, part of salvation is being healed. But a lot of Christians miss that part. God says our bodies were healed when Jesus took the stripes on His back. We believe Him instead of the lying devil who says we will never recover. In Matthew 11:28-30 Jesus said, "*Come to Me, all you who labor and are heavy laden, and I will give you rest. Take My yoke upon you and learn from Me, for I am gentle and lowly in heart, and you will find rest for your souls. For My yoke is easy and My burden is light," (NKJV, Matt. 11:28-30).*

Rest is peace (*shalom*) and prosperity. Peace is an all-inclusive word that encompasses prosperity, safety, health, protection, fruitfulness, and abundance. Peace and rest are not only for Heaven but also for the here and now on the earth. It is not something coming one day. It's here, and it's yours! Jesus is the Prince of Peace, and He dwells in your heart through the person of the Holy Spirit. His peace is supernatural. It's already done. All you have to do is walk in faith, and it's yours. Your days should not be full of trouble. That doesn't mean trouble will not come, but you can stand up and tell trouble to go, to leave. You do not have to live a life of worry and anxiety. Peace is yours. Prosperity is yours. Even when trouble comes, it should not take away your peace. Peace is what you have as a saint of God, as a child of God. You are a citizen of the heavenly kingdom of God. Believe it!

The Gospel is that Jesus Christ came and died so that you could experience the shalom of God. He was beaten and crucified so we could have peace. All who believe and come under the rule of the Messiah can have peace. You will have the blessings of God. It's the guarantee of His covenant of peace. It belongs to the saints of God. So, no matter how bad the news gets, don't let the devil take your peace and your shalom away from you. You will learn what authority you have over demons and the devil and evil forces.

When God says that He will protect you, believe Him instead of the lying devil who tells us God sometimes will let bad things happen to teach us a lesson. The devil is the one telling you that. I know that Father God is not going to do some evil campaign to teach His children a lesson. Everything good is from God our Father, so we hang on to the truth of God's Word by faith.

I believe that Our Father God provides for our every need. I believe that His Holy Spirit is bringing our family and friends to salvation. I believe that there is absolutely nothing to fear because 365 times in the Bible, in one form or another, we are told, "Fear not." Did you know that fear is what the enemy uses to keep us from seeking deliverance and being set free to find rest in Christ. The day you can be set free from all your spiritual enemies and then be equipped to stay free is a wonderful day! Fight the good fight of faith! (1 Timothy 6:12).

I know in my heart that this study will send you on your way. Everything that you will study and learn in this book is based out of the Bible, backed up with Scripture, and the first book I read about being a new Christian, *First Things First* by Russell Board, who blessed me with the Truth which started me and my husband on our new journey.

Since the beginning, I personally have used the New King James Version (NKJV), The Dake Annotated Reference Bible NKJV, and the Amplified Bible Classic Edition (AMPC). We have taught this lesson to many believers who have wanted to rededicate their lives and to new believers who now have a solid, strong foundation in Jesus Christ, and some have gone on to do bigger things for our Lord. The Lord has placed on my heart to share this study with you. I am not one to sugarcoat anything. This is the truth backed up with Scripture so you will become an overcomer. Your strength comes from reading the Bible, hearing the Word, and listening to the Holy Spirit. Know what your authority in Jesus Christ is. Be strong and courageous! You can do all things through Christ who strengthens you! He who lives in you is greater (mightier), than he [that lying devil] who is in this world.

I encourage you to highlight, write in, circle passages, make notes, whatever it takes to be free from evil and to take authority over your life. My Bibles and every single book I own that made a difference in my life, I have written in and circled words and quotes. Some books I have had coiled at a local print shop because they were falling apart. My daily Bible I have had restored. Extra note pages and four ribbons were added. I have so many notes written in it that I can't be without it.

My prayer for you is:

Father God, I thank you that my friend here holding this book will be greatly blessed. I ask that the Holy Spirit would radically expand their understanding of who You are and to have a divine relationship with You daily. Help them to see Your personality and role as "My Helper" like never before. Show them the truth in Your Word which will bring freedom. Show them that You have given them authority and power over the enemy. Father, let Your perfect love and powerful promise cast out fears. Help them to be spiritually in tune to hear the Lord's still, small voice that speaks to them continually with words of life, peace and love. Train them to see Your point of view in all things.

In Jesus' name, Amen

Chapter 1

Now That I'm SAVED.... What in the World are They Talking About!

Saving us is the greatest and most
concrete demonstration of
God's love,
the definitive display of His grace
throughout time and eternity.

Since no man is excluded
from calling upon God,
the gate of salvation
is open to all. There is nothing
else to hinder us from entering,
but our own unbelief.

Chapter 1

Now That I am Saved … What in the World are They Talking About!

Why do I need to be saved? For me personally, growing up in an alcoholic family, there was no moral code, and I couldn't stand the lifestyle, the shame, and the darkness. One day, while walking home from school, I had to walk through my small town in Northern California. I had noticed a sign for the first time walking by a bar that said "Spirits". I thought, *Why would anyone want to drink spirits?* I knew that alcohol played with your mind and created a terrible, out-of-control, mean monster. It was destroying me; the shame and embarrassment was overwhelming. I was extremely sad and felt unloved, unwanted, and rejected. There definitely was no responsibility, no training or love, and I desperately wanted something different, not only for myself but for my parents; I wanted them to stop drinking. I remember saying as a young person that I didn't want to be like these people. The hardest part was that I was being judged by the sins of my parents, not only at school but in my neighborhood as well. I was becoming a loner.

When we read the Bible, it is clear to us that the entire human race is guilty of sin, and there are no exceptions. Sin has infected the entire human race in different stages of moral character. It doesn't matter which ethnic group you are from or what the color of your skin is, we are all guilty. In the Bible, it says our salvation is provided only through Jesus Christ, no other. Some may think it is a sign of weakness, but that isn't true whatsoever. For me, the Bible is an instruction manual written from the Father who knows all about His child, even numbering the hairs on your head (Matt. 10:30). He protects His child and rescues him when he gets into trouble (Isa. 41:10; Psa.46:1). He teaches you the way that you should go (Hos. 11:1-3, Psa. 32:7-8) and supplies all of your needs (Matt. 6:33). It will truly be a strength that will build you up, as a Father should, and it will surpass your understanding only to make you stronger, wiser, and thankful in all areas of your life as it has mine. As we all know, sin has continued to advance to different degrees in different people. There are obvious differences in moral character from person to person. Sin is present in everyone, and it is deadly. We are all sinners.

The Amplified Bible says:

> *"10 As it is written, None is righteous, just and truthful and upright and conscientious, no, not one.*
> *11 No one understands [no one intelligently discerns or comprehends]; no one seeks out God.*
> *12 All have turned aside; together they have gone wrong and have become unprofitable and worthless; no one does right, not even one!*
> *13 Their throat is a yawning grave; they use their tongues to deceive (to mislead and to deal treacherously). The venom of asps is beneath their lips.*
> *14 Their mouth is full of cursing and bitterness.*
> *15 Their feet are swift to shed blood.*
> *16 Destruction [as it dashes them to pieces] and misery mark their ways.*
> *17 And they have no experience of the way of peace [they know nothing about peace, for a peaceful way they do not even recognize].*
> *18 There is no [reverential] fear of God before their eyes.*
> *23 Since all have sinned and are falling short of the honor and glory which God bestows and receives," (Amplified Class Edition, Rom. 3:10-18, 23).*

Doesn't that sound like what is going on today in this world? God, in His infinite love, gives us an opportunity for choice. You have to make that choice.

The underlying reason for the increasing corruption of societies is that they have no fear of God, that is, they think they will not have to answer to God for their immorality.

Sin, The Fall - What is it and how did it happen?

The story of the heavens and the earth, then, is the story that leads from creation to rebellion (sin), then on to grace and blessings to salvation and redemption that will end in new heavens and a new earth when Christ makes all things new (Rev. 21:1-2). This is a story that begins with God as Creator (Gen. 1) and ends with God as re-Creator (Rev. 21). This story begins in a garden (the Garden of Eden) and ends in a city (the New Jerusalem).

In the beginning, God creates the formation of the solar system, the preparation of the land for habitation, and the creation of life on the earth. All of the eight acts of creation are accomplished in six days. Everything that God made was good (Gen. 1). All things were designed by God to operate according to the laws He established.

It Begins With the Garden

It all happened in the garden. It wasn't an ordinary garden. God made this place especially for his new creatures—humans. This garden was a place filled with goodness, where the land produced with abundance and the creatures God made could be fruitful. It was a place God Himself could go to enjoy the cool of the afternoon in the company of his creatures. The air was clean and the water that flowed was clear.

> *"The LORD God planted a garden eastward in Eden," (New King James Version, Gen. 2:8).*

Let's look at the words used here. God plants the garden in Eden. The descriptions of the planting and the garden are very different from how Genesis 1 describes the process of creation. Here, God's involvement is more personal: He is a gardener. Although He never stops being the great King of Genesis 1, who organizes His created Kingdom, the metaphor here is easier for us to understand. Gardeners care for and nurture their plants; they are deeply involved with their gardens. Gardening requires time, attention, work, and love.

Why did God put such care into preparing this garden?

- The garden is the model of what God's original intentions were for creation. It is the standard that allows us to see how things should be and how the world should function.

- The garden is a place where God's creatures, the man and the woman, would be able to flourish. It provided the place and space for humans to develop their talents and their full potential to be the creatures that God wanted them to be: loving, relational creatures who would contemplate God and His creation and be filled with praise and gratitude. They could be God's friends, caretakers of this special creation, and fulfill the potential of creation.

- Most importantly, the garden is a temple for the Lord. What makes the temple, or the tabernacle, or the garden important is God's presence. A temple is a meeting place where humans encounter God's presence. God walked in the garden! This is a beautiful image that expresses God's direct presence in His temple. God is not an absent gardener.

The Human in the Garden

The Scriptures use the metaphor of the gardener for God when talking about the garden. But the metaphor changes when the Scriptures talk about humanity: God becomes a potter—He forms man from the dust of the ground. Once again, God's care and hands-on involvement show the importance that the creature would have to Him.

Unlike the material of the potter, however, God did not use clay to make Adam. God used dust.

> "And the LORD God formed man of the dust of the ground, and breathed into his nostrils the breath of life; and man became a living being."
> Genesis 2:7 (NKJV)

Dust? Pottery is made with clay. Why did God use dust? The term 'dust' is probably not a reference to the raw materials that God used when forming Adam. Rather, dust is an important term used in ancient Hebrew writing. Remember, this story was originally written in ancient Hebrew. Ancient Hebrew did not have periods or other punctuation marks to help readers understand the text. In Genesis 2:7, we find that God formed the man (*'adam*) out of the ground (*'adamah*). Those words are not necessarily connected, (I thought they might have been), but the similarity of sounds connects them. In this case, Adam is connected to the ground. In Genesis 1, humans are connected to God. They are made in God's image and likeness, but they are not gods. Genesis 2 makes it clear that humans are creatures of the earth, the ground.

In Genesis 2:7, there is a repetition of sound that is not apparent in English but is easy to identify in ancient Hebrew: *"from the dust of the ground and breathed into his nostrils the breath of life."* The word for nostril (*'aphim*) is similar to the word for dust (*'aphar*). The connection is that just as dust rises to life from the ground to become "living dust", so it will go back down to the ground when life is extinguished (Gen. 3:19).

God breathes into this creature, and the man becomes a "living being" or a "living creature" (*nephesh haya*). Notice that animals are also each described as a "living creature" (*nephesh haya*, Gen. 2:19). What distinguishes humans from animals is being created in the image and the likeness of God.

"Let Us make man in Our image, according to Our likeness," (NKJV, Gen. 1:26)

"Then the LORD God took the man and put him in the garden of Eden to tend and keep it," (NKJV, Gen. 2:15).

The word for 'work' in Hebrew used here, *'eved'*, is the same word used for both 'worship' and the 'work' of the priests in the tabernacle and the temple. If the garden was a natural temple for the Lord, then Adam's original world was that of a priest. The priests' main role in Israel was to preserve the order of the temple and the worship. God gave humanity an extraordinary task: to preserve the order and harmony of creation, as described in Genesis 1. We see this task in action when Adam names the animals and takes care of the garden. In other words, God made humans His representatives on Earth. Among other important things, being created in God's image means that we represent God in His creation. We have been given the task of keeping the order and harmony of His creation.

The LORD God made
all kinds of trees grow
out of the ground—trees
that were pleasing
to the eye and good for food.
In the middle of the garden
were the tree of life
and
the tree of the knowledge
of good and evil.
Genesis 2:9 (NIV)

The Two Trees in the Garden

As with the man whom God made from the ground, God made *"all kinds of trees grow out of the ground," (New International Version, Gen. 2:9).* Genesis calls our attention to two of these trees: the tree of life and the tree of the knowledge of good and evil. God allows the man to eat from every tree in the garden (including the tree of life) except for the tree of the knowledge of good and evil.

The Scriptures do not yet explain the purpose of the tree of life. However, we learn later in Genesis 3:22 that eating from this tree prolongs life; the verse affirms that the fruit of the tree would give perpetual life, a life so long as to seem endless.

In other places in the Bible, the tree of life is associated with wisdom (Prov. 3:18; 11:30; 13:12; 15:4). From the book of Proverbs, we know that one of the functions of wisdom is that it allows for a long and abundant life: *"Long life is in her [wisdom's] right hand; in her left hand are riches and honor," (NIV, Prov. 3:16).* Regarding the other tree in the garden, we read of this one prohibition to the man: *"You must not eat from the tree of the knowledge of good and evil," (NIV, Gen. 2:17).* What is so wrong with knowledge of good and evil? Why does God forbid the man to eat the fruit of this tree?

The expression "good and evil" is a well-known literary device called merism. For example, the expression "morning and night" does not refer only to the morning and the night; it also refers to all the time in between. In other words, the whole day. Also, the expression "heavens and earth" refers to both the heavens and earth and everything in between the heavens and the earth—the entire creation. The expression "good and evil" refers to more than just absolute goodness and absolute evil—the two extremes—it also means everything in between.

In our culture, knowledge is often seen as a mental activity, like scientific or rational knowledge. In the culture of the Old Testament, knowledge meant experiential learning—what we come to understand or appreciate based on our experiences. The term "knowledge of good and evil" seems to refer to the ability to discern between good and evil that allows one to make proper decisions—in other words, **wisdom**.

But the sort of wisdom available from this prohibited tree is a characteristic of God, a kind of knowledge that only He can possess (Job 15:7-9; Job 40; Prov. 30:1-4). For humans to take the fruit from this tree would be essentially a shortcut—an attempt to gain God-like wisdom without learning or experience and without God.

Companions for Adam

God did not intend the man to be alone. God created humans to be in relationships. For that reason, God formed creatures to be company to the man. God brought these animals to Adam, and Adam named them. But they were not "suitable help" for man.

So, God makes another special creation (Gen. 2:21-22). Just as Adam was taken from the ground, the woman was taken from the man. The man is taken from dust, but the woman is taken from a rib of the man. God took the woman from the side ribs, instead of the head or the feet, showing that this companion stands side by side with the man, rather than above or below him. God considers her to be the right companion for the man. It is not that God was experimenting with creation, trial and error. Rather, God created male and female, and together made them in His image and likeness.

Jesus' Family Tree: Seeing God's Faithfulness in the Genealogy of Christ (Rose Publishing)

Sin, the Fall

The third chapter of Genesis tells the story of how the first man and woman broke the law of God with disastrous results. The disobedience and sin of Adam and Eve caused them to lose the state of innocence and the realm of dominion in and for which they had been created. This event plunged them and all of mankind into a state of sin and corruption and allowed the loss of their intended rule and purpose. Adam and Eve were created by God in a state of sinless perfection so they could glorify God, reflecting His righteousness on the earth, and enjoying fellowship and union with Him. Their calling was to exercise dominion, or control, over God's creation through their own labors and those of their offspring in faithful response to the Word of God. As a specific test of this loyalty, God commanded them not to eat of *"the tree of the knowledge of good and evil," (NIV, Gen. 2:17).* Adam and Eve were to demonstrate their willingness to live *"by every word that proceeds from the mouth of the LORD," (New King James Version, Deut. 8:3; [of God] Matt. 4:4).* God warned them clearly that their disobedience would result in death.

Just because it

looks

pleasant to the

eye—

nice to touch,

beautiful and

delicious—

doesn't mean that

it's

GOOD

for you!

The fall from their original state of innocence and intended purpose occurred when Satan approached Eve through the serpent who tempted her to eat of the forbidden fruit. Satan called into question the truthfulness of what God had spoken about the tree and its significance. He urged Eve to discover, through trial and error, whether it was in her best interest to do what God had forbidden. Eve's sin did not consist of being tempted, but in "believing and acting on Satan's lie." Her rejection of God's command occurred when she was deceived and ate of the forbidden fruit. The New Testament holds the man, Adam, at least equally if not more responsible in that his action was "consciously disobedient", taking and eating the fruit as an assertive decision not as the result of deception (1 Tim. 2:14; Rom. 5:17-18). The term 'Fall' should not be interpreted to suggest that their sin was accidental. The temptation was <u>purposeful</u>, and their submission to it involved <u>their willing consent</u>.

The immediate consequence of the Fall was death, the death of their union with God, the death of their dominion under His rule, and the setting in motion of the death process in their physical bodies. For the first time, Adam and Eve experienced fear in the presence of the Lord God, and they hid when He approached (Gen. 3:8-10). Because of their unbelief and rebellion, they were removed from the garden that God had provided as their home.

From that time on, man would experience pain and encounter resistance as he worked at the task of earning his daily bread. Physical death with the decay of the body is not a natural process. It entered the human experience as God's curse upon sin.

Furthermore, God's Word reveals that Adam did not sin simply as a private person, but as the representative of all members of the human race (Rom. 5:12-21). His sin set loose the death syndrome as a genetic reality, transmitting to all the successive generations, and through the Fall, all persons receive a fallen, corrupt nature. It is their nature that inevitably asserts itself through the actions of every human being and stands as the root which begets all personal violations of God's commandments. For this reason, Adam was the head and representative of the whole human race; his sin affected all future generations (Rom. 5:12-21). Associated with this guilt is a fallen nature passed from Adam to all of his descendants. Out of this fallen nature, twisted from the original order of God's benevolent intent, arises all the sins that people commit (Matt. 15:19); no person is free from involvement in sin (Rom. 3:23).

Every human born, with the exception of Jesus Christ, has inborn tendency to rebel against God's Law. To sin is not just to make a small mistake or to break some rules. To sin is to go against the very nature of God Himself. In the Bible, sin is portrayed as a real and positive evil. Sin is more than unwise, inexpedient, calamitous behavior that produces sorrow and distress. It is a violation of God's Law—the universal standard of righteousness (Psa. 119:160) occasioned by ignorance, disobedience, or rebellion.

Ongoing violation of the Law of God in thought, word, and deed shows the sinfulness of the human heart, and sin is capable of compounding its evil even unto the most deprived actions conceivable. Because sin is actually a contradiction to the holiness of God, whose image mankind bears, even the least severe actions of sin are subject because they evidence the original sin's ruination of the divine order. Mankind sins by choice but also is sinful by birth. Apart from Jesus Christ, all are *"dead in trespasses and sins," (NKJV, Eph. 2:1).* When we rebel, we become a law unto ourselves and substitute our own self-made laws for the laws of God. We wreck our own lives and the world we live in. Sin is simply doing what you please (Isa. 53:6). This may sound simple enough until we realize that it is a rejection of God's authority over His creation. When we sin, we rebel against the One who created and sustains our lives, claiming for ourselves the right to determine how to run things. In effect, we attempt to push God off His throne and take His place.

Sin is rooted in pride and selfishness. These things are, first of all, inward conditions. They eventually result in outward actions, but the source of our problem is located inside us, in "what" we are, not just what we do. (Matt. 5:21-22, 27-28). We sin because we are sinners.

> *"If we say we have no sin [refusing to admit that we are sinners], we delude and lead ourselves astray, and the Truth [which the Gospel presents] is not in us [does not dwell in our hearts]. If we [freely] admit that we have sinned and confess our sins, He is faithful and just (true to His own nature and promises) and will forgive our sins [dismiss our lawlessness] and [continuously] cleanse us from all unrighteousness [everything not in conformity to His will in purpose, thought, and action]. If we say (claim) we have not sinned, we contradict His Word and make Him out to be false and a liar, and His Word is not in us [the divine message of the Gospel is not in our hearts]," (Amplified Classic Edition, 1 Jn. 1:8-10).*

What are the results of sin?

All of humanity is under the wrath of God for breaking His laws. We stand condemned with no excuse to offer (Eph. 2:1-3). We face a destiny of eternal punishment in Hell, the place God has set aside for those who refuse to live by His Law. They are hard-hearted and hard-headed and refuse to repent. They believe they are "good people".

God warned Adam and Eve that disobedience to His Law would result in death. Death entered the world after their sin, and we are all subject to it. But more than this, we are now born into the world in a state of spiritual death.

God created us to have communion with Him and to have a relationship with Him. But with sin came separation from God; rebellion cut us off from Him. Because of sin, the spirit in man or woman (that part of him or her which relates to and communes with God) is dead, and humanity has lost the consciousness of God. In this state of spiritual death, we can neither see, know, nor please God.

Sin is deceitful. Why are we so foolish in thinking we would find freedom in having nothing to do with God and His laws? Are we the boss, telling God to move over as we sit on the throne? The fact is, sin leads to slavery as we find that we become slaves to sin itself. (Read what Jesus says about it in John 8:34). We are trapped in bondage and strongholds from which we cannot escape. The natural state of sinful mankind is an unhappy one: guilty, spiritually dead, and enslaved to sin.

Is there anything that I can do to save myself from sin and the results?

There is nothing that you can do to save yourself. You cannot change the past. Even if you were never to commit another sin from this day forward, the sins from your past would remain to condemn you. Sin is an inward condition, a problem that afflicts our very nature. This infection is in our hearts and it needs to be cured. This is beyond our ability. We need help!

What did God do about our condition?

Against this dark background of sin and its reality, the gospel comes as Good News of deliverance that God has provided through His Son, Jesus Christ. Jesus, the God-Man, bore the penalty of our sins when He suffered and died on the cross. Jesus, the human-divine Son of God, suffered death as a mortal man; though He was righteous and innocent, He was punished in our place (Isa. 53:4-6). After three days, He was raised from the dead in victory over sin and Satan, having broken the bonds that held us captive (Acts 2:23-24). God did this in order to reunite us with Himself, to restore the relationship that our sin had broken. God did not and could not overlook our sin. He placed our sins on Himself and paid the price to make amends for it and redeem us from the curse (Eph. 1:7). God the Son came to Earth and died in order to bring us back to Himself (2 Cor. 5:19-21). His resurrection proved and sealed His defeat from death, Hell, and the grave.

What is grace?

We are saved by God's grace. This means that it is all God's doing. There is nothing in us that deserves the salvation God offers us; it is a free gift that flows to us from God's unfathomable love. Our attempts to be or to do good can add nothing to what Christ has already done. He is the Savior, and He alone saves (Eph. 2:8-9) This is a simple statement of how men are resurrected "*spiritually*" from the death of their sins.

Not one Scripture teaches unconditional grace or that God gives grace to men who disobey the Gospel. If so, then God is obligated to save all, even sinners who disobey if He saves even one (Rom. 2:11). God is obligated to saints only when they walk in the light and remain true to the Gospel (1 Jn. 1:7). He is not obligated to sinners until they come to full obedience of the Gospel. Grace teaches men to deny ungodliness and worldly lusts and to live soberly, righteously, and godly here and now (Titus 2:11-12). If men do not obey its teaching, grace can go no further.

Grace: Unmerited help given to people by God (as in overcoming temptation); freedom from sin through divine grace; a virtue coming from God.

How do I receive the salvation God has provided in Jesus Christ?

Even though God has done everything necessary to provide for our salvation, it does not come to us automatically. We must receive the gift God offers. How do I do this?

A Call to Repentance — The first step is the *necessity* of repenting from sin! Repentance is *mandatory* to become a child of God, not optional. No one can come into a genuine relationship with Jesus without starting with genuine repentance and having fully repented of known patterns of sin. Jesus' first instructions are, *"Repent, for the kingdom of heaven is at hand," (New King James Version, Matt. 4:17).*

Jesus knew repentance was the necessary and critical step to having a lasting relationship with God. Again, repentance is not optional. Jesus also made this statement to a group of people: "*Unless you repent you will all likewise perish," (NKJV, Lk.13:3).*

Here is the truth: There is no turning to God without repentance. The New Testament presents a clear message: there is no salvation without repentance from sin. You cannot marry Jesus while still in relationship with the world. You have to die to your old life in order to begin your new one. The Baker Encyclopedia of the Bible states that repentance is "literally a change of mind, not about individual plans, intentions, or beliefs, but rather a change in the *whole personality* from a sinful course of action to God" (emphasis added).

Believe— You must believe that this forgiveness is YOURS in Christ and trust in Him alone to save you. Place your trust in God's truth, take Him at His word, and trust in Him for salvation. The belief that saves is one that rests in the finished work of Jesus Christ; it trusts God alone for salvation (John. 3:16).

Submit— I must put my life in His hands, for only then can He save me. Jesus is both Savior and Lord.

It takes only a moment's prayer to call upon the name of the Lord and receive the salvation that is yours in Jesus Christ.

(Read Romans 10:9-13, NKJV)

*9 That if you ***confess with your mouth** the Lord Jesus and ***believe** in your heart that God has raised Him from the dead, you will be saved.*
*10 For with the ***heart** one believes unto righteousness, and with the mouth confession is made unto salvation.*
11 For the Scripture says, 'Whoever believes on Him will not be put to shame.'
12 For there is no distinction between Jew and Greek, for the same Lord over all is rich to all who call upon Him.
13 For 'whoever calls on the name of the LORD shall be saved.' "

***Note: believe,** *pisteuo* (pist-yoo-oh): Strong's #4100; the verb form of *pistis*, "faith". It means to trust in, have faith in, be fully convinced of, acknowledge, rely on. *Pisteuo* is more than credence in church doctrines or articles of faith. It expresses reliance upon and a personal trust that produces obedience. It includes submission and a positive confession of the lordship of Jesus.

Oral confession declares, confirms, and seals the belief in the ***heart**. God offers salvation to every individual regardless of ethnic background. Salvation comes through believing in Jesus. No amount of good works can ever be sufficient to win God's approval.

FAITH'S CONFESSION. Here is the most foundational lesson in the importance and power of faith's confession found anywhere in the Bible. The principle is established at the very beginning of our life in Christ. Just as salvation (God's righteous working in our behalf) is appropriated by heart belief and spoken confession, so His continuing working in our lives is advanced by the same means.

The word ***confess** has a meaning of "a binding public declaration by which a legal relation is contractually established". Thus, as our words "contract" from <u>our</u> side the salvation God has fully provided from <u>His</u> by Christ's saving work and power, so we have a principle for all of life.

Beginning in this spirit of saving faith, let us grow in active faith, believing in God's mighty power for all our needs, speaking with our lips what our hearts receive and believe of the many promises in His Word. Let us accept God's "contracts" for all our needs by endowing them with our confessed belief, just as when we were saved (Acts 4:33; 1 Cor. 11:23-26).

What happens when I put my faith in Jesus Christ?

God made the first move when Christ became man to die for our sins. He makes the next move as well when He causes us to hear and understand the gospel of salvation in Christ and draws us to Himself by His Holy Spirit (read Jn. 6:44). When we respond to His call in repentance and faith, believing and receiving this Gospel, God moves again. When God saves us, several things happen:

- We are *justified* (read Rom. 3:23-26). This means that we are declared innocent in God's sight. Christ has taken our sin upon Himself and, in return, we are clothed with His righteousness (read 2 Cor. 5:21). All of our sin is removed from us and forgotten (read Psa. 103:12), and we stand before God blameless.

- We are *regenerated* (read Eph. 2:1, 2 Cor. 5:17). Our spirits, which were dead because of sin, are given a **new birth through the Holy Spirit of God (read Jn. 3:3-8). We become spiritually alive, and our communion with God is restored. The heart that was infected with sin is cleansed and made new. We are united with Christ and given new life, His life in us. New birth, the begetting of new life, the rebirth of the human spirit to a restored relationship with God by an act of God's Holy Spirit through Jesus Christ. In regeneration, a person's sinful nature is changed, and he is renewed to life and salvation in God by faith. Being born of the Spirit is essential before a person can enter the Kingdom of God. Every biblical command to man to undergo a radical change of character from self-centeredness to God-centeredness is, in effect, an appeal to be "born again" (Psa. 51:5-11; Jer. 31:33; Zech. 13:1). Regeneration changes a person's desires because "newness of life" is begotten in the person (Rom. 6:4, 7:6), as well as a right relationship with God in Christ.

  Note: (read Jn. 3:1-5) Upon repentance, a new order of life opens to the believer in Jesus Christ. Jesus used the figure of "new birth" to dramatically indicate three things:

1. Without new birth, there is no life and no relationship with God (Jn. 14:6).

2. In new birth, new perspective comes as we "see the Kingdom of God" (Jn. 3:3), God's Word becomes clear, and the Holy Spirt's works and wonders are believed and experienced—faith is alive.
3. Through new birth, we are introduced—literally we "enter" (Jn. 3:5)—to a new realm, where God's new Kingdom order can be realized (*for you*) (2 Cor. 5:17). New birth is more than simply being "saved". It is a requalifying experience, opening up the possibilities of our whole being to the supernatural dimension of life and fitting us for beginning in God's Kingdom order.

- We are *adopted* into God's family (read Rom. 8:14-17). With our new birth, we are reborn into the family of God. He takes us to Himself and counts us as His children. We have a new relationship with God and can truly call Him "Father" as His Holy Spirit comes to dwell within us and mark us as His possession (read Eph. 1:13-14). How great is God's grace which goes even beyond justifying and cleansing us to making us His very own children (read 1 Jn. 3:1). As a repentant sinner, you are a member of the family of God, as if you had been born into the family—the placement as a son with all the rights and privileges of a son.

For what purpose am I saved?

When we receive God's gift of salvation in Christ, it is only the first step in a never-ending journey together with God. God saves us for a purpose in order that we may love, serve, and glorify Him throughout our lives in this world and beyond (read Eph. 2:10). God's ultimate goal is that we become like Christ, conformed to His image (read Rom. 8:29). This is so great and glorious as to be almost beyond our comprehension, but it is true. God is at work in me and in you, to make us more and more like Jesus. Everything that He does in us and for us, everything He brings into our lives, has this glorious end in view. And we can be confident that the work God has begun in us, He will carry to completion, for His own glory (read Phil. 1:6). After reading Philippians 1:6, understand that by sharing your faith in Jesus, you gain a fuller understanding of your inheritance in Christ.

Notes:

Chapter 2

The Body, Soul, and Spirit

For You formed
my inward parts;
You covered me
in my mother's womb.
I will praise You, for I am
fearfully and wonderfully made; Marvelous
are Your works,
And that my soul knows very well.

Psalms 139:13-14

Chapter 2

The Body, Soul, and Spirit

Our Body

The body is wonderfully made (Psa. 139:14). The Bible teaches that the body is God's good gift to man (Gen. 2:7). In the Old Testament, the word 'body' sometimes means "corpse" (Num. 6:6). Occasionally, the reference is to the body as the part of man that is involved in reproduction (Deut. 28:4).

In the New Testament, these Old Testament meanings are carried forward. Paul teaches that the body is often the instrument of sin.

> *"Shun immorality and all sexual looseness [flee from impurity in thought, word, or deed]. Any other sin which a man commits is one outside the body, but he who commits sexual immorality sins against his own body," (Amplified Classic Edition, 1 Cor. 6:18).*

The body must die as a penalty for sin (Rom. 7:24), and that sin dishonors a person's body (Rom. 1:24). On the other hand, believers in Christ may *"put to death the deeds prompted by the body," (AMPC, Rom. 8:13)* and present their bodies as holy sacrifices which pleases God.

> *"I APPEAL to you therefore, brethren, and beg of you in view of [all] the mercies of God, to make a decisive dedication of your bodies [presenting all your members and faculties] as a living sacrifice, holy (devoted, consecrated) and well pleasing to God, which is your reasonable (rational, intelligent) service and spiritual worship," (AMPC, Rom. 12:1).*

Since human life requires a body, sometimes the term 'body' symbolizes the whole person. Both Jesus and Paul used the word in this way.

"The eye is the lamp of the body. So if your eye is sound, your entire body will be full of light. 23 But if your eye is unsound, your whole body will be full of darkness. If then the very light in you [your conscience] is darkened, how dense is that darkness!" (AMPC, Matt. 6:22-23)

"Your eye is the lamp of your body; when your eye (your conscience) is sound and fulfilling its office, your whole body is full of light; but when it is not sound and is not fulfilling its office, your body is full of darkness," (AMPC, Lk. 11:34).

The Bible reveals only introductory ideas regarding our state or existence after the death of our human body, but the real promise of an eternal body is given. At death, we do not become wandering souls or "unclothed" spirits.

1 *For we know that if our earthly house, this tent, is destroyed, we have a building from God, a house not made with hands, eternal in the heavens.*
2 *For in this we groan, earnestly desiring to be clothed with our habitation which is from heaven,*
3 *if indeed, having been clothed, we shall not be found naked.*
4 *For we who are in this tent groan, being burdened, not because we want to be unclothed, but further clothed, that mortality may be swallowed up by life.*
5 *Now He who has prepared us for this very thing is God, who also has given us the Spirit as a guarantee.*
6 *So we are always confident, knowing that while we are at home in the body we are absent from the Lord.*
7 *For we walk by faith, not by sight.*
8 *We are confident, yes, well pleased rather to be absent from the body and to be present with the Lord," (New King James Version, 2 Cor. 5:1-8).*

However, the fullest completion of salvation's purpose, in terms of our physical bodies, will be realized at the return of Christ (1 Thess. 4:13-18). Then we shall receive our "glorified" bodies—eternal bodies like unto Christ's after His resurrection (Phil. 3:21; 1 Cor. 15:35-58; 1 Jn. 3:2).

Our Soul

Man's soul is the seat of the emotions, passions, desires, appetites, and all feelings. It is a word with two distinct meanings in the Bible:

1. That which makes a human body alive. The word used in the New Testament for soul occurs in reference to "life" in Mark chapter 8 for example.

> *35 "For whoever desires to save his life will lose it, but whoever loses his life for My sake and the gospel's will save it.*
> *36 For what will it profit a man if he gains the whole world, and loses his own soul?" (NKJV, Mk. 8:35-36).*

The same idea regarding physical life is also present in the Old Testament. For example, the soul of a dying person departed at death (Gen. 35:18). The prophet Elijah brought a child back to life by stretching himself upon the child three times and praying that God would let the child's soul come back into him (1 Kings 17:19-23).

2. The use of the word 'soul' as it refers to the inner life of man is the seat of his emotions and the center of human personality. The first use of the word in the Old Testament expresses this meaning: *"And the LORD God formed man of the dust of the ground, and breathed into his nostrils the breath of life; and man became a living being (soul)," (NKJV, Gen. 2:7).* This means more than being given physical life, but the statement that man became a "living soul" indicates his uniqueness as a fully conscious, coherent, responsible, moral being with a capacity for a spiritual relationship with God.

The soul is described as the seat of many emotions and desires: the desire for food (Deut. 12:20-21), love (Song 1:7), longing for God (Psa. 139:14), and memory (Lam. 3:20).

In the New Testament, Jesus spoke of His soul as being *"exceedingly sorrowful,"* (Matt. 26:38). Mary, the mother of Jesus, proclaimed that her soul *"magnifies the Lord" (Lk. 1:46).* John prayed that a believer would *"prosper in all things and be in health, just as your soul prospers," (3 Jn. 2).*

The word 'soul' (Greek) *psuche, psyche*: *Strong's* #5590: Breath, the soul. (a) the vital breath, breath of life, (b) the human soul, (c) the soul as the seat of affections and will, (d) the self, (e) a human person, an individual. Also *nephesh:* Strongs (Hebrew) #5315 A life, a living being; soul, self, person, mind, personality; inner desires and feelings. This noun, occurring more that 750 times, is a highly significant Bible term. "Soul" is the word usually chosen in translations for *nephesh*, but "heart," "person," "life," and "mind" are occasionally best suited to a particular context. Unlike the English word 'soul', which usually describes only the inner person and is contrasted with the outer person, *nephesh* describes the whole person as a unit, that is a life, a living creation. The charts on pages 28 and 29 may help describe the distinction between the soul and spirit (Heb. 4:12).

The soul [Greek word *psyche*]. It is the psychological part of you—your mind, will, and emotions. This part of you was not born again. It may be affected by the new birth in your spirit, but it was not born again. Your soul must be transformed by the renewing of your mind through the Word of God (Rom. 12:2). Your will has to be submitted to God (James 4:7).

In fact, your soul needs to be saved (delivered) by receiving with meekness the engrafted Word (James 1:21). Your body has to be brought under subjection (1 Cor. 9:27). We also know that sickness, which can be a spirit (Lk. 13:11) and is an oppression of the devil (Acts 10:38), can be in the bodies of born-again believers.

Although Christians don't have demons in their born-again, recreated spirits, many times they can and do have demons in their souls or physical bodies. These areas of a believer are being progressively sanctified and preserved blameless according to 1 Thessalonians 5:23. If you will receive this revelation, don't fall for the lie that Christians can't have demons. That is what the devil wants you to believe. If you don't believe you need help, you won't seek any, even though you may know from experience there is something in you that is driving and controlling you.

Our Spirit

The chart may help show how the human spirit, dead through sin (Eph. 2:1-3), is brought to life by the power of new life in Christ (2 Cor. 5:17). Only the Spirit, by the new birth, can renew and recover that which was destroyed by the Fall (Jn. 3:5-6). To reach our highest human potential, to have abundant life, we must accept Jesus Christ by faith.

Man's spirit is the seat of the intellect, will, and conscience. It is capable of all divine powers, only in a lesser degree. The inner man, consisting of soul and spirit, is eternal (see 1 Pet. 3:4b).

Man was made a little lower than angels (Psa. 8:5; Heb. 2:7). He was made a 3–fold being—body, soul, and spirit (1 Thess. 5:23; Heb. 4:12).

Material and spiritual natures of man are clearly distinguished in Scripture:

- Soul and spirit not dust (Gen. 2:7).
- Spirit leaves body at death (2 Sam. 12:19-23; 1 Kings 17:20-22; Job 14:10; Eccl. 12:7; Lk. 8:49-56; 16:22; 23:43; Acts 5:10; 2 Cor. 5:8; 12:3-4; Phil. 1:21-24; Heb. 12:23; James 2:26: 2 Pet. 1:13-15; Rev. 6:9-11).
- Soul and spirit are in man's body, but are not the material of the body (Job 14:22; 32:8; Prov. 20:27; Zech. 12:1; 1 Cor. 2:11; 7:34).
- The body can be killed but not the soul (Matt. 10:28; Lk. 12:5).
- The spirit can be willing but the flesh powerless to execute (Matt. 26:38-41).
- Both flesh and spirit are to glorify God (1 Cor. 6:20).
- Both the flesh and spirit can be filthy or holy (2 Cor. 7:1).
- The inner man is eternal; the body mortal (2 Cor. 4:16-18).
- The inner man is fully conscious after leaving the body (Matt. 10:28; 17:3; Lk.16:19-31; 20:38; Jn. 11:25-26; Acts 2:27; Eph. 3:15; 4:8-10; 2 Cor. 5:8; 12:1-4; Phil. 1:21-24; Heb. 2:14-15; 12:23; 1 Pet. 3:4b; Rev. 6:9-11).
- Souls can be dead while the bodies are alive (Matt. 8:22; Eph. 2:1-9; 1 Tim. 5:6; Rev. 3:1).
- Souls of the righteous have eternal life even after the body dies (Jn. 3:16; 5:24; 6:47, 53, 63, 11:25-26; 14:19).
- Souls of the righteous go to Heaven at death (2 Cor. 5:8; Eph. 3:14-15; Phil. 1:21-24; Heb. 12:23; Rev. 6:9-11). Their bodies go to graves (Dan. 12:2; Jn. 5:28-29).
- The body is the house of the inner man (Job 4:19; 14:22; 32:8; Zech. 12:1 1 Cor. 2:11; 2 Cor. 5:1-8; Phil. 1:21-24; 2 Pet. 1:13-15). The soul and spirit design; the body executes. Man, through his **body,** has material or world consciousness; through the **soul**, self-consciousness; and through the **spirit**, God-consciousness.

Universal instinct to worship God and meet certain standards that will better the future and eternal existence proves immortality of the body. Nature causes the birds to go north and south and to know when to mate. The ants, bees, and all other creatures know by instinct how to carry on their own peculiar life for the future. Everything in creation obeys its natural instinct, except unregenerated man, refusing to believe in the existence of God. He is capable of choosing to better himself or to degenerate to unnatural living, falling below a normal or desirable level in physical, mental, or moral qualities now and forever. He has outstanding instincts to worship and prepare for eternal life. Is man the only creature that nature lies to and fools? Why don't animals have the same natural craving for immortality? This proves man capable of worship and preparing for eternity to better himself (1 Jn. 3:1-3; 2 Cor. 7:1; Heb. 12:14-15; Gal. 5:24; 2 Cor. 5: 17-21).

Man was created to live forever physically, as well as in soul and spirit. Sin cut him off from this and hindered the original plan. Jesus came to restore all to man. Being constituted to live bodily forever proves the possibility of immortality. Man's creation in God's own image and likeness demands it; the eternal purpose of God demands it; and the eternal plan of God provides for it; but sinners forfeit their part in the glorious plan by sin (Prov. 1:22-23; Matt. 25:31-46; Rom. 6:16-23; 8:12-13). Even they will exist bodily forever as an eternal monument of God's justice to all coming generations throughout all eternity (Isa. 66:22-24; Rev. 14:9-11; 20:10-15; 21:8, 22:15).

The Intermediate State

By this, it is meant the state of the dead between death and the resurrection of the body. After the body goes back to dust at physical death (Gen. 3:19; Eccl. 3:19-21; James 2:26), it remains dead (separated from the inner man) until the future resurrection day when the body will be made immortal (1 Cor. 15:35-54). The soul and spirit continue alive, being immortal either in Heaven or Hell, until the resurrection day when the body will be made immortal.

At physical death, the soul and spirit leave the body (James 2:26). If one is a converted person, his soul and spirit go to Heaven immediately at death to await the resurrection of the body (Lk. 20:38; Jn. 11:25-26; 2 Cor. 5:8; Eph. 3:15; 4:8-10; Phil. 1:21-24; Heb. 12:22-23; Rev. 6:9-11). If he is unsaved, his soul and spirit go to Hell at death to await the resurrection of the body (Lk. 16:19-31; 2 Pet. 2:9; Rev. 20:11-15; Isa. 14:9).

The Dake Annotated Reference Bible pages 685-686 / Deliverance and Spiritual Warfare Manual - by John Eckhardt Spirit, Soul, Body page 71

THE STRUCTURE OF A PERSON

Body

Soul

Spirit

BODY

World – Consciousness

Senses: See, touch, taste, smell, hear
May yield to indulgence, sensuality.

Well-being: Physical systems, strength, disorder
May become diseased or afflicted.

Appearance, Action: May become self-serving or God-pleasing.

SOUL

Self - consciousness

Intellect: the mind, thought, reason.
May yield to unbelief and/or confusion, etc.

Emotion: feelings, temperament, concerns.
May yield to bitterness, lust, anger, etc.

Will: choices, actions
May yield to disobedience.

SPIRIT

God-consciousness

Faith: assurance, stability
Fed by the Word of God.

Hope: confidence expectancy
Sustained by looking unto Jesus.

Love: communication motivation
Nurtured by the flow of the Holy Spirit.

THE SALVATION OF A PERSON

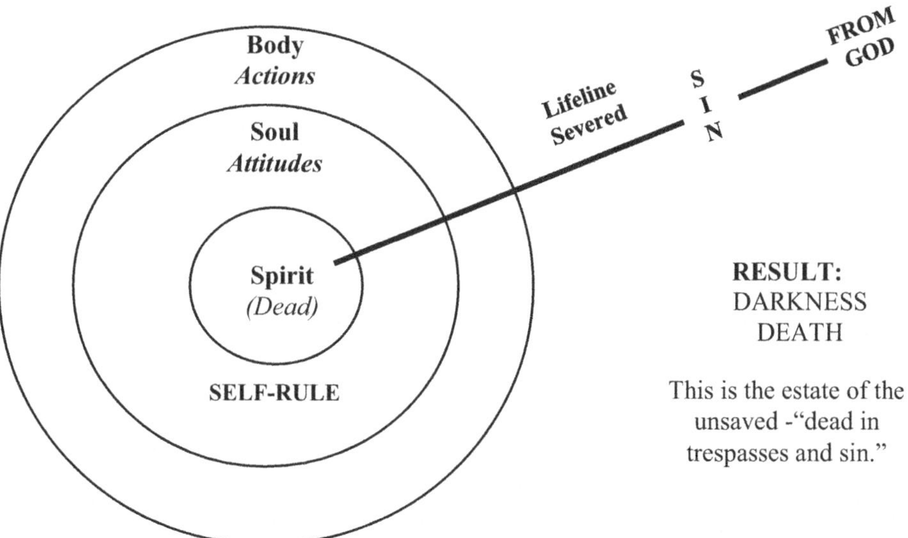

RESULT:
DARKNESS
DEATH

This is the estate of the unsaved -"dead in trespasses and sin."

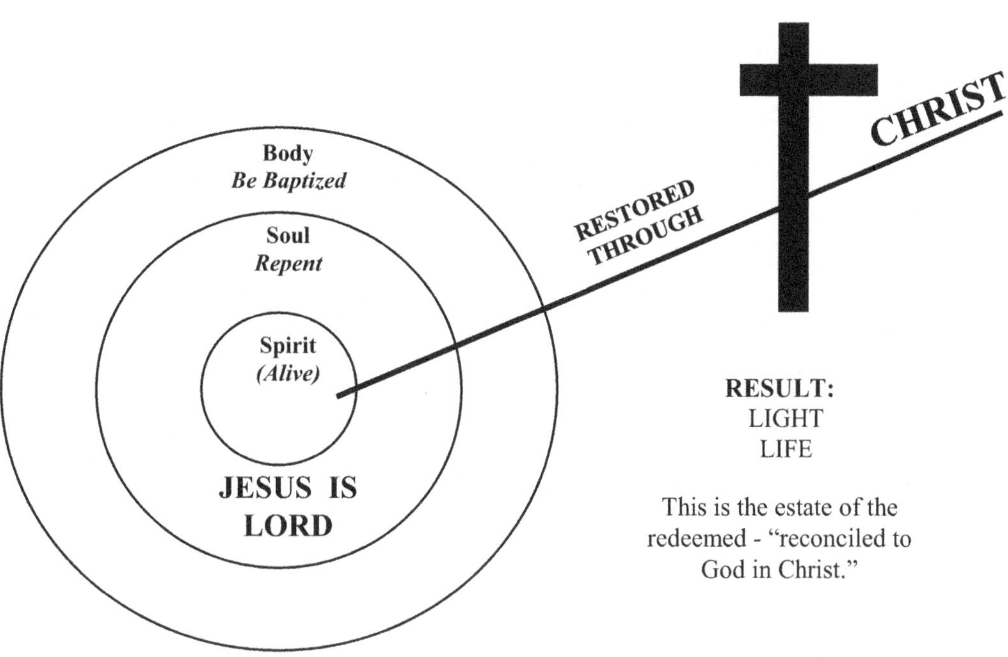

RESULT:
LIGHT
LIFE

This is the estate of the redeemed - "reconciled to God in Christ."

Notes:

Chapter 3

Father God

To know God

as our Father—

Our almighty, loving Father –

is the highest,

richest, and most

rewarding aspect of our

Whole relationship

with Him.

Chapter 3

Father God

Now that you are a member of God's family, you need to know God and your relationship to Him.

The study of God is called *theology*. Our Father is the First Person of the Holy Trinity.

The study of God can be extremely exciting, learning about the One who created us and the world that we live in. The reason so many people lead aimless, empty lives is because they do not know God, the Source of life, and sadly do not know what life is all about. If you do not know Him, how would you know the will for your life. What is the purpose of your life?

Theology is essential because knowing God is essential! God the Father is the source of truth and love (Jn. 17:17; 1 Jn. 4:16).

Ephesians 3:14-15 states, *"For this reason I bow my knees to the Father of our Lord Jesus Christ, from whom the whole family in heaven and earth is named," (NKJV).*

These two verses show that God's overall household or family is both in Heaven and on Earth. Through creation, God is the Father of both the angelic world (Job 1:6; 38:7) and humans (Mal. 2:10; Lk. 3:38). Almighty God is responsible for everything that exists; thus, He rightfully is a Father to all who have life (1 Tim. 6:13). So, it was natural for the apostle Paul to refer to God as the head of a vast family.

God reveals to us that He was also a Father to the children of Israel, that is, Abraham's family grown large through Isaac and Jacob. God refers to Israel as His firstborn (Exod. 4:22), meaning He is the One who gave these former slaves life and identity as a nation, calling them His own. In Jeremiah 31:9, God says, *"For I am a Father to Israel, and Ephraim is My firstborn," (NKJV).*

Jesus Christ is the Son of God in a unique and special way. He is identified as the *"Son of the Most High God," (Mk. 5:7).* Psalm 2:7 says, *"You are My Son, today I have begotten You,"*

(NKJV). Jesus referred to God as His Father on numerous occasions. The very well-known John 3:16 states, *"For God so loved the world that He gave His only begotten Son," (NKJV).*

Adam and Eve were created by God from the dust of the ground and given life by God, but they did not have a mother, nor were they conceived. Jesus Christ is the only Being that was born of a virgin by God's own Spirit overshadowing Mary, resulting in a conception (Lk. 1:35). Jesus is literally the only begotten Son of God. All other humans have a physical father. So, God is a Father to Jesus in a way that He is not to any other living being.

This aspect of the Gospel message reveals how, through repentance, baptism, and the receiving of God's Holy Spirit (Acts 2:38), God Almighty can actually become our Father in a very personal way. He becomes our Father, and we become His children, when we are spiritually converted. Romans 8:14 tells us, *"For as many as are led by the Spirit of God, these are sons of God," (NKJV).*

We begin our spiritual life as babes (1 Pet. 2:2), but we are to grow in Christian maturity until our death or until Christ returns (1 Thess. 4:15-17). Through this new life based on God's Spirit living in us, we can begin to not only grasp spiritual truths and values (1 Cor. 2:9-11), but also have a very personal, close relationship with God our Father. Paul says that we are now able to address Him as *"Abba, Father," (NKJV, Rom. 8:15).*

God reveals through the New Testament that we can have a warm, affectionate, personal relationship with Him that goes far beyond just acknowledging Him as the One who created us and who gives us beneficial rules to make our lives happy and complete. We are children in God's eyes and enjoy the special connection and love only a father and his children can enjoy. We are not just servants having a master, but sons and daughters having a Father.

With our Father, there is mercy, loving-kindness, compassion, forgiveness, healing, deliverance, and redemption. With Jesus, in John 10:31-38, He talks about the work He is doing. He made it clear in this passage that these were the works of the Father.

God's mercy was being manifested through Jesus—God's mercy, compassion, loving-kindness on Israel; His love was saving them, healing them, delivering them, and restoring them. Jesus demonstrated to them, and to us, that He is the representation of God our Father, who is concerned about people who are hurting, sick, wounded, bleeding, and dying. This same manifestation of mercy now comes to you.

How does God reveal Himself?

God shows Himself to us in several ways:

Creation — We can know something of God from the world He has made. This is called general revelation. The universe bears witness to the wisdom, power, and glory of God, its Creator (Psa. 19:1-4; Rom. 1:20). Our minds testify to His intelligence, and our consciences testify to His righteousness. Every time we open our eyes, we are presented with His handiwork; every time we take a breath we are reminded of His faithfulness in sustaining our lives.

Scripture — The knowledge of God we gain from creation is limited, but God has given additional special revelation of Himself in the Bible. Through the Holy Spirit, God inspired the authors (prophets and apostles) of Scripture to record certain of His words and deeds, giving us a more complete picture of Himself (2 Tim. 3:16, 2 Pet. 1:20-21). It is the written will of God revealed by the Holy Spirit. Only the Scriptures reveal the mind of God.

Special Visitations — The Bible tells of how God sometimes appeared to men in dreams, visions, and other extraordinary experiences. These were often powerful and life-changing events (Isa. 6:1-8). God still shows Himself in such ways at times and places of His own choosing—vision experiences similar to dreams through which supernatural insight or awareness is given by revelation. The difference between a dream and a vision is that dreams occur only during sleep, while visions can happen while a person is awake (Dan. 10:7). Visions never supersede Scripture, but like dreams, prophecies are to be tested by the Word (2 Pet. 1:16-21) and judged or (1 Cor. 14:29) evaluated by mature believers.

Jesus Christ — He is the second person of the Trinity. The fullest and most complete revelation of God is found in Jesus Christ (Heb. 1:1-3). Jesus is called the Word because He is the perfect expression of what God reveals to us of Himself (Jn. 1:1). In Christ, God Himself took upon human form in order that we might look upon the invisible God (Jn. 1:14, Col. 1:15). In Christ, God spoke with a human voice and was seen, heard, and touched by human hands (1 Jn 1:1-2). If we want to see God, we need only look at Jesus (Jn. 14:7-10).

The Holy Spirit — The Holy Spirit is the third person of the Trinity who exercises the power of the Father and the Son in creation and redemption because the Holy Spirit is the source of the power by which believers come to Christ and see with new eyes of faith. He guides believers into all truth with what He hears from the Father and the Son (Jn. 15:26). The most direct and intimate knowledge of God comes from His Holy Spirit dwelling within us. In the Holy Spirit, God draws near to us and makes Himself known to our hearts (Jn. 15:15-23). The Holy Spirit also reveals to Christians the deep things of God (1 Cor. 2:10-12)—*"The work of the Holy Spirit,"* (John 16:5-15). What a precious privilege, to know God in such a close and intimate way! In the Amplified Bible, it says it beautifully.

> *"5 But now I am going to Him Who sent Me, yet none of you asks Me, Where are You going?*
> *6 But because I have said these things to you, sorrow has filled your hearts [taken complete possession of them].*
> *7. However, I am telling you nothing but the truth when I say it is profitable (good, expedient, advantageous) for you that I go away. Because if I do not go away, the Comforter (Counselor, Helper, Advocate, Intercessor, Strengthener, Standby) will not come to you [into close fellowship with you]; but if I go away, I will send Him to you [to be in close fellowship with you].*
> *8 And when He comes, He will convict and convince the world and bring demonstration to it about sin and about righteousness (uprightness of heart and right standing with God) and about judgment:*
> *9 About sin, because they do not believe in Me [trust in, rely on, and adhere to Me];*
> *10 About righteousness (uprightness of heart and right standing with God), because I go to My Father, and you will see Me no longer;*
> *11 About judgment, because the ruler (evil genius, prince) of this world [Satan] is judged and condemned and sentence already is passed upon him.*
> *12 I have still many things to say to you, but you are not able to bear them or to take them upon you or to grasp them now.*
> *13 But when He, the Spirit of Truth (the Truth-giving Spirit) comes, He will guide you into all the Truth (the whole, full Truth). For He will not speak His own message [on His own authority]; but He will tell whatever He hears [from the Father; He will give the message that has been given to Him], and He will announce and declare to you the things that are to come [that will happen in the future].*
> *14 He will honor and glorify Me, because He will take of (receive, draw upon) what is Mine and will reveal (declare, disclose, transmit) it to you.*
> *15. Everything that the Father has is Mine. That is what I meant when I said that He [the Spirit] will take the things that are Mine and will reveal (declare, disclose, transmit) it to you," (Amplified Classic Edition, Jn. 16:5-15).*

Who are the members of the Trinity?

The trinity consists of God the Father, God the Son, and God the Holy Spirit (Matt. 28:19). All are divine and co-equal. Looking at 1 Corinthians 12:4-7, it offers some insight into how the Three work together as One. Verse 4 - Spiritual gifts by the Holy Spirit. Verse 5 - God the Son as the agent through whom creation and redemption were accomplished. The Son administrates. Verse 6 - God the Father operates or initiates. Verse 7 - The Holy Spirit manifests. God the Holy Spirit is a power by whom creation and redemption were affected. Yet all of them work together for the same purpose.

> For an example … let's say that you were going to build a house. What would you need to do first? Hire an architect, a foreman, and workers (subcontractors) to actually build the house. In this example … God the Father is the Architect, Jesus is the Foreman, and the Holy Spirit represents the Workers who build the house. He "manifests" creation. All three roles are essential to the construction of any house.

The Scripture states clearly that the triune Godhead operates coequally, coeternally, consistently as one unit. We also might view this unity of activity with an eye toward the special function of each member of the Trinity.

Titles and offices of the Father, the Son, and the Holy Spirit reveal their character, work, and separate parts in the plan of God that are being carried out by the THREE separate and distinct persons of the Divine Trinity. They reveal that the Father has the HEADSHIP part, the Son has the CREATIVE and REDEMPTIVE part, and the Holy Spirit the DIRECT POWER of operation. All three persons of the Trinity have worked and are still working in perfect harmony in the creation, redemption, and eternal good of all.

All three Person of the Godhead are eternal. The Father exists and has existed forever. With Him always existed His expression, the Son. Always the Father loved the Son, and the Son loved and served the Father. From the relationship of love exists the Spirit of God, who is eternal and has existed forever. The Father did not exist first, then later the Son, and still later the Spirit. They all three have existed from before there was anything that could begin—three distinct Persons all functioning as One. The Father spoke from Heaven, the Son was fulfilling all righteousness, and the Spirt descended upon the Son like a dove (Matt. 3:16, 17). God the Son has existed eternally in a loving and submissive relationship with God the Father

> *1 "In the beginning [before all time] was the* ****Word (Christ)****, and the Word was with God, and the Word was God Himself.*
> *2 He was present originally with God.*
> *3 All things were made and came into existence through Him; and without Him was not even one thing made that has come into being," (AMPC, Jn. 1:1-3)*

> ***Note:** The **Word** refers to **Christ** (also in Jn. 1:14; Rev. 19:13) and proves His pre-existence (Mic. 5:1-2; Rev. 1:8,11; 2:8; 22:13-16). He is an eternal Being as are also the Father and the Holy Spirit (Psa. 90:1-2; Heb. 9:14). They make the Divine Trinity (1 Jn. 5:7). Not only was the Word with God, but He was God and always will be as much divine as the other two members of the Trinity (Psa. 45:6-7; Isa. 9:6-7; Jn. 1:1; Heb. 1:8-12; Rev. 1:8, 11; 22:13-16). (The Dake Annotated Reference Bible page 159)

God the Son became incarnate as the Man Jesus Christ, fully divine and fully human. He lived in perfect obedience to God the Father and worked miracles through the power of the Holy Spirit. He died in our place to make amends (atone, atonement) for our sins, was raised by the Father through the Holy Spirit, and now reigns as King over all. From His throne, at the right hand of the Father, He pours forth the Holy Spirit upon His people (Acts 2:32-33).

The existence of the Trinity is a mystery that one day we will understand clearly. For now, we know that the Bible teaches it and Jesus revealed it, and the Christian Church from the beginning has confessed and safeguarded this precious truth (1 Cor. 12:4-6; 2 Cor. 13:14; Eph. 4:4-6; 2 Thess. 2:13, 14).

What is God like?

He is the substance of all human virtues. He is all wise and all knowing. He can do anything and everything we cannot do, and He is everything good that we would like to be. God is a Spirit: eternal and ever-living. He has no beginning or end. He is a Person who is totally self-aware—"I am"; totally moral—"I ought"; and totally self-assertive—"I will". He is the essence of love, and He is loving. He is also a righteous judge— totally fair and just.

God is the Father of all creation, the Creator of all. He is all powerful and sustains the universe. He exists outside the universe, yet He is present throughout the universe and is its ruler. He exists in nature, but He is not nature, nor is He bound by the laws of nature. He is the source of all life and everything that is.

Although we cannot fully understand God, we still can know Him. We know Him through the ministry of the Holy Spirit, who makes a personal relationship with Christ and growing knowledge of Him possible by faith (Jn. 15:26-27; 16:7-15). We also learn of Him through a study of His revealed Word—the Bible.

God may be described in terms of His attributes, the inherent characteristics of His person or being. The Bible reveals both natural and moral attributes of God.

The Natural Attributes:

- God Is *Spirit*. Jesus taught that "God is Spirit" (Jn. 4:24). God has no body, no physical or measurable form, thus God is invisible. He became visible in human form in the person of Jesus Christ, but His essence is invisible.

- God Is *Changeless*. Progress and change may characterize some of His works, but God Himself remains unchanged (Heb. 1:12). He does not change; otherwise, He would not be perfect or complete. What we know of God can be known with certainty. He is not different from one time to another.

- God Is *All Powerful (Omnipotent)*. God's power is unlimited. He can do anything that is not inconsistent with His nature, character, and purpose (Gen. 17:1; 18:14). The only limitations on God's power are imposed by Himself (Gen. 18:25). "Impossible" is not in God's vocabulary. God creates and sustains all things, yet He never grows weary (Is. 40: 27-31).

- God Is *All knowing (Omniscient)*. God possesses all knowledge (Job 38:39; Rom. 11:33-36) because God's presence reaches everywhere at one and the same time. He knows everything simultaneously – past, present, and future. God even knows the thoughts and motives of every heart, as is evident from many Scripture passages (see Job 37:16, Psa. 147: 5, Heb. 3:13).

- God Is *Everywhere (Omnipresent).* God is not confined to any part of the universe but is present in all His power at every point in space and at every moment in time (Psa. 139:7-12). God does not belong to any one nation or generation. He is the God of all the earth, the heavens, and beyond the universe itself (Gen. 18:25).

- God Is *Transcendent.* Though He has created all things and His presence pervades the entirety of His creation, He is beside and beyond it, unlimited to it and uncontained by it. Thus *pantheism*, which makes God a life force within all things, is in **error**, as is any system which reduces Him to a "force" rather than a Person.

- God Is *Eternal.* Eternity refers to God's relation to time. Past, present, and future are known equally to Him (2 Pet. 3:8, Rev. 1:8). Time is like a parade that man sees only a segment at a time. But God sees time in its entirety. (Entirety - the whole of something).

The Moral Attributes:

The second is moral attributes, describing God's character—His essential nature.

- God Is *Holy.* The word 'holy' comes from a root word that means "to be apart from, different than, separate." It refers to God as separated from or exalted above all other things (Isa. 6:3). Holiness involves perfection, purity, majesty, and glory. God is perfect in righteousness, pure, and uncontaminated by any form of evil. He is supreme in value and worth. Holiness refers to God's moral excellence or absolute completeness. Being holy, God calls for holiness in His own children, and what He calls for, He supplies. Holiness is God's gift that we receive by faith through His Son, Jesus Christ (Eph 4:24). He lives in unapproachable light (1 Tim. 6:16) and is the source and model of all goodness and truth.

- God Is *Righteous.* Righteousness, as applied to God, refers to His affirmation and administration of what is right as opposed to what is wrong. His righteousness infuses His moral laws in the Ten Commandments, laid down to guide the conduct of humankind. Righteousness also refers to God's administration of justice. He brings equity to the violated and punishment upon the disobedient (Gen. 18:25, Deut. 32:4, Rom. 2:6-16). Finally, God's righteousness is redemptive, as in His declaring the believer to be in a state justified in Christ through His death and resurrection (Rom. 1: 16-17, 3:24-26).

- God *Is Love.* Love is the central, quintessential description of the nature of God. God's love for man seeks to awaken a responsive love of man for God. Divine love runs like a golden thread through the entire Bible. There we discover God giving Himself and all He possesses to His creatures in order to win their response and to possess them and share Himself with them. God loved and gave; He loved and sought just as a shepherd seeks his sheep. God loved and suffered, providing His love by giving His all on the cross for the redemption of humanity. God, in His love, wills ultimate good for all His creatures (Gen. 1:31, Psa. 145:9, Mk. 10:18). (1 Jn. 4:8) God's heart is a heart of love. Every instance of human love we experience or witness—the love of a mother for her child, the love between husband and wife, the love which binds two people in friendship—all are pale imitations of the love which overflows from the heart of God. God's love is abundant enough to envelop the vilest sinner and redeem him back to Himself. The love of God is measured by the depths of His sacrifice for us on the cross of Calvary (Jn. 3:16).

Who can understand such love as this? Who can refuse it?

- God *Is Truth.* All truth, whether natural, physical, or spiritual, is grounded in God. Thus, any seemingly inconsistent teaching between natural and physical sciences and God's revelation of Himself is only a temporary misconception of man's based on his limited perspective and incomplete knowledge. Fullness of truth ultimately will be verified and magnified in alignment with God's revelation.

- God *Is Wisdom.* God's wisdom is revealed in His doing the best thing, in the best way, at the best time, for the best purpose. Some people have knowledge but little wisdom, while at times it seems the most wise have little knowledge. In contrast, God is "the only wise God" (1 Tim. 1:17), being *all* wise as well as *all* knowing. In creation, history, human lives, redemption, and finally and ultimately in Christ, His divine wisdom is revealed. The promise of James 1:5 affirms our human privilege of asking for and renewing wisdom from God.

- God Is *Personal.* God is not just some "force" that permeates and energizes the universe which we can manipulate or use for our purposes. He is not a vague "influence" but a Person who thinks, feels, speaks, plans, and acts. He is not less personal than we are, but more so (Psa. 94:7-10). He has distinct character and will; He can be pleased or offended, known or ignored, obeyed or disobeyed, loved or despised.

However complete our effort at describing God through His attributes, our understanding of Him will continue to increase through our earthly pilgrimage, finally to be completed in eternity when we stand in His presence.

NOTES:

Chapter 4

Powerful Names of God

The Bible tells us that
God will meet all
our needs.
He feeds the birds of the air
and clothes the grass
with the splendor of lilies.
How much more,
then,
will He care for us,
who are made in
His image?

Chapter 4

Powerful Names of God

God is the only One who never changes. His character, His name remains the same through all generations. He is fully trustworthy, always powerful, forever loving, and constantly present with us. Studying what God's Word says about all that, He can help us to understand His very nature and character even more.

He is the God of miracles and nothing is impossible for Him. He split the seas and delivered His people straight through away from all their enemies. He offered His protection through desert days, and lovingly led them in the wilderness to the promised land. He provided a way for us to be saved through His Son Jesus Christ, and He gave us His Spirit to help us today. Hold on to the promise that His love is everlasting. His mercies and grace are new every morning.

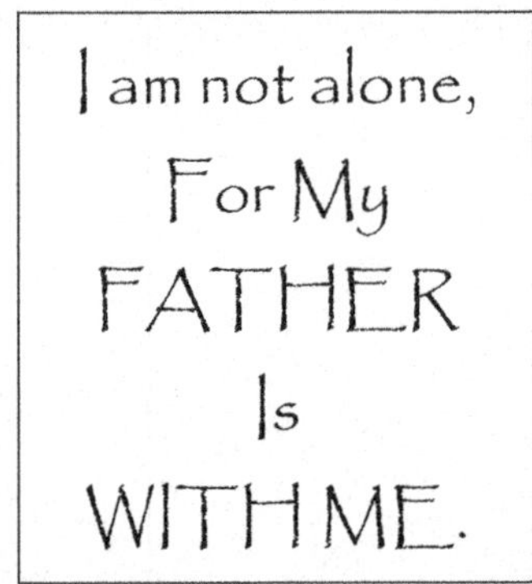

We are going to examine the titles or designations given to God throughout the Bible. In the ancient world, knowing another's name was a special privilege that offered access to that person's thoughts and life. God favored his people by revealing Himself by several names which offered special insight into His love and righteousness.

Elohim

Elohim means "God" - This name refers to God's incredible power and might. The word 'Elohim' appears more than 2,500 times in the Old Testament. It refers to God the Creator, the One and only God. He is supreme, strong, and mighty. Elohim, which is a plural form in Hebrew, reveals that God has more than one part of His being. We call those distinct parts "the Father," "the Son," and "the Holy Spirit". He is sovereign. He is the One we can completely trust. He is the Mighty One over all of nature, this world, and the heavens above, our creative God who has worked wonders by His hands. God reminds that He is Elohim every single day. His amazing power is at work in every sunrise, every sunset, in the way He holds the stars in the sky, and carries His people through difficult times. You can be assured you are held by an almighty God. You never have to fear; God's hands are strong and secure (Gen. 1:1, 2 Kings 19:15, Psa. 19:1).

Jehovah/Yahweh

Jehovah means "I AM," The One Who Is the Self-Existent One. Yahweh means "the Lord" - from the verb "to be", meaning simply but profoundly, "I am who I am" and "I will be who I will be". The four-letter Hebrew word (called the tetragrammaton) *YHWH* was the name by which God revealed Himself to Moses at the burning bush (Exod. 3:14). This bush itself was a vivid symbol of the inexhaustible energy and activity of God, who burns like a fire with love and righteousness yet remains the same and never diminishes.

God's name, Yahweh, is one of authority. It is one that holds great power, and says to all who hear, "I AM the one, true God. Follow me." God is still the "Great I AM" for He never changes. We can trust His loving leadership in our lives, just as Moses did. He calls us for his specific purposes, reminding us that He knows our way and He has a plan. God never changes. His promises never fail. When we are faithless, He is faithful. We need to obey Him.

As the author of life and salvation, God's "I AM" expresses the fact that He is the infinite and original personal God who is behind the existence of everything and to whom everything must finally be traced. This name, "I AM who I AM" signals the truth that nothing else defines who God is but God Himself. What He says and does is who He is. The inspired Scriptures are the infallible guide to understanding who God is by what He says about Himself and what He does.

God had already disclosed Himself to Abraham, Isaac, and Jacob as Yahweh. Each of them had called on the name of the Lord, Yahweh (Gen. 12:8, 13:4, 26:25, Exod. 3:15) as the God who protects and blesses.

Abba

Abba means "Daddy, Father". Abba is the most intimate form of God's name, showing you His character as your loving Daddy. He is the One who can be fully trusted, the One you can lean on, the One who cares about all that concerns you. Just as a godly father's presence in our daily lives is one of protection, security, and unconditional love, the constant presence of our heavenly Father is what gives us the strength and covering we need for this life's journey. He deeply loves each of us as His children. He gives us the privilege of being called his own sons and daughters. He provides the way for us to call out to Him and the assurance, beyond a doubt, that He hears and will answer. In our most difficult to painful times in life, we can call out to our heavenly Father and know that He is for us and His arms will hold us securely (Gal. 4:6).

Adonai

Adonai means “The Lord My Great Lord”. God is the Master and majestic Lord. God is our total authority. Adonai (plural) is derived from the singular Adon (Lord). This term was pronounced in substitution of *YHWH* (considered too sacred to be uttered).

El

El means “The Strong One”. He is more powerful than any false god. God will overcome all obstacles. We can depend on God. El occurs more than 200 times in the Old Testament (including compounds). Names such as Isra-*el* (wrestles with God), Beth-*el* (House of God), and *El*-ish (God is salvation) (Exod. 15:2, Num. 23:22, Deut. 7:9, Mk. 15:34).

Elyon

Elyon means “God Most High”. Elyon is a name used through the Old Testament revealing God is above all gods, that nothing in life is more sacred. He is greater than any force of darkness in this world. God is still in control. He never will lose His power and might, though the world feels dark many days. He has conquered death and sin. He is mighty. He is Lord. He is exalted over all (Gen. 14:17-22, Psa. 78:35, Dan. 4:34, Acts 16:17).

El Roi

El Roi means “The God Who Sees Me”. There are no circumstances in our lives that escape His fatherly awareness and care. God knows us and our troubles. Hagar called the Lord by this name beside a fountain of water in the wilderness. God knows all of our thoughts and feelings. Jesus knew the thoughts of those around Him, demonstrating that He is El Roi (Gen. 16:11-14, Psa. 139:7-12, Matt. 22:18, 26:21, 34, Lk. 5:21-24).

Jehovah-Jireh

Jehovah-Jireh means “The Lord Will Provide”. Just as God provided a ram as a substitute for Isaac, He provided His son, Jesus, as the ultimate sacrifice. God will meet all our needs. Abraham called the place “The Lord will provide” where God provided a ram to be sacrificed instead of his son, Isaac. Jesus said that He was the bread of life and anyone who comes to Him will be provided for (Gen. 22:13, 14, Psa. 23, Mk. 10:45, Rom. 8:2, Jn. 6:35).

Jehovah-Nissi

This name means "The Lord Is My Banner" in honor of God's defeat of the Amalekites (Exod. 17:15, 16). God gives us victory against the flesh, the world, and the devil. Our battles are His battles of light against darkness and good against evil (Deut. 20:3, 4, Isa. 11:10-12, Eph. 6:10-18).

Jehovah-Shalom

This phrase means "The Lord Is Peace", the name Gideon gave the altar which he built in Ophrah (Jdg. 6:22-24). God defeats our enemies to bring us peace. Jesus is our Prince of Peace. God brings inner peace and harmony. Isaiah tells us that the Messiah will also be known as the "Prince of Peace", our Jehovah-Shalom (Num. 6:22-27, Isa. 9:6, Heb. 13:20).

Jehovah-Shammah

This name expresses the truth that "The Lord Is There", "The Lord My Companion". God's presence is not limited or contained in the tabernacle or temple, but is accessible to all who love and obey Him. God revealed to Ezekiel that the name of the New Jerusalem shall be "The Lord Is There". Through Jesus Christ, the Spirit of God dwells in us (Ez. 48:35, Psa. 46, Matt. 28:20, 1 Cor. 3:16, Rev. 21).

Jehovah-tseboath [Sabaoth]

This name translates as "The Lord of Hosts", "The Lord of Armies". This was used in the days of David and the prophets, witnessing to God the Savior who was surrounded by His hosts of heavenly power (1 Sam. 1:3). The Lord of the hosts of Heaven will always fulfill His purposes, even when the hosts of His earthly people fail (1 Sam. 17:45, Psa. 46:7, Mal. 1:10-14; Rom. 9:29).

Jehovah-Elohe-Israel [Yisrael]

This name means "Lord God of Israel", "God, the God of Israel". It appears in Isaiah, Jeremiah, and the Psalms. Other names similar to this are *Netsah Israel*, "The Strength of Israel" (1 Sam. 15:29) and *Abir Yisrael*, "The Mighty One of Israel" (Isa. 1:24). The God of Israel is distinct and separate from all false gods of the world. This was the name of the altar that Jacob (Israel) erected after his encounter with God and God's blessing upon him (Gen. 32: 24-30, 33:19, 20, Exod. 5:1, Psa. 68:8, Psa. 106:48).

Jehovah—Mekaddishkem

This name means "The Lord Who Sanctifies". God sets us apart as a chosen people, a royal priesthood, holy unto God, a people of His own. He cleanses our sin and helps us mature. We have been set apart, made holy, and redeemed by the blood of Jesus Christ, our Jehovah-Mekaddishkem. Therefore, we are to continue to live our lives holy and pleasing to God (Exod. 31:12, 13, 1 Pet. 1:13-25, Heb. 13:12, 1 Thess. 5:23, 24).

Jehovah-Rapha

This name means "The Lord Who Heals". God has provided the final cure for spiritual, physical, and emotional sickness in Jesus Christ. God can heal us. Jesus demonstrated that He was Jehovah-Rapha in His healing of the sick, blind, lame, and through the casting out of demons. Jesus also heals His people from sin and unrighteousness (Exod. 17:15, 16, Psa. 103:3, 147:3, Lk. 5:31, 32, 1 Pet. 2:24).

Jehovah-Rohi

This means "The Lord is My Shepherd". The Lord protects, provides, directs, leads, and cares for His people. God tenderly takes care of us as a strong and patient shepherd. Jesus is the good shepherd who laid down His life for all people (Psa. 23:1-3, Isa. 53:6, Jn. 10:14-18, Heb. 13:20, Rev. 7:17).

Jehovah-Tsidkenu

This means "The Lord Our Righteousness". Jesus is the King who would come from David's line and is the one who imparts His righteousness to us. All people sin and fall short of God's glory, but God freely makes us righteous through faith in Jesus Christ (Rom. 3:22, 23). God promised to send a King who will reign wisely and do what is just and right. The people will live in safety (Jer. 23:5, 6; 33:16, Ezek. 36:26, 27, 2 Cor. 5:21).

Yah, or Jah

This means; "I AM", "The One Who Is", "The Self-Existent One". God never changes. His promises never fail. When we are faithless, He is faithful. God promises His continuing presence. It is a shorter form of *Yahweh*. It is often used when combined with other names or phrases. *Hallelujah* means "Praise Yah (the Lord). *Elijah* means "God is Yah (the Lord)" and *Joshua* means "Yah (the Lord) is my salvation" (Exod. 3:14, 15:2, Psa. 46:1, Psa. 68:4, Isa. 26:4).

El Olam

This means "The Eternal God", "The Everlasting God". He is the Beginning and the End, the One who works His purposes throughout the ages. He gives strength to the weary. Jesus Christ possesses eternal attributes. He is the same yesterday and today and forever. He obtained eternal redemption for us (Gen. 21:33, Psa. 90:1, 2, Isa. 40: 28, Rom. 1:20, Heb. 9:12, 13:8).

El Shaddai

This means "The All Sufficient One", "The God of the Mountains", "God Almighty". God is the all-sufficient source of all of our blessings. God is all-powerful. Our problems are not too big for God to handle. Some scholars suggest that *Shaddai* refers to God's power evident in His judgment. Others suggest that *El Shaddai* means "God of the Mountains". God refers to Himself as *"El Shaddai"* when He confirms His covenant with Abraham (Gen. 17:1-3, 35:11, 48:3, 49:25, Psa. 90:2).

Immanuel

This means "God With Us", "I AM". Jesus is God in our midst. In Him, all the fullness of deity dwells in bodily form. This name indicates that Jesus is more than man. He is also God. Isaiah said that the child born to the virgin would be called "Immanuel". He is the radiance of God's glory and the exact representation of His nature (Isa. 7:14, 8:8-10, 9:6, Matt. 1:23, Heb. 1:3).

NOTES:

Chapter 5

The Ten Commandments and You

God

blesses those who

remain in

a covenant

relationship with Him.

He is

their God

and they become

His

holy people.

Chapter 5
The Ten Commandments and You

PERSONAL APPLICATION: Exodus 20:1-17

1. God blesses those who remain in a covenant relationship with Him. He is their God and they become His holy people.

2. God explains in great detail what is acceptable to Him.

3. God delivers those who find themselves in bondage. The deliverance may not come instantaneously, but it will come to those who wait and make preparation for His deliverance. That deliverance is based upon obedience to God's expressed will and upon moving when He says to move. When He says you have been delivered and to sin no more, that is His condition—SIN no more.

There are some interesting facts about the 10 commandments. God spoke the commandments and then Israel begged that His voice be heard no more lest they die (Deut. 5:22-29). God then stopped speaking with an audible voice to the whole nation and spoke only to Moses, giving the rest of the commands which Israel should obey.

In verse 7 of Exodus 20, the commandment is against all false swearing, (using God's name in vain, such as: I swear to God, God damn, Jesus Christ as in cursing) blasphemy, and all profane, vain, trivial, light, and irreverent use of God's name in ordinary life. It also refers to using God's name in false religions, witchcraft, conjuring, and abuse of the sacred and holy name whatsoever. The right use of His name is confined to that which is sacred: prayer, praise, prophecy, teaching, worship and communion with God and saints (Mal. 3:16).

Below is a modern example of the Ten Commandments. The first four are having "respect for God" and five through ten having "respect for people."

The Modern Version of the Ten Commandments and You
RESPECT FOR GOD
"You shall love the Lord your God with all your heart."

Commandment	Bible Example	Modern Example
1. You shall have no other gods before me.	The Exodus Exodus 34:11-14	Put God first! Today a "god" may be anything a person allows to rule his daily life: deities of other religions, superstitions, horoscopes, bad habits or addictions, friends, heroes, desire for money, fame or power.
2. You shall not make for yourself an idol.	Golden Calf Exodus 32:1-8	Put your faith in God only. You are not to worship or serve any man-made thing that is thought to have supernatural power: statues of gods of other religions, crystals, pictures, jewelry, amulets, charms, rabbit's foot, or objects thought to have power or "good luck".
3. You shall not misuse the name of the Lord your God.	Don't use God's name in a false oath. Lev. 19:12	Treat God's name with respect. Don't use God's name lightly in making promises or in any other way. This is the name that raised people from the dead, caused the blind to see, and made the paralyzed to walk. It is a powerful name and needs to be used with the right attitude.
4. Remember the Sabbath day by keeping it holy.	God provides enough on the sixth day for the seventh. Exodus 16:23-30	In Jesus' time, very religious people obeyed this commandment by refusing to do any kind of work—even to the point of not helping people in need. Jesus said that Sabbath was made for man's benefit. People should rest from their normal work, but also be available to do good to others. Today, Christians set aside the day to worship God and meet with other Christians.

RESPECT FOR PEOPLE

Commandment	**Bible Example**	**Modern Example**
5. Honor your father and your mother so that you may live long in the land the Lord your God is giving you.	Jesus was obedient to Mary and Joseph. Luke 2:51	Treat your parents with respect no matter what. Your parents have made many sacrifices to raise you. They have changed diapers, lost sleep, bought food, toys and clothes, paid doctor bills and changed their schedules to help you. Even if you don't get along with your parents, they deserve your gratitude. If your parents ask you to do something wrong, respectfully tell them no and suggest a good alternative that they might consider.
6. You shall not murder.	Each person is made in God's image. Genesis 9:6	Personal revenge belongs to God. God will make things right in the end. God has set up governments and rules to deal with murderers. Life and death are in God's hands. Examples: no revenge killing, murder, suicide, abortion or euthanasia (mercy killing). Jesus said we should love our enemies and pray for them.
7. You shall not commit adultery.	Joseph runs from temptation. Genesis 39:1-13	Stay true to your husband or wife. Marriage vows made before God should be kept in spite of difficulties: sex only within marriage relationship, no rape or incest, avoid sexual temptation (provocative videos, movies, television, magazines, computer games or programs, pictures and books). Jesus said that even thinking about another person lustfully is wrong.
8. You shall not steal.	Achan Steals. Joshua 6:17-19 Joshua 7:1-5	Respect the possessions of others. Don't take things that don't belong to you. Examples: shoplifting (taking candy, toys, or anything from the store), taking money or valuables from others, cheating on tests and taxes, photocopying music or any printed material without permission.
9. You shall not bear false witness against your neighbor.	Honesty toward neighbors. Leviticus 19:13	Be trustworthy. Don't falsely accuse or blame someone else. Don't lie about them or to them. Don't gossip. Don't lie to God and to yourself by believing you are perfect. Keep your promises.
10. You shall not covet… anything that belongs to your neighbor.	Life is more than possessions. Eccl. 5:9-18; 6:12	Be content with what you have. Don't long for things that belong to others. Example: their house, car, job, bike, toys, jewelry, clothing, or friends. Ask God to give you what you need. He promises that He will take care of your needs! Seek wisdom and good character, not riches.

The Ten Commandments

Exodus 20:1-17 (New King James Version)

1 "And God spoke all these words, saying:
2 'I am the LORD your God, who brought you out of the land of Egypt, out of the house of bondage.
3 'You shall have no other gods before Me.
4 'You shall not make for yourself a carved image—any likeness of anything that is in heaven above, or that is in the earth beneath, or that is in the water under the earth;
5 you shall not bow down to them nor serve them. For I, the LORD your God, am a jealous God, visiting the iniquity of the fathers upon the children to the third and fourth generations of those who hate Me,
6 but showing mercy to thousands, to those who love Me and keep My commandments.
7 'You shall not take the name of the LORD your God in vain, for the LORD will not hold him guiltless who takes His name in vain.
8 'Remember the Sabbath day, to keep it holy.
9 Six days you shall labor and do all your work,
10 but the seventh day is the Sabbath of the LORD your God. In it you shall do no work: you, nor your son, nor your daughter, nor your male servant, nor your female servant, nor your cattle, nor your stranger who is within your gates.
11 For in six days the LORD made the heavens and the earth, the sea, and all that is in them, and rested the seventh day. Therefore the LORD blessed the Sabbath day and hallowed it.
12 'Honor your father and your mother, that your days may be long upon the land which the LORD your God is giving you.
13 'You shall not murder.
14 'You shall no commit adultery.
15 'You shall not steal.
16 'You shall not bear false witness against your neighbor.
17 'You shall not covet your neighbor's house; you shall not covet your neighbor's wife, nor his male servant, nor his female servant, nor his ox, nor his donkey, nor anything that is your neighbor's.' "

In verse 11, it is explained in chapter 24 and explains the Sabbath.

Honor your parents. This is the first commandment of the ten with a promise (Eph. 6:2-3). It implies a shorter life, proving there is no set time to die and suggesting that man basically determines his own length of life and destiny (Psa. 91; 1 Cor. 11:30).

Verse 13 - this law does not prohibit killing as punishment for crimes, or killing in war, which God Himself commanded these same people to do, but it does prohibit killing for malice, and premeditative and willful destruction of man who was made in the image of God. All violence, a plan or a scheme, assault and battery, hatred and anger, vengeance, and danger to human life in general was forbidden.

In verse 14, this commandment prohibits all unlawful sexual relationships and upholds the sacredness and divine appointment of marriage for the propagation and multiplication of the human race.

In verse 15, this commandment prohibits secret and open removal of the property of another, any injury done to it, and carelessness about that which belongs to a neighbor.

In verse 16, this prohibits false testimony in courts of justice, and lying about the acts, words, and property of a neighbor.

The last commandment, in verse 17, prohibits the inward desire of the heart from longing for, scheming, and putting forth any effort to acquire anything that belongs to another.

The Beatitudes

Matthew 5:3-12 (NKJV)

3 " 'Blessed are the poor in spirit, For theirs is the kingdom of heaven.
4 Blessed are those who mourn, For they shall be comforted.
5 Blessed are the meek, For they shall inherit the earth.
6 Blessed are those who hunger and thirst for righteousness, For they shall be filled.
7 Blessed are the merciful, For they shall obtain mercy.
8 Blessed are the pure in heart, For they shall see God.
9 Blessed are the peacemakers, For they shall be called sons of God.
10 Blessed are those who are persecuted for righteousness' sake, For theirs is the kingdom of heaven.
11 Blessed are you when they revile and persecute you, and say all kinds of evil against you falsely for My sake.
12 Rejoice and be exceedingly glad, for great is your reward in heaven, for so they persecuted the prophets who were before you.' "

What do the Beatitudes mean?

Jesus surprised His disciples by telling them what kind of people would be blessed by God. His list of traits are called Beatitudes, meaning "to bless" or "to make happy".

Poor of Spirit

This word was taken from a Greek word meaning "to crouch". It can mean lowly, afflicted, helpless, powerless to solve a problem, lacking wealth and education, or begging. Is there a problem or situation in your life that is beyond your control? Are you reduced to begging God for help? God promises to help the poor of spirit.

Mourn

The word means "to wail". This is deeper than sadness; it is despond and despair. Do you know anyone who is crushed with the disappointments of life? God promises to comfort.

Meek

Meekness means humility, a gentleness of spirit, or a mild disposition. A meek person is one who trusts God and accepts today's circumstances as God's best for them, even if situations in their lives are painful, frightening, frustrating, or annoying. Two of the most powerful people in the Bible, Jesus and Moses, were considered "meek" (Num. 12:3, Matt. 11:29, 21:5).

Hunger and thirst after righteousness

These people eagerly desire (or crave) righteousness. Righteousness is holy and upright living, conforming to God's standard.

Merciful

These people are kind, even to those who treat them without respect. They forgive. God is kind to us, even though sometimes we treat Him and His commands without respect. Isaiah 55:7 says, *"Let the wicked forsake his way and the unrighteous man his thoughts; Let him return to the LORD, and He will have mercy on him, and to our God, for He will abundantly pardon," (NKJV).* Is there someone you need to pardon? If we refuse to forgive, God will not forgive us.

Pure of Heart

This person approaches life with innocence and blamelessness. Psalm 73:1 says, *"Truly God is good ... To such as are pure in heart," (NKJV).*

Peacemakers

These are people who want peace. They do not stir up fights or arguments. They do not look for reasons to complain or to say bad things about others. James 3:18 says, *"Now the fruit of righteousness is sown in peace by those who make peace," (NKJV).*

Persecuted for righteousness

These people are teased, harassed, harmed, or bothered by others because they choose to do what is right. Jesus said, *"A servant is not greater than his master. "If they persecuted Me, they will also persecute you," (Jn. 15:20, NKJV).* He said, *"Rejoice in that day and leap for joy! For indeed your reward is great in heaven," (NKJV, Lk. 6:23).* You will have a great reward when you suffer for the Lord.

Reference Book: Modern Ten Commandments and the Beatitudes Rose Book of Charts, Maps, and Time Lines

NOTES:

Chapter 6

My Savior is Jesus

"I have complete confidence that

God is able

to take care of any situation and provide

an answer to any question or problem -

He has all the resources

of the universe to draw upon in

helping each one of us

through any type of crisis if

we will trust Him."

Charles Stanley

Chapter 6

My Savior is Jesus

Who is Jesus Christ?

Jesus Christ is a man. He is unlike any other person who ever lived. He was born into the world a helpless infant, and grew from childhood into adulthood. He laughed and cried. He worked, grew tired, and rested. He felt the full range of emotions any human being is subject to: sorrow and joy, fear and frustration, love and anger. As a man, Jesus experienced everything you and I experience in this life. Even though He never sinned, He still suffered the consequences of the sins of others. He knew disappointment, rejection, and betrayal. He faced every temptation that we face and to an even greater degree for He resisted unto the end (Heb. 4:15).

As a real man, Jesus died a real death. The cross He hung upon had real splinters. Real nails pierced His flesh and held Him there. Real blood drained from His veins and dripped to the earth. Jesus lived as a man and died as a man.

- *His birth.* Jesus, the human, divine Son of God, supernaturally incarnate being born of the Virgin Mary, was fathered by no man but God Himself (Luke 1:26-35). Jesus was born in Bethlehem, a town about six miles south of Jerusalem, toward the end of Herod the Great's reign as king of the Jews (37-4 B.C.). Early in His life, He was taken to Nazareth, a town of Galilee. There, He was brought up by His mother, Mary, and her husband, Joseph, a carpenter by trade. He was known as "Jesus of Nazareth" or "Jesus of Nazareth, the son of Joseph" (Jn. 1:45). Jesus was His mother's firstborn child; He had four brothers (James, Joses, Judas, and Simon) and a number of sisters (Matt. 13:55, Mk. 6:3). In this Scripture, it is proof that Jesus learned the carpenter trade and worked at it, perhaps up until He entered the ministry. Joseph apparently died before Jesus began His public ministry. The only incident noted from Jesus' first thirty years (after his infancy) was His trip to Jerusalem with Joseph and Mary when He was twelve years old (Lk. 2:41-52). Since He was known in Nazareth as "the carpenter" in Mark 6:3, He may have taken Joseph's place as the family breadwinner at an early age.

*Jewish law and custom required every father to do four things for a firstborn son:

1. Circumcise him (Gen. 17:10-14).
2. Redeem him (Exod. 13:2, 12; Num. 3:42-51).
3. Teach him the law (Deut. 6:6-9; 11:19-20).
4. Teach him a trade. This was founded upon the maxim: "He who teaches not his son to do some work is as if he taught him robbery."

- *His life.* Jesus is the only person who lived who never committed a single sin (1 Pet. 2:22). He lived a life of love and perfect righteousness; even his enemies could find nothing of which to accuse Him (Mk. 14:55).

- *His words.* (Jn. 7:46) He was untrained and from a little-known family in a small town, yet He debated and refuted the most highly regarded scholars of His day (Luke 20:26, 40), and they could not find fault with His simple reasoning. Nothing He said gave an excuse to deliver Him to death. The people who heard Him speak were astonished at His teachings. He had a unique wisdom and authority in His voice (Matt. 7:28-29). Jesus' perfect revelation of the Father is also expressed when He is described as the Word (*logos*) of God (Jn. 1:1-18). In the New Testament, Christ is portrayed as the personal wisdom of God (1 Cor. 1:24, 30), the One through whom all things were created (1 Cor. 8:6, Col. 1:16, Heb. 1:2). Though He wrote nothing, Jesus' words have been recorded by eye witnesses and reproduced in more languages and have sold more copies than any book ever written. His words have stood the test of time, changing individual lives and guiding whole civilizations for over 2000 years.

- *His deeds.* Jesus did things no man before or since has done (Jn. 21:25). He performed miracles of every sort showing His power over disease (Matt. 4:23), Satan and demons (Luke 11:14), the forces of nature (Mk. 4:41), even death itself (Jn. 11:43-44). He had the spiritual gifts of knowledge and discernment, which He possessed to the fullest measure (Lk. 5:22, 1 Cor. 12:4-11). For a time, Jesus' healing aroused great popular enthusiasm throughout Galilee. However, the religious leaders and teachers found much of Jesus' activity disturbing. He refused to be bound by their religious ideas. He became friends with social outcasts. He insisted on healing sick people on the Sabbath day. He believed that healing people did not profane the Sabbath but honored it, because it was established by God for the rest and relief of human beings (Luke 6:6-11). This is the true will of God.

- *His death and resurrection.* Being perfectly righteous, Jesus was the only person whose death was wholly avoidable and undeserved. Though He didn't have to die, Jesus chose to suffer a shameful and tortuous death on the cross, dying in our place. His death wrought changes in the heavens (Mk. 15:33), on the earth (Mk. 15:38), and in the hearts of men (Mk. 15:39). Jesus did not remain dead, but came forth out of the tomb on the third day. He alone conquered death, Hell, and the grave. He is the Lamb of God who died for mankind's sin, Lord of Life who rose from the dead, and the Ascended Lord, our Great High Priest, who intercedes now for His people at the right hand of God's throne from which He will come to Earth a second time to receive His redeemed Church and judge the earth in righteousness. He is the Founder of the Christian Church and the central figure of the human race.

- *His work.* His three-fold office was as prophet, priest, and king. As prophet, He is the perfect spokesman of God to the world, fully revealing God's character and will. As priest, Jesus has offered to God by His death a sufficient sacrifice for the sins of the world. Now, from that sacrifice he exercises a ministry of intercession on behalf of His people, you and me. As king, He is "the ruler over the kings of the earth," (Rev. 1:5), the one whose rule over the whole world will be revealed.

- *His finished work.* This is the work of atonement or redemption for the human race which He completed by His death on the cross. It is so perfect that it requires neither repetition nor addition. Because of this, He is called *"Savior of the world," (NKJV, 1 Jn. 4:14)* and *"the Lamb of God who takes away the sin of the world," (NKJV, Jn. 1:29).* His finished work broke Hell's powers. Colossians 2:15 speaks of the *"principalities and powers"* as those evil powers which have controlled humanity. There was no hope of successful resistance against them until Christ confronted them when it looks as if death and Hell had conquered Him too. But on the cross, He conquered death itself, along with all other hostile forces. In His victory, all who believe in Him have a share. *"Thanks be to God, who gives us the victory through our Lord Jesus Christ," (NKJV,1 Cor. 15:57).* This saving work includes the reconciliation of sinners to God (2 Cor. 5:19, Col. 1:20).

- *His present work.* The Holy Spirit was sent to dwell in His people (Jn. 16:7). The fulfillment of this promise from the Father was announced by Peter on the Day of Pentecost (Acts 2: 33). This promise can be traced back to John the Baptist, who prophesied that Jesus would *"baptize you with the Holy Spirit," (NKJV, Mk. 1:8).* Paul, spoke of *"Christ who died, and furthermore is also risen, who is even at the right hand of God, who also makes intercession for us," (NKJV, Rom. 8:34; also see Heb. 7:25).* Jesus' presence with God the Father as His people's representative provides the assurance that their requests for spiritual help are heard and granted. This is a powerful incentive for His followers. No good thing that Jesus seeks for them is withheld by the Father. The exaltation of Christ is presented in the New Testament as the fulfillment of Psalm 110:1, *"Sit at My right hand till I make Your enemies Your footstool."* This means that Christ reigns from His present place of exaltation and must do so until all His enemies are overthrown. Those enemies belong to the spiritual realm. *"The last enemy that will be destroyed is death," (NKJV, 1 Cor. 15:26).*

- *His place in history.* No one had greater influence upon the course of history, no name has inspired so many acts of heroism, mercy, and devotion. His birth marks the dividing of history, from BC & AD, for after His coming nothing has been the same.

JESUS CHRIST IS GOD

Christianity is the only religion whose Founder not only claimed to show the way to God, but actually claimed to *be* God. Indeed, He is the only man who could make such a claim and be believed.

The human-divine Son of God, supernaturally incarnate, was born of the Virgin Mary; He is the Lamb of God who died for mankind's sin and is the Lord of Life who rose from the dead, the Ascended Lord, our Great High Priest who intercedes now for His people at the right hand of God's throne from which He will come to Earth a second time to receive His redeemed Church and judge the Earth in righteousness.

When Jesus made His declaration before the high priest and His colleagues, He did so in response to the question: *"Are You the Christ the Son of the Blessed?" (NKJV, Mk. 14:61). "He replied, 'I am,' " (NKJV, Mk. 14:62). "It is as you said," (NKJV, Matt. 26:64).*

Jesus was acclaimed as the Son of God at His baptism (Mk. 1:11). He also was given this title by the angel Gabriel at the annunciation: *"That Holy One who is to be born will be called the Son of God," (NKJV, Lk. 1:35).* The Gospel of John especially makes it clear that the Father-Son relationship belongs to eternity, that the Son is supremely qualified to reveal the Father because He has His eternal being *"in the bosom of the Father," (NKJV, Jn. 1:18).*

"Doubting Thomas" had to see with his own eyes and touch Him. *(NKJV, Jn. 20:27-28).* John declared that the Word existed not only *"in the beginning"* where He was *"with God"* but also actually *"was God," (NKJV, Jn. 1:1).* Not only did Christ exist before the worlds were made, it was through Him that they were brought into being (Jn. 1:3). Christ is the eternal Word of God through whom creation was spoken into existence. He is both Creator and Sustainer of all things (Col. 1:16-17).

Jesus claimed a special relationship with God the Father, a unity that could only mean that He, too, was divine (Jn. 10:30). He claimed for Himself the authority to forgive sins (Mk. 2:5) and accepted worship that is due God alone (Jn. 10:38). For these things, He was put to death as a blasphemer (Jn. 19:7), and He refused to save Himself by denying that He was more than a man (Luke 22:70).

Jesus's disciples came to recognize His divinity, and offered Him their worship (Luke 24:52) and obedience. They gave their lives to make Him known to the world. Millions of Christians since have believed their testimony and have come to know for themselves that Jesus Christ is God (Jn. 20:31).

JESUS CHRIST IS THE SAVIOR

The angel who appeared to Mary and told her of her coming childbirth said that she was to name her child "Jesus" (Luke 1:31). The name means "the Lord saves" for Jesus was to be the One through whom God would save mankind from the destruction of sin. Jesus was also given the title "Christ," meaning "anointed one". He was the One whose coming was foretold by the prophets, who would be anointed by God to bring about the salvation of His people.

This was the purpose of Jesus' coming into the world. This was the reason He was born, the reason He lived, the reason He died, the reason he rose from the grave. It is the reason He carries on even now a ministry of intercession before the Father in Heaven (Heb. 7:25). He was given the task of saving a lost mankind, and He accomplished it completely (Jn. 19:30). Through Jesus, the door is open for anyone to be saved from sin and to return to God. He is the Savior.

He is called *"Savior of the world," (NKJV, 1 Jn. 4:14)* and *"the Lamb of God who takes away the sin of the world!" (NKJV, Jn. 1:29).* If we reject Jesus, we reject any hope of salvation, for there is no salvation apart from Him. He is the Savior, and there is no other (Acts 4:12, Jn. 14:6). There is but one mediator, one link between man and God, the God-man Jesus Christ (1 Tim. 2:5). There is but one way back to God for lost men and women (Jn. 14:6). We must come God's way or not at all.

JESUS CHRIST IS THE LAMB OF GOD, THE LION AND KING

John the Baptist publicly identified Jesus as *"the Lamb of God who takes away the sin of the world!" (NKJV, Jn. 1:29, 36).* There are other places in the New Testament Jesus is called a lamb (Acts 8:32; 1 Pet. 1:19; Rev. 5:6). In the Book of Revelation, it speaks of Jesus as a lamb twenty-seven times.

The strongest image from the Old Testament is the suffering servant who *"was led as a lamb to the slaughter," (NKJV, Isa. 53:7)* and who *"bore the sin of many," (NKJV, Isa. 53:12).* This vivid description of Jesus was a pointed announcement of the atonement He would bring about on man's behalf.

Jesus is called not only the Lamb but also the Lion (Rev. 5:5). In strength and majesty He shall conquer all of His enemies. Actually, they are already vanquished. When Christ returns in power and glory, all will bow and acknowledge Him as Lord, those on Earth and those under the Earth (Phil. 2:10-11). He shall be the Judge and Ruler of all the nations (Rev. 19:15-16) and shall reign as King of kings forever (Rev. 11:15).

Though He is not yet universally recognized as King, even now Jesus has been given all authority in Heaven and on Earth (Matt. 28:18). All who now resist Him do so in vain. They continue only by His grace as he patiently gives them time to repent and uses their resistance for His own purposes. All must submit to His will either voluntarily or not.

Jesus is Lord of all the world and all of life. He is Lord not only of the Church, but of every institution, government, and individual. He reigns not only over the "religious" parts of our lives, but over every part: our homes and our jobs, our time and our money, our communities and our nations.

There is nothing that is not under Jesus' authority, nothing that is not to be submitted to His Lordship. We must seek to do His will in all things, and seek to see His will done in all areas of life, in all parts of the world. For Jesus is Lord of all.

'Worthy is the Lamb who was slain
To receive power and riches and wisdom,
And strength and honor and glory and blessing!' "
And every creature which is in heaven and on the earth
and under the earth and such as are in the sea,
and all that are in them, I heard saying:
'Blessing and honor and glory and power
Be to Him who sits on the throne,
And to the Lamb, forever and ever!' "
(NKJV, Rev. 5:12-13)

NOTES:

Chapter 7

Jesus Is

Jesus said to him,

"I am the way,

the truth, and the life.

No one comes to

the Father

except through

Me."

John 14:6

Chapter 7

Jesus is:

God: *"In the beginning was the Word, and the Word was with God, and the Word was God," (NKJV, Jn. 1:1).*

One with God: *" 'I and My Father are one,' " (NKJV, Jn. 10:30).*

Eternal: *"He laid His right hand on me, saying to me, 'Do not be afraid; I am the First and the Last,' " (NKJV, Rev. 1:17b).*

Omnipresent: Omnipresent means present everywhere. *"And He put all things under His feet, and gave Him to be the head over all things to the church, which is His body, the fullness of Him who fills all in all," (NKJV, Eph. 1:22, 23).*

Omniscient: Omniscient means all-knowing. *"Lord, You know all things." (NKJV, Jn. 21:17).*

Life giving: *"In Him was life, and the life was the light of men," (NKJV, Jn. 1:4).*

Often in the scriptures, Jesus is called or compared to God's names found in the Old Testament. Jesus would call attention to His divine nature by comparing Himself to several names used for God the Father. Here are a few examples of Jesus being compared to Father God:

El Olam: The Beginning and the End: *"I am Alpha and the Omega, the Beginning and the End, the First and the Last," (NKJV, Rev. 22:13).*

Jehovah-Jireh: The Lord will Provide: *"Jesus said to them, 'I am the bread of life. He who comes to Me shall never hunger, and he who believes in Me shall never thirst,' " (NKJV, Jn. 6:35).*

YHWH-Rohi: *" 'I am the good shepherd. The good shepherd gives His life for the sheep,' " (NKJV, Jn. 10:11)*

YHWH-Tsidkenu: The Lord is Righteousness: *"For He made Him who knew no sin to be sin for us, that we might become the righteousness of God in Him," (NKJV, 2 Cor. 5:21).*

YHWH-Rapha: The Lord Who Heals: *"Who Himself bore our sins in His own body on the tree, that we, having died to sins, might live for righteousness— by whose stripes you were healed," (NKJV, 1 Pet. 2:24).*

El Shaddai: The All Sufficient One: *"My grace is sufficient for you, for My strength is made perfect in weakness," (NKJV, 2 Cor. 12:9).*

Immanuel: God With Us: *" 'They shall call His name Immanuel,' which is translated, 'God with us', " (NKJV, Matt. 1:23).*

YHWH-Shalom: The Lord is Peace: *" 'Peace I leave with you, My peace I give to you,' " (NKJV, Jn. 14:27).*

NOTES:

Chapter 8

Who is the Holy Spirit?
Why is He my Helper?

Your spiritual transformation
is primarily the work of the
Holy Spirit.
He is the Master Sculptor.
He is the Potter –
You are the Clay.

Chapter 8

Who is the Holy Spirit? Why is He my Helper?

Who is the Holy Spirit?

The Holy Spirit is probably the least understood member of the Trinity. The Holy Spirit is not just a vague, impersonal force or influence. He is a Person who *speaks* (Acts 10:19), *hears* (Jn. 16:13), and *acts* (Jn. 16:14). He can *be lied to* (Acts 5:3), *grieved* (Eph. 4:30), and *blasphemed* (Matt. 12:31). The Holy Spirit is not just an emanation from God. He is God, in co-equal union with God the Father and God the Son.

Let's look at Acts 10:38 to see the distinct identification of the Father, the Son, and the Holy Spirit.

> "God *anointed* Jesus *of Nazareth with the* Holy Spirit *and with* power, *who went about doing good and healing all who were oppressed by the devil, for God was with Him," (NKJV).*

In this verse, we witness the Father anointing Jesus with the Holy Spirit—three distinct Persons working together for one common purpose. Here is another example:

> *"When He had been baptized, Jesus came up immediately from the water; and behold, the heavens were opened to Him, and He saw the* Spirit of God *descending like a dove and alighting upon Him. And suddenly a* voice came *from heaven, saying, 'This is My beloved Son, in whom I am well pleased,' " (NKJV, Matt. 3:16-17).*

The Holy Spirit. Father God on the throne.

This being Jesus' baptism, you will notice the members of the Godhead manifest as three distinct Persons. First, *Jesus* was baptized by John. The *Spirit of God* descended on Him, and finally *God the Father* declared from Heaven, "This is My beloved Son in whom I'm well pleased." All three members were working together for the same purpose.

If God the Father is God transcendent (matchless, beyond compare/comparison), dwelling in the highest Heaven above all creation, then the Holy Spirit is God immanent, present everywhere in the midst of creation. If Jesus is Emmanuel, God with us, then the Holy Spirit is the Comforter, God within us.

The Holy Spirit means a lot more than we could ever imagine. In Him, He brought all power, the peace and presence of God. He came ***to live in us*** and to have fellowship with us constantly.

> Jesus told His disciples, " '*However, I am telling you nothing but the truth when I say it is profitable (good, expedient, advantageous) for you that I go away. Because if I do not go away, the Comforter (Counselor, Helper, Advocate, Intercessor, Strengthener, Standby) will not come to you [into close fellowship with you]; but if I go away, I will send Him to you [to be in close fellowship with you],' " (Amplified Classic Edition, Jn. 16:7).*

What they didn't understand at the time was that Jesus was with them, yes, but the Holy Spirit would come to live in them. He is the same Holy Spirit—Comforter, Counselor, Helper, Advocate, Intercessor, Strengthener and Standby—who lives in us today. We have all of His authority, strength, comfort, creativity and help. It is available to us right now when we need it. All we have to do is ASK.

What does the Holy Spirit do?

The Holy Spirit is the divine agent who carries out the Father's will in His dealing with believers. His activity begins even before conversion when He convicts the sinner of his guilt and draws him to Christ (Jn. 16:8). Then it is the Holy Spirit who regenerates the repentant sinner, reviving the dead spirit within and giving new life (Jn. 3:5-6). Next, He takes up residence within the believer and dwells there (Rom. 8:9), His presence a seal of ownership marking him as God's property (2 Corinthians 1:22).

The Holy Spirit is the source of the power by which believers come to Christ and see with new eyes of faith. From then on, it is the Holy Spirit who directs and empowers every step of our Christian life. It is impossible to overestimate His activity within us and on our behalf. Jesus said that the Holy Spirit would take His place, becoming to all believers everything that Jesus was to His twelve disciples (Jn. 14:16).

Do not overlook the importance of the Holy Spirit. Scripture is clear about not only His vital role, but also His divine actions. Here are some of the countless things the Spirit of God continues to do today. The Holy Spirit appears in the Gospel of John as the power by which Christians are brought to faith and helped to understand their walk with God. He brings a person to new birth: *"That which is born of the flesh is flesh, and that which is born of the Spirit is spirt," (New King James Version, Jn. 3:6); "It is the Spirit who gives life," (NKJV, Jn. 6:63).* The Holy Spirit is the Helper, Comforter, or Advocate whom Jesus promised to the disciples after His ascension. He guides believers into all truth with what He hears from the Father and the Son (Jn. 15:26). It is a remarkable fact that each of the persons of the Godhead serves the others as all defer to one another. The Son says what He hears from the Father (Jn. 12:49-50); the Father witnesses to and glorifies the Son (Jn. 8:16-18, 50, 54); the Father and Son honor the Holy Spirit by commissioning Him to speak in Their name (Jn. 14:16, 26); the Holy Spirit honors the Father and Son by helping the community of believers.

- He helps us (Rom. 8:26)
- He guides us (Jn. 16:13)
- He teaches us (Jn. 14:26)
- He speaks (Rev. 2:7)
- He reveals (1 Cor. 2:10)
- He instructs (Acts 8:29)
- He testifies of Jesus (Jn. 15:26)
- He comforts us (Acts 9:31)
- He calls us (Acts 13:2)
- He fills us (Acts 4:31)
- He strengthens us (Eph. 3:16)
- He prays for us (Rom. 8:26)
- He prophesies through us (2 Pet. 1:21).
- He bears witness to the truth (Rom. 9:1)
- He brings joy (1 Thess. 1:6)
- He casts out demons (Matt. 12:28)
- He brings freedom (2 Cor. 3:17)
- He helps us to obey (1 Pet. 1:22)
- He calls for Jesus' return (Rev. 22:17)
- He transforms us (2 Cor. 3:18)
- He lives in us (1 Cor. 3:16)
- He frees us (Rom. 8:2)
- He renews us (Titus 3:5)
- He produces fruit in us (Gal. 5:22-23)
- He gives gifts (1 Cor. 12:8-10)
- He leads us (Rom. 8:14)
- He convicts (Jn. 16:8)
- He sanctifies us (2 Thess. 2:13)
- He empowers us (Acts 1:8)
- He unites us (Eph. 4:3-4)
- He seals us (Eph. 1:13)
- He gives peace (Rom. 14:17)

The Holy Spirit's attitude and ministry are marked by generosity. His chief function is to illumine Jesus' teaching to glorify His Person, and to work in the life of the individual believer and the Church. It is important to note that the Holy Spirit never draws attention to Himself.

> *"But when He, the Spirit of Truth (the Truth-giving Spirit) comes, He will guide you into all the Truth (the whole, full Truth). For He will not speak His own message [on His own authority]; but He will tell whatever He hears [from the Father; He will give the message that has been given to Him], and He will announce and declare to you the things that are to come [that will happen in the future]," (Amplified Classic Edition, Jn. 16:13).*

This quality of generosity is very noticeable in the Gospels of Matthew, Mark, and Luke, where the Holy Spirit prepares the way for the births of John the Baptist and Jesus the Son (Matt. 1:20; Lk. 1:15, 35, 41). At the baptism of Jesus, the Spirit of God is manifest in the form of a dove. This completes the presence of the Godhead at the inauguration of the Son's ministry (Matt. 3:16-17; Mk. 1:9-11; Lk. 3:21-22, Jn. 1:33). As you look back, it is broken down for you. I love how Mark 1:9-11 in the AMPC Bible says it:

> *"In those days Jesus came from Nazareth of Galilee and was baptized by John in the Jordan. And when He came up out of the water, at once he [John] saw the heavens torn open and the [Holy] Spirit like a dove coming down [to enter] into Him. [also see Jn. 1:32] And there came a voice out from within heaven, You are My Beloved Son; in You I am well pleased," [also see Psa. 2:7; Isa. 42:1].*

Now Jesus is filled and full with the Holy Spirit as He is led into the wilderness to be tempted (Luke 4:1). His claim, He is anointed by the Spirit of the Lord in fulfillment of Old Testament prophecy (Isa. 61:1; Lk. 4:18-19). Luke 4:18-19 (AMPC) reads,

> *"The Spirit of the Lord [is] upon Me, because He has anointed Me [the Anointed One, the Messiah] to preach the good news (the Gospel) to the poor; He has sent Me to announce release to the captives and recovery of sight to the blind, to send forth as delivered those who are oppressed [who are downtrodden, bruised, crushed, and broken down by calamity], To proclaim the accepted and acceptable year of the Lord [the day when salvation and the free favors of God profusely abound]," [also see Isa. 61:1, 2].*

During Jesus' ministry, Jesus refers to the Spirit of God (Matt. 12:28-29; Lk. 11:20) as **the power** by which He is casting out demons, thereby invading the stronghold of *Beelzebub (*Beelzebub is identified in the New Testament as the devil, "prince of the demons") and freeing those held captive. The Spirit works with the Father and Son in realizing the redeeming power of the Kingdom of God. God's Kingdom is not only the reign of the Son but also the reign of the Spirit, as all share in the reign of the Father.

He is the Person who bears witness to us that we are children of God (Rom. 8:16-17). He *"makes intercession for us with groaning which cannot be uttered," (Rom. 8:26-27).* The Holy Spirit also reveals to Christians the "*deep things of God," (1 Cor. 2:10-12)* and "*the mystery of Christ," (Eph. 3:3-5).* The Holy Spirit acts with God and Christ as the pledge or "*guarantee"* by which believers "*are sealed for the day of salvation" (2 Cor. 1:21-22),* and by "*which they walk and live," (Rom. 8:3-6)* and "*abound in hope with power," (Rom. 15:13).*

Since the Holy Spirit is the present avenue on Earth of expressed power of the Godhead, and Spirit-filled Christians show the fruit of the Spirit, it is imperative that one does not ***grieve the Spirit*** since no further appeal to the Father and the Son on the day of redemption is available.

> *"And do not grieve the Holy Spirit of God [do not offend or vex or sadden Him], by Whom you were sealed (marked, branded as God's own, secured) for the day of redemption (of final deliverance through Christ from evil and the consequences of sin)," (AMPC, Eph. 4:30).*

Do not grieve the Holy Spirit. What does that mean?

Here is a quote from John Bevere, a minister and author, from his book *The Holy Spirit*:

> "We must never forget that the Spirit has taken up permanent residence in us. When you walk into a movie, you are taking Him—the God of the universe who is holy and infinite in might— with you. He's always with you because He promised to never leave nor forsake you. But you will find that when you drag Him into situations that grieve Him, He will suddenly become quiet. What should our response be when we have caused the Spirit sorrow? We should immediately ask for forgiveness, but it must be a deep, sincere apology."

When we read 2 Corinthians 7:11 to the Corinthian church, their disobedience caused a break in their fellowship with God. *"Just see what this godly sorrow produced in you! Such earnestness, such concern to clear yourselves, such indignation, such alarm, such longing to see me," (New Living Translation).*

While we believers are in right standing with God, we still have to re-establish communion with the Holy Spirit when we have saddened Him. Just as the Apostle Paul did with the Corinthians until they were truly sorry, so the Holy Spirit persists in convicting us because He is zealous for our genuine fellowship. Godly sorrow produces a genuine earnestness to clear things up and a longing in your soul to be reconnected in communion. I am very thankful that the Holy Spirit is quick to forgive!

Let's look for a moment and consider the working of the Spirit in the Old Testament. The Spirit is the energy of God in creation (Gen. 1:2; Job 26:13; Isa. 32:15). God endows man with personal life by breathing into his nostrils the breath of life (Gen. 2:7). The Spirit strives with fallen man (Gen. 6:3), and comes upon certain judges and warriors with charismatic power (Joshua in Num. 27:18; Othniel in Judg. 3:10; Gideon in Judg. 6:34; Samson in Judg. 13:25; 14:6). However, the Spirit departs from Saul because of his disobedience (1 Sam. 16:14).

As we look forward to the ministry of Jesus Christ, the Holy Spirit inspired Isaiah to prophesy: *"The Spirt of the Lord will rest on Him," (NLT, Isaiah 11:2).* The Holy Spirit inspired Jesus with wisdom, understanding, counsel, might, knowledge, fear of the Lord, righteousness, and faithfulness. (Isa. 11:2-5). This is also the 7-fold anointing of the Messiah, (the 7 Spirits of God; Isa. 11:2). Here, we come full cycle to the New Testament where Jesus claims the fulfillment of this prophecy in Himself (Isa. 61:1-2; Lk. 4:18-19).

Be Careful not to Grieve Him

"And do not bring sorrow to God's Holy Spirit by the way you live.
Remember, he has identified you as his own …
(NLT, Eph. 4:30)

Fellowship with the Holy Spirit is priceless! His manifest presence is life-giving in every area of living. For Kathryn Kuhlman, this was a way of life. Millions heard her speak about God's love and the power of His Spirit, many experiencing His miraculous healing. In her book, the ***Greatest Power in the World***, Kuhlman explains how the Spirit can be grieved:

> "…. Even though the Holy Spirit is the mighty power of the Trinity, He is sensitive and easily grieved. There is no doubt that this wonderful person may be grieved by bitterness, by wrath, anger, evil speaking. In other words, He can be grieved by anything in the life of an individual that is contrary to meekness, long-suffering, forbearing one another in love, and endeavoring to keep the unity of the Spirit in the bond of peace."

It is very important to understand what grieves (saddens) the Spirit and causes Him to draw back from manifesting His presence in our lives. Carefully read Ephesians 4, which provides the context of what it means to grieve the Holy Spirit. (Pay close attention to verses 1-6 and 17-32).

NOTES:

Chapter 9

How Do I Strive For Holiness?

"God doesn't want you
to become a god;
He wants you
to become godly –
Taking on His values,
His attitude,
His character."

Chapter 9

How do I strive for holiness?

Now that you have been adopted into the family of God, He wants us to go much further with Him. And this is only the beginning of what God wants to do in our lives. This may surprise you, but the plan God has for our lives encompasses our past, our present, and our future (Rom. 8: 29-30).

> "God doesn't want you to become a god;
> He wants you to become godly –
> Taking on His values,
> His attitude and His character"

Can I live a holy life? (Matt. 5:8)

If it were not possible to live a holy life, God would not have commanded it. He said, "*You shall be holy, for I the LORD your God am holy," (New King James Version, Lev. 19:2).* To be holy means to be separated to God. God's nature itself defines holiness. Being set apart to God makes us holy.

We are ***not*** made holy by doing good things. We ***are*** made holy by faith in Christ, just as we are saved by faith. Little by little, as we grow and live with the Lord, we will become more like Christ (2 Cor. 3:18).

As we look to the Lord Jesus, think about Jesus, study about Jesus, pray to the Father and seek to follow the Lord's example, we become like Him. We begin to think like Him and act like Him. We become like Him because we are *set apart* to Him. This is true holiness.

Jesus said, *"Blessed are the pure in heart, for they shall see God," (NKJV, Matt. 5:8).* We can achieve a degree of purity in this life. It comes from God as we grow closer to Him and are more like Him. Although perfection is not totally attainable in this life, it is something we should constantly strive toward and aim for, for Christian maturity and holy living constitute being a responsible son or daughter of God. Holiness is also practical.

Holiness is one of the essential elements of God's nature required of His people. Holiness may also be rendered "sanctification" or "godliness". Holiness is separation from everything profane and defiling and, at the same time, it is dedication to everything holy and pure.

Justification – Justification is God's act of removing the guilt and penalty of sin while at the same time making a sinner righteous through Christ's atoning sacrifice. Justification, then, is based on the work of Christ, accomplished through His blood (Rom. 5:9) and brought to His people through His resurrection (Rom. 4:25).

When God justifies, He charges the sin of man to Christ and credits the righteousness of Christ to the believer (2 Cor. 5:21). *"Through one Man's righteous act the free gift came to all men, resulting in justification of life," (NKJV, Rom. 5:18).* Because this righteousness is *"the righteousness of God"* which is *"apart from the law," (NKJV, Rom. 3:21),* it is thorough; a believer is *"justified from all things," (NKJV, Acts 13:39).* God is "just" because His holy standard of perfect righteousness has remained unlowered, but has been entirely fulfilled in Christ. Further, He is the "justifier" because this righteousness is freely given to the believer (Rom. 3:26; 5:16).

Sanctification – To sanctify is to literally "set apart" for a particular use in a special purpose or work and to make holy or sacred. It is the work of God's grace by which the believer is separated from sin and becomes dedicated to God's righteousness. Accomplished by the Word of God (Jn. 17:7) and the Holy Spirit (Rom. 8:34), sanctification results in holiness or purification from the guilt and power of sin. Sanctification is *instantaneous* before God through Christ (1 Cor. 1:3) and progressive before man through obedience to the Holy Spirit and the Word (1 Thessalonians 4:1-8).

Sanctification as separation from the world and setting apart for God's service is a concept found throughout the Bible.

Sanctification is the atonement. As the process by which God purifies the believer, sanctification is based on the sacrificial death of Christ. We are sanctified by God the Father (Jude 1), God the Son (Heb. 2:11), and God the Holy Spirit (2 Thess. 2:13; 1 Pet. 1:2). Perfect holiness is God's command (1 Thess. 4:7) and purpose. As Paul prayed, *"Now may the God of peace Himself sanctify you completely," (NKJV, 1 Thess. 5:23).* Sanctification is a process that continues during our lives as believers (Heb. 10:14).

The believer has work to do also. Numerous commands in the Bible imply that believers also have a responsibility in the process of sanctification. We are commanded to *"be holy"* (Lev. 11:44; 1 Pet. 1:15-16), to *"be perfect"* (Matt. 5:48), and to *"present your members as slaves of righteousness for holiness,"* (Rom. 6:19). Paul made a strong plea for purity (1 Thess. 4:3-5).

These commands imply obedience on our part and dependence upon grace to grow. As we believe in Jesus, we are *"sanctified by faith in"* Him (Acts 26:18). Through the Holy Spirit, we must also *"put to death the deeds of the body," (NKJV, Rom. 8:13).* Paul itemized the many *"works of the flesh"* from which we must separate ourselves (Gal. 5:19-21).

Glorification – The process of glorification is where God removes all spiritual defects of the redeemed. It first involves the believer's sanctification, where they are made and are being made holy. It is a continual process where the Holy Spirit works to mold believers to the image of Christ. Glorification is the end goal of every Christian's life journey.

What we need to understand and realize is what God's purpose is for you, so you can cooperate with Him and not hinder what He is trying to accomplish in your life. God wants to conform you to the image of Christ. Everything that He brings into our lives or brings us through has this end in view. Knowing what God is up to, we should give ourselves fully to accomplish this purpose. You cannot just sit back and wait. You must focus on the goal that God has in mind for you by devoting our time and energy to Him. Aim to achieve the goal God has set for you. Spare no cost in this quest. Spare no effort in your pressing toward the mark of knowing Christ (Phil. 3: 12-14).

Why do we need to be sanctified?

"What shall we say then? Shall we continue in sin that grace may abound? Certainly not! How shall we who died to sin live any longer in it?" (NKJV, Rom. 6:1-4). We should walk in newness of life. God wants nothing less than holiness for His people, that is, holiness in conduct that springs from holy thoughts, emotions, desires, and determination. It is a willful holiness that exists to produce and perform what is right and recognize and shun what is not.

To summarize the above: Sanctification means a separation to God from the profane, secular, and carnal use to a sacred, religious, and spiritual use. The word means "setting apart". One begins to become sanctified when he begins to consecrate (devote) his life to God, and the process is continued as he continues in his dedication.

What did God do about the problem of our sin nature?

God wants us to have victory over sin that dwells within us. He wants you and I to be an overcomer. God dealt with this problem through the death of Christ on the cross. The Gospel comes as the Good News of the deliverance that God has provided through His Son. Jesus bears the penalty of sin in place of His people (Mark 10:45). He also redeems us from lawlessness and begets an inner desire and ability for good works in service to God and others (Rom. 8:1-16; Titus 2:14).

Also, that sin will no longer have us in its power (Rom. 6:6-7) though we can never say in this life that we are free from all sin because we have a continual choice day after day whether to yield ourselves to sin or to God (James 3:2; 1 Jn. 1:8, 10). We also should never say, "This one sin has defeated me. I give up." The power of Christ's resurrection at work within us (Rom. 6:4, 5, 11) is greater than the power of any ***sin***, no matter how long-established it has been in our lives. To be ***under law*** is to be under a system of trying to earn salvation in our own strength by obeying the law, but to be ***under grace*** is to be justified and to live by the indwelling resurrection power of Christ. We can die to sin, not because of the law forbidding it, but through all the resources that grace provides.

What must I do in order to experience deliverance from sin?

In the Book of Romans, it reveals a new, victorious method for our dealing with sin. Living free of sin's rule is now possible because we are no longer slaves of sin but have become slaves of God, able to choose righteousness rather than being bound to the old nature. Obedience to the Word of God gains a new nature of holiness. Say "No!" to sin whenever it confronts you. Recognize that you are really free from its demands. Believe with conviction that it is your old, sinful nature, not your new nature in Christ, that manifests itself in acts of sin.

The believer's two natures often baffle and confuse him or her. The wisdom found in Romans will help in managing this conflict by identifying which aspects of behavior result from the Holy Spirit's life and which result from the fleshly nature's activity. So, we can navigate our new life with Spirit-induced wisdom and understanding.

The Word of God illuminated by the Holy Spirit is the only true means for transforming the human heart. Salvation by faith is a specific occasion, while the **renewing of the mind by the Word is a continuing process**. The disciple devotes himself to God's Word to be transformed

into a holy person, radiantly Christ-like and radically different from the world. Spiritual disciples devour God's Word because in it is the key to a more dynamic relationship with our living Lord and a greater availability to the Holy Spirit.

Is sanctification a one-time experience or a long process?

It is both! God's work in us transforms us into the image of Christ, and this continues throughout all of our life.

Sanctification really happens in four stages:

1. When we are born again, our sins are forgiven (Jn. 3:7).
2. Sanctification as a crisis experience—our heart is purified, the power of sin is broken; we *"reckon ourselves indeed dead unto sin,"* (James 4:8; Rom. 6:11; Acts 15:9).
3. Spiritual growth—day by day we grow to be more like Christ (Heb. 6:1; Jn. 17:17).
4. Glorification—we will finally be perfect when we see Jesus face to face (1 Jn. 3:2).

What happens if I sin?

Sin breaks our fellowship with God and puts us in danger of leaving the path and wandering away from God again. Acts of sin or rebellion will take away the joy of your salvation. Sin should be confessed immediately, so that your relationship with God can be restored. *"If we confess our sins, He is faithful and just to forgive us our sins and to cleanse us from all unrighteousness," (NKJV, 1 Jn. 1:9).* <u>Sin is serious business</u>. It must never be taken lightly for it is deadly and can destroy the soul. For it is written, *"Therefore, to him who knows to do good and does not do it, to him it is sin," (NKJV, James 4:17).* What this means is sin is not only actively committing evil deeds, it is also passively failing to do what you know God wants you to do.

Do the good you know to do, regardless of the cost. Not to do so is sin! But, we need not despair, for God's grace is greater than our sin (Rom. 5:20-21). If we return to Him in repentance and faith, He will restore us.

What is the simplest way to understand sanctification?

The sanctified life is described most clearly and simply in Galatians 2:20, *"I have been crucified with Christ; it is no longer I who live, but Christ lives in me; and the life which I now live in the flesh, I live by faith in the Son of God, who loved me and gave himself for me," (NKJV).* The sanctified life is an exchanged life; I trade my sinful life for Christ's righteous one. I die in Him; He lives in me.

Holiness is living in the world without partaking of the spirit of the world, and it is the Christian's call. When the Spirit of God reveals to us the true spiritual poverty in which the world exists, it becomes easier to overcome the lures seeking to attract us back into that condition. When we understand the fullness of our inheritance in Christ, the world's offer seems poor indeed. When we truly set our affection on God, the lusts of the flesh are reduced as a problem.

First Things First Author Russell A. Board

FOR A DEEPER STUDY

READ HEBREWS = ENCOURAGING YOU TO STAND FAST IN YOUR FAITH

(The **highlighted** words are "***action words***" that offer specific steps you can take to let God guide your life - at all times.)

In the book of **Hebrews** the ***action invites you*** to;
2:1-4 **Give your full attention** to God's Word and your relationship with Jesus.

3:1 **Let** Jesus and His Word be the foundation and sustainer of your thinking.

4:8-11. **Devote your whole heart** to obeying God and His Word. **Trust** Him to do the things He says He will do.

4:12, 13 **Allow** the Word of God to judge the intents and thoughts of your heart.

4:14. **Be tenacious** in holding on to God's promises. **Aggressively pursue** God, **study** His Word, and **build up** your faith.

4:16. **Draw near** to God with confidence when in need. **Believe** He understands your suffering.

5:12-14 **Recognize** that it is only through a sustained daily effort to apply God's Word to your life that you will become mature.

6:11,12. **Turn** from laziness and **patiently endure**, sustaining diligence in your pursuit of Christ-likeness.

9:11-15 **Celebrate daily** that you have gained access to God through the shed blood of Jesus Christ.

10:22 **Continually draw near** to God with a blameless heart and faith.

11:6 **Seek God** diligently. **Believe** that He will reward you for it.

12:1-3. **Discard** any attitude or practice that hinders your walk with Christ. **Model** your life after Jesus. **Give careful thought and study** to the life of Jesus for encouragement in your struggle with sin.

12: 4-10. **Embrace** God's discipline. **Know** that it is evidence that He is training you as His child.

12:11. **Accept** God's correction as necessary for spiritual growth.

12:25. **Never reject** a message because it makes you uncomfortable. **Accept** <u>correction</u> from God's Word.

13:7. **Honor**, **consider**, and **imitate** those God has put over you to lead you.

13:17,18. **Obey** church leadership. **Recognize** and **cooperate** with leadership to make their job easier. **Pray** for them continuously and faithfully.

FOR A DEEPER STUDY, READ 1 JOHN = <u>EXHIBITING LOVE IS CLEAR EVIDENCE THAT ONE IS A CHRISTIAN</u>

Fellowship with God requires walking in the light and obeying the commandments of God (1:6, 7; 2:3-5). The one *"who practices righteousness is righteous, just as He is righteous,"* (3:7) while *"whoever does not practice righteousness is not of God,"* (3:10). The love of the Father and the love of the world are totally incompatible (2:15-17) and no one born of God is in the habit of practicing sin (3:9; 5:18).

The personal application here, which is very important to a believer, consists of three tests that prove the genuineness of Christianity:

1. The **test of belief** (4:2)
2. The **test of obedience** (2:3)
3. The **test of love** (4:20).

The one who professes to be a Christian, but who cannot pass the test of belief (2:22), the test of obedience (1:6) and the test of love (4:20) **is a liar**. John brings all three tests together in 5:1-5 where he indicates that a profession of Christianity is false unless it is characterized by correct belief, holy obedience, and brotherly love. The same tests are valid today.

In the book of 1 John, he shows the *truth in action*: letting the LIFE of the Holy Spirit bring faith's works alive in you. The scriptures below from 1 John are a breakdown of the *truth in action*––walking in the truth, walking in the light.

1:5-10. **Be open** and transparent in all you do. **Admit** your weakness to God. **Trust** Him to cleanse and forgive.

2:3-6. **Recognize** that only those who obey Jesus really know Him. **Understand** that obedience is the first evidence of love for God. **Know** and **believe** that only those who are learning to live like Jesus know and love Him.

2:9-11. **Recognize** that hate for others means that you are in darkness.

2:15-17. **Do not** set your affections on or live sacrificially on behalf of anything that 1) appeals to your fleshly appetites, 2) appeals to your covetousness or greed, or 3) fosters pride or arrogance.

2:18,19. **Recognize** that the devil brings about all separation and division in the body of Christ.

2:24, 25. Let **God's Word live in you** so that **you can live in God and have eternal life!**

2:29 **Understand** that the best evidence for new birth is in <u>*your conduct*</u> and <u>*behavior.*</u>

3:1, 2 **Look forward** to seeing Christ at His coming. **Know** you will be **transformed** into His likeness when He comes.

3:4-9 **Know** that continued, willful sinning in life contradicts a genuine conversion.

3:7-15. **Understand** that righteousness manifests itself in behavior. **Understand** that righteousness manifests itself in <u>righteous</u> behavior. **Practice** righteousness. **Love** your brother.

3:11-15 **Know** that continued hatred 1) is impossible for those in Christ and 2) no murderer or hater of men has eternal life.

3:16-18 **Know** that love 1) denies its own interests on behalf of others, and 2) is expressed practically.

3:21-24. **Base** your confidence on the witness of the Holy Spirit and growing obedience in your life.

4:1-6 **Exercise** discernment when listening to **any** teaching. **Make sure** all teaching conforms to God's Word.

4:4 **Be assured** that victory is already ours in Christ.

4:7-19 **Understand** that fear shows an absence of love. **Know** that Christ's presence always results in love.

5:1-8 **Understand** that one who is born again 1) loves other believers and 2) obeys the Word of God and the Holy Spirit.

5:4 **Know** that those who are born again can never be conclusively defeated.

5:14,15 **Practice** the principles of faith-filled prayer. Faith is based on your knowledge of God's Word and His character. 1) Know that God hears all prayers that are in accord with His will, and 2) The New Testament elsewhere bases the assurance on asking in Jesus' name (John 14:13, 14; 15:16; 16:23, 24), abiding in Christ and allowing His words to abide in you (John 15:7). 3) Let him ask in faith, with no doubting. For let not that man suppose that he will receive anything from the Lord; he is a double-minded man, unstable in all his ways (James 1:6-8). 4) God wills and cares that we pray. Genuine prayer is not an attempt at precise means of getting God to meet our desires and demands but rather, by surrendering our will to His, we open the doorway to His fullest blessings being released in our lives.

5:16,17 **Pray** for your brother who is in sin. **Know** that all lawlessness is sin.

5:21. **Do not** allow anything to lessen, not even slightly, your worship, service, or devotion to God.

NOTES:

Chapter 10

What is Baptism in the Holy Spirit?

In the Upper Room –
"The baptism
in the Holy Spirit
comes by grace
through faith.
You must **believe**
that **the promise** is
for you also."

Chapter 10

What is baptism in the Holy Spirit?

The most amazing proof of the truth of Christianity lies in the fact that a band of lowly fishermen who, according to the standards of religious leaders of that day, were *"ignorant and unlearned men," (Acts 4:13)* yet were able to go forth against the severest opposition and, under God, bring into existence the most powerful religious movement of all history. With the baptism **in** the Holy Spirit, they were filled with the Spirit. They were not destitute of knowledge for they had *divine knowledge.*

The disciples actually received the Holy Spirit before Jesus ascended into Heaven, "*He breathed on them and said to them, 'Receive the Holy Spirit,' " (NKJV, John 20:22).* But they were not clothed with power until they had been filled with the Spirit on the day of Pentecost. Before Jesus ascended into Heaven after His resurrection, He *commanded* His disciples to "wait" in Jerusalem to receive the gift promised by His Father.

> *"And being assembled together with them, He* ***commanded*** *them not to depart from Jerusalem, but to wait for the Promise of the Father, 'which,' He said, 'you have heard from Me; for John truly baptized with water, but you shall be baptized with the Holy Spirit not many days from now,' " (NKJV, Acts 1:4-5).*

Notice here that Jesus commanded them not to depart from Jerusalem until the promise had come. Why? Because the empowerment of the Spirit is essential to all Kingdom work. The disciples were ready and eager to share the good news of His resurrection. They had firsthand evidence of Christ's victory over death. And Jesus spent days with His disciples; this we learn as we read Acts 1:3. They were ready to get into action! But Jesus looked at them and said, "Don't start your ministry. Don't start preaching the Gospel all over the world, and don't start any churches until you have been clothed with the Spirit's power from on high" (Luke 24:49 paraphrased by author).

On the day of Pentecost, about ten days after Jesus' ascension, some 120 believers were gathered for prayer. These followers of Jesus, both men and women, were engulfed or baptized in God's presence. This revealed presence is also seen in the reference to a "rushing mighty wind". The Holy Spirit is not a "mighty wind". He is a Person. However, the manifestation of His arrival in the upper room took the form of a "mighty wind". When they received the promised gift—the baptism **in** the Holy Spirit—they were filled! (Acts 2:1-4). The Greek word for 'filled' in Acts 2:4 means "*satiated*". According to the dictionary, '*satiate*' means "to supply to excess". Those in the upper room were filled to excess with the Holy Spirit. All of them experienced a greater degree of God's manifest presence in their lives. In addition to the manifestations of fire and wind, another sign of the infilling of the Spirit was the fact that the believers began to speak in other tongues.

As a crowd had gathered to see what was happening,

> *"And there were dwelling in Jerusalem Jews, devout men, from every nation under heaven. And when this sound occurred, the multitude came together, and were confused, because everyone heard them speak in his own language. Then they were all amazed and marveled, saying to one another, "Look, are not all these who speak Galileans? And how is it that we hear, each in our own language [tongue] in which we were born?" (NKJV, Acts 2:5-8).*

The crowd (multitude) was astonished that the Galileans who were considered untrained or unlearned were speaking in many different languages. This expression of God's Spirit was a sign to those who were not yet followers of Jesus. Peter made it clear to them that the good news of salvation has been made available to all who "*call on the name of the LORD,*" *(NKJV, Rom. 10:13).* He also made it abundantly clear that the promise (the gift of the Holy Spirit) was not limited to a certain group or a certain time, but was for all who would put their faith in Christ (Acts 2:37-39).

What is the baptism **in** the Holy Spirit? It is compared to baptism in water (Acts 1:5), suggesting the image of being immersed or covered. The Holy Spirit already dwells within us **if** we are Christians, but baptism means receiving the Spirit in an abundant measure, even to overflowing.

> An example of this: Picture a glass filled with water, that is the first measure of the Holy Spirit when you were first saved. Take the glass filled with the water and drop it into a glass pitcher full of water. Now it is submerged, overflowing and completely covered in the Holy Spirit.

We **yield** ourselves totally and the Holy Spirit fills us completely. A process of **yielding** refers to an assertive, prayerful, heartfelt quest for God. The baptism in the Holy Spirit is not a denomination or a movement but an experience that brings on *"spiritual power"* for intensified service. An anointing signifies being **chosen** and **empowered** to serve God.

While the reactions and responses of people receiving the baptism in the Spirit may vary, the initial evidence is "speaking in tongues", that is, the Holy Spirit gives words to speak in a language we do not know so that we praise God without knowing what we are saying. **The most important manifestation of the Holy Spirit's infilling, however, is what follows: a life yielded to God, directed and empowered by His Spirit for powerful and effective witnessing** (Acts 1:8).

The first thing one thinks of in attaining a victorious Christian life is the need of power. We need power to be able to witness effectively to others and to carry out our chief function as Christians. The purpose of the baptism ***in*** the Holy Ghost is to give us this power.

In Romans 8:1, 2, and 13, we are told that the Holy Spirit frees us from the law of sin and death. Without the Spirit, man's attempts to live a holy life are futile and vain. He cannot, in his own strength, live an overcoming life. He will fail again and again as Paul describes in his experience in Romans 7. Indeed, man's self-righteousness is as filthy rags in the sight of God. Now every Christian has the Spirit of Christ to some degree. Otherwise, he is not a follower of the Lord at all (Rom. 8:9). But the experience as received on the day of Pentecost represents a fuller measure of the Spirit. He was *with* the believer, but now He is ***in*** him. It is the Holy Spirit that gives a man power to live a holy life. Also, in John 7:37-39, the experience received on Pentecost was the *"rivers of living waters"* that Jesus spoke about.

Anyone who has received the baptism of the Holy Ghost intuitively knows that the Bible is the Word of God! Of course, the believer may receive the Holy Spirit and still be subject to mistakes. It is possible for him to do wrong since God never takes away man's free will (Read 1 Tim. 1:19-20, 2 Tim. 2:17-18). But if he yields to the Spirit's leading, the Spirit of the Lord will keep him from serious error. Again, be careful not to grieve the Holy Spirit (Ephesians 4) as mentioned in Chapter 8.

First, the Bible definitely declares, *"**Be filled** with the Spirit," (NKJV, Eph. 5:18)*. An analysis of the Greek verb translated "**be filled**" shows that it is in the present tense, indicating that this blessing is one that we may experience and enjoy now. The fact that the verb **is a command** does not leave the responsive disciple an option in the matter. Being filled with the Holy Spirit is something done for you and to which you submit.

The baptism or infilling of the Holy Spirit is an experience subsequent to Christian conversion, one that comes about through a process of yielding the complete person into the guidance and indwelling of the Holy Spirit. The Holy Spirit is operative in every believer and in the varied ministries of the Church. Still, every believer must answer the question of Acts 19:2, *"Have you received the Holy Spirit since you believed?"*

The ultimate purpose of this experience was for empowered witnessing (Act 1:8) and a deeper dimension of Christian commitment for the achievement of happiness (Eph. 5:19), gratitude (Eph. 5:20), humility (Eph. 5:21) and fruitfulness (Gal. 5:22-23).

Our part is to be filled, to pray, to study God's Word, and to learn to develop our own sensitivity and obedience to the Holy Spirit's lead.

> *"I will give them one heart [a new heart] and I will put a new spirit within them; and I will take the stony [unnaturally hardened] heart out of their flesh, and will give them a heart of flesh [sensitive and responsive to the touch of their God]," (Amplified Classic Edition, Ezek. 11:19).*

How to Receive the Baptism in the Holy Spirit

> *"For the promise [of the Holy Spirit] is to and for you and your children, and to and for all that are far away, [even] to and for as many as the Lord our God invites and bids to come to Himself," (AMPC, Acts 2:39).*

The baptism in the Holy Spirit comes by grace through faith. You must believe that the promise is for you also.

Those who desire to receive the Holy Spirit should fully repent of their sins. Peter told the people this in his sermon preached on the day of Pentecost.

> *Repent (change your views and purpose to accept the will of God in your inner selves instead of rejecting it) and be baptized, every one of you, in the name of Jesus Christ for the forgiveness of and release from your sins; and you shall receive the gift of the Holy Spirit," (AMPC, Acts 2:38).*

A person may not have victory over all bad habits, but they can give up loving them. In their heart, they can turn from what they knows to be evil. Anyone who still loves his sins or still loves the world is not ready to receive the Holy Spirit.

John the Baptist preached in Luke 3:16 the baptism of repentance and told people to prepare for the One Who was to come, Who would baptize them in the Holy Spirit and fire. But John went further than this. He said "*Prepare the way of the Lord, make His beaten paths straight," (AMPC, Lk. 3:4).* There is such a thing as preparing the way of the Lord. Jesus cannot walk with those who follow crooked paths. John the Baptist, who was the first preacher of the baptism in the Holy Spirit should emphasize so strongly that people should prepare their ways before the Lord. It is not the matter of making one's self better; the important thing is that there is a deep desire to draw close to God. "*Draw near to God and He will draw near to you," (New King James Version, James 4:8).* God is looking for people that really want Him, not just His blessings.

It is God's plan if the heart is hungry to receive immediately. When Paul was converted on the Damascus road, he was permitted to spend three days and nights in prayer. It was a time of heart searching and getting his bearings for the new life that was before him. When the Lord told Ananias to go and lay hands on him that he might receive the Holy Spirit and when hands were laid on Paul, he received the Holy Spirit instantly.

Jesus said, "*Blessed are those who hunger and thirst for righteousness, For they shall be filled," (NKJV, Matt. 5:6).* We only have to ask Christ to baptize us. Sometimes it is instant and other times, hands are laid on you. But we are to be encouraged to ask in faith, for it is Father God's desire to give us this gift (Luke 11:13).

Tongues allow our spirit to worship freely without being constrained by the limited vocabulary of our minds. Every believer should be encouraged to seek and want this gift. We only have to ask Jesus Christ to baptize us.

> Prayer: Father God, I believe in my heart that you raised Jesus from the dead. I confess with my mouth (say it out loud) "Jesus is my Lord." Jesus, come into my heart. Please, forgive all of my sins and make me a child of God. Fill me with Your Holy Spirit with the evidence of tongues so that I will have Your power to live for you. Thank you for your free gift of eternal life! In Jesus' name, I pray. Amen!

Begin to worship Him in English as you fix your eyes on Him in Heaven with joy and gratitude for who He is and for all He has done for you. Once English (or your native language) becomes limited, choose *not* to speak in English anymore, and continue to worship. Begin to speak *not* using English and believing in childlike faith you are being filled and formed by the Spirit who flows within. It is as simple as that. Our Father would not give you a gift that is impossible to open and use. Don't make this hard. It must be easy enough for a child to do otherwise it is no longer Christianity.

> *"16 But Jesus called them to Him and said, 'Let the little children come to Me, and do not forbid them; for of such is the kingdom of God.*
> *17 Assuredly, I say to you, whoever does not receive the kingdom of God as a little child will by no means enter it,' (NKJV, Lk. 18:16-17).*

Father God gave speaking in tongues to you to enjoy, to energize and refresh your spirit, to build you up, to have power to witness, to produce health and joy to your entire being. Your spirit is speaking mysteries to God.

Never forget that the gift of tongues is a vital aspect of the empowerment of the Holy Spirit as well as a beautiful part of our intimate relationship with God. So, my hope for you is the same as Paul's: My prayer is for you to embrace this remarkable gift and grow in the power and presence of the Spirit every single day.

Notes:

Chapter 11

The Four Types of Tongues

When you speak in other tongues,
no one understands what
you're saying, because
you're speaking to God.
It's a direct communication
between Your spirit and God.
You're speaking the language that only
He understands.

Praying in tongues charges your spirit,
brings on the power –
like a battery charger
charges a battery.

Chapter 11

The Four Types of Tongues

There is a two-fold function of the gift of tongues.

The Bible describes four basic functions of "tongues". It is for **personal edification** and for **public exhortation**. In the experience of the baptism in or the infilling of the Holy Spirit, "tongues" functions as a sign of the Holy Spirit's presence. Jesus prophesied it as a sign (Mark 16:17). Paul referred to it as a sign (1 Cor. 14:22). And Peter noted its uniformity as a sign-gift in confirming the validity of the Gentiles' experience in the Holy Spirit. (Compare Acts 10:44-46 with 11:16-17 and 15:7-9). Speaking in tongues is a properly expected sign affirming the Holy Spirit's abiding presence and assuring the believer of an invigorated living witness. It is not viewed as a ***qualification for*** fullness of the Holy Spirit but as on ***indication of*** that fullness.

One: Personal Edification: A private affair for self-edification.

> *"2 For one who speaks in an [unknown] tongue speaks not to men but to God, for no one understands or catches his meaning, because in the [Holy] Spirit he utters secret truths and hidden things [not obvious to the understanding]. 3 But [on the other hand], the one who prophesies [who interprets the divine will and purpose in inspired preaching and teaching] speaks to men for their upbuilding and constructive spiritual progress and encouragement and consolation. 4. He who speaks in a [strange] tongue edifies and improves himself, but he who prophesies [interpreting the divine will and purpose and teaching with inspiration] edifies and improves the church and promotes growth [in Christian wisdom, piety, holiness, and happiness]," (Amplified Classic Edition, I Cor. 14:2-4).*

In 1 Corinthians 14:2, Paul's assertion clearly establishes the primary purpose for tongues as the gift of the Spirit for private worship. It is a unique God-ward and not a man-ward gift, unless interpreted so the hearers may understand (reading v. 5). Tongues are intended for personal prayer and to give praise to God. The use of tongues is a means of private self-edification. This practice does not denote selfishness but rather spiritual strengthening. Praying in tongues is praying from the spirit instead of the intellect, and the same is true of singing praises. For Paul, praying and singing, both in tongues and in everyday language, were normal and regular parts of daily prayer and praise. There is no suggestion of hysteria, emotionalism, or abnormality of any kind. Paul thanked God for the self-edification afforded by the full measure of the gift in his own devotional life when you read 1 Corinthians 14:18 (AMPC). When you do not know what to pray for, your spirit prays in an unknown tongue, which is a perfect prayer to God, building you up (v 14).

> *"For if I pray in an [unknown] tongue, my spirit [by the Holy Spirit within me] prays, but my mind is unproductive [it bears no fruit and helps nobody]," (AMPC, I Cor. 14:14).*

You may be asking, "What am I supposed to do?"

"Then what am I to do? I will pray with my spirit [by the Holy Spirit that is within me], but I will also pray [intelligently] with my mind and understanding; I will sing with my spirit [by the Holy Spirit that is within me], but I will sing [intelligently] with my mind and understanding also," (AMPC, 1 Cor. 14:15).

Two: Tongues for Intercession

This is the act of petitioning God or praying on behalf of another person or group. The Spirit also helps in our weaknesses.

> *"26 So too the [Holy] Spirit comes to our aid and bears us up in our weakness; for we do not know what prayer to offer nor how to offer it worthily as we ought, but the Spirit Himself goes to meet our supplication and pleads in our behalf with unspeakable yearnings and groanings too deep for utterance.*
> *27 And He Who searches the hearts of men knows what is in the mind of the [Holy] Spirit [what His intent is], because the Spirit intercedes and pleads [before God] in behalf of the saints according to and in harmony with God's will," (AMPC, Rom. 8:26-27).*

What weakness is Paul referring to? The answer is, *"For we do not know what we should pray.. but the Spirit Himself makes intercession for us with groanings which cannot be uttered," (NKJV, Rom. 8:26).* Our weakness is that we are limited to our understanding of what is going on with that person, situation, or world event. Therefore, we are truly limited in our understanding and we do not know how to pray. But when we rely on and intercede in the Spirit (who knows all things), He prays the perfect will of God through us. The Holy Spirit knows the perfect will of

God for all situations. He will intercede through you or me, as we yield to partner with Him in prayer. The Spirit searches all things and knows all things. Great peace accompanies the knowledge that we are allowing the Holy Spirit to pray through us.

Clarification About Private Tongues

There are occasions when believers who are all filled with the Spirit pray together in tongues. In these times, it is appropriate for all of them to pray together in the Spirit. There are other times when believers should refrain from praying publicly in their prayer languages. Paul made this statement:

> *"Therefore, if the whole church comes together in one place, and all speak with tongues, and there come in those who are uninformed or unbelievers, will they not say that you are out of your mind?" (New King James Version, 1 Cor. 14:23).*

Two groups are identified in this passage. First, Paul mentions *unbelievers*. This refers to those who have not received Jesus Christ as their Lord, those who are outside the faith. The second group is the *uninformed*. These people are believers in Jesus, but they have not been taught about the language of the Spirit. A person belonging to either group would be uncomfortable in an atmosphere where others pray together in tongues. They could easily think of those speaking, "Are you out of your mind?"

However, there are times when a church calls for a believers' prayer meeting. In these meetings, all are *informed* and *believers*. It is perfectly fine for all to pray in tongues as a group when gathered in ministry to the Lord or for intercession.

In other words, Paul is not saying that there is never an appropriate time or place for a group of believers to gather and speak together in what we might call "private tongues". He is simply making the distinction that in "public", when *unbelievers* or the *uninformed* are present in our midst, our expressions of tongues must be appropriate to our environment.

> "39 *So [to conclude], my brethren, earnestly desire and set your hearts on prophesying (on being inspired to preach and teach and to interpret God's will and purpose), and* ***do not forbid or hinder speaking in*** *[unknown]* ***tongues.***
> *40 But all things should be done with regard to decency and propriety and in an orderly fashion," (Amplified Classic Edition, 1 Cor. 14:39-40).*

Paul knew that the Church would mishandle the amazing gift of tongues. So, he urged us, "Use the right type of tongue in the right setting, and do not forbid speaking in tongues because certain believers have misappropriated this extraordinary gift of the Spirit." Unfortunately, the Church is ignorant of many things of the Spirit. This is tragic, because the Holy Spirit is the One who has been sent to empower the Church. God has chosen His Church as the vehicle by which He advances His Kingdom. If we do not wake up to the power that comes with our position in Christ, we will be no different than a king who refused to exercise the power of his throne.

Being baptized in the Holy Spirit with the evidence of speaking in tongues does not mean that you will start prophesying in your church. Remember it is **your prayer language, for self-edification**.

Here are the following reasons for speaking with tongues:

1. Speaking with tongues as the Holy Spirit gives utterance is the unique spiritual gift identified with the Church of Jesus Christ. All other gifts, miracles, and spiritual manifestations were in evidence during Old Testament times, before the Day of Pentecost. This fact came into evidence and became uniquely identified with the Church and was ordained by God for the Church (1 Cor. 12:28; 14:21).
2. Speaking with tongues is a specific fulfillment of prophecies by Isaiah and Jesus. (Compare Isa. 28:11 with 1 Cor. 14:21, and Mk. 16:17 with Acts 2:4; 10:46; 19:6; and 1 Cor. 14:5, 14-18, 39).
3. Speaking with tongues is a proof of the resurrection and glorification of Jesus Christ (John 16:7; Acts 2:26 AMPC).
4. Speaking with tongues is an evidence of the baptism in or the infilling of the Holy Spirit (Acts 2:4; 10:45-46; 19:6).
5. Speaking with tongues is a spiritual gift for self-edification (1 Cor. 14:4; Jude 1:20).
6. Speaking with tongues is a spiritual gift for spiritual edification of the church when accompanied by interpretation (1 Cor. 14:5).
7. Speaking with tongues is a spiritual gift for communication with God in private worship (1 Cor. 14:15).
8. Speaking with tongues is a means by which the Holy Spirit intercedes through us in prayer (Rom. 8:26; 1 Cor. 14:14; Eph. 6:18).
9. Speaking with tongues is a spiritual means for rejoicing (1 Cor. 14:15; Eph. 5:18-19).
10. Paul's application of Isaiah's prophecy seems to indicate that speaking with tongues is also intended as a means of "rest" or "refreshing" (Isa. 28:12; 1 Cor. 14:21).

11. Tongues follow as one confirmation of the Word of God when it is preached (Mark 16:17, 20; 1 Cor. 14:22).

Three: Public Demonstration as a sign

This type of tongues is for public demonstration, ***a sign***.

> *"Thus [unknown] tongues are meant for a [supernatural] sign, not for believers but for unbelievers [on the point of believing], while prophecy (inspired preaching and teaching, interpreting the divine will and purpose) is not for unbelievers [on the point of believing] but for believers," (AMPC, 1 Cor. 14:22).*

These tongues occur when the Holy Spirit transcends our intellect (our mind) and gives us the ability to speak another language of this earth, a language that we do not know how to speak from our own experience or education. This is a type of tongue that operated through the disciples on the Day of Pentecost.

> *"Now there were then residing in Jerusalem Jews, devout and God-fearing men from every country under heaven.*
> *6 And when this sound was heard, the multitude came together and they were astonished and bewildered, because each one heard them [the apostles] speaking in his own [particular] dialect.*
> *7 And they were beside themselves with amazement, saying, Are not all these who are talking Galileans?*
> *8 Then how is it that we hear, each of us, in our own (particular) dialect to which we were born?*
> *9 Parthians and Medes and Elamites and inhabitants of Mesopotamia, Judea and Cappadocia, Pontus and [the province of] Asia,*
> *10 Phrygia and Pamphylia, Egypt and the parts of Libya about Cyrene, and the transient residents from Rome, both Jews and the proselytes [to Judaism from other religions],*
> *11 Cretans and Arabians too–we all hear them speaking in our own native tongues [and telling of] the mighty works of God!" (AMPC, Acts 2:5-11).*

These Jews heard the believers speaking in each of their native earthly tongues. This demonstration was a sign that God was at work among those who believed the Gospel of Jesus, because there was no way the untrained Galileans could perfectly declare the wonders of God in so many languages. Many came to know Jesus because of this expression of the Spirit's power. The primary purpose of tongues as a sign is to grab the attention of one who is not yet a believer.

Four: Tongues for Interpretation

This type of tongue is also for public ministry. Unlike tongues as a sign, these tongues are heavenly languages that are not spoken anywhere on the earth. *Tongues for interpretation* are the type of tongues Paul referred to as a **spiritual gift** when he said, "…to another *different kinds of tongues*, to another *the interpretation of tongues,*" *(New King James Version, 1 Cor. 12:10).*

Heavenly tongues (which account for three of the four types of New Testament tongues) cannot be translated, for they transcend our human understanding, but they can be interpreted. Any expression of tongues that falls under *tongues for interpretation* should always come with an interpretation. Without this interpretation, the church cannot be edified, and this tongue is exclusively given for the church's edification (see 1 Corinthians 14).

> *"So God has appointed some in the church [for His own use]: first apostles (special messengers); second prophets (inspired preachers and expounders); third teachers; then wonder-workers; then those with ability to heal the sick; helpers; administrators; [speakers in] different (unknown) tongues.*
> *29 Are all apostles (special messengers)? Are all prophets (inspired interpreters of the will and purposes of God)? Are all teachers? Do all have the power of performing miracles?*
> *30 Do all possess extraordinary powers of healing? Do all speak with tongues? Do all interpret?" (Amplified Classic Edition, 1 Cor. 12:28-30).*

Paul is speaking of the public gifts which God has ordained for ministry in the church. Are all apostles? No. Are all prophets? No. Are all teachers? No. Do all speak in or interpret tongues *as a public ministry*? No. Paul's point is that we should all flourish in specific gifts that God has placed on our lives. Not everyone in the church will operate in tongues *as* a public ministry.

The Difference Between the Two Public Tongues

Later in Pauls' letter to the Corinthians, he explains the difference between the two types of public tongues:

"Thus [unknown] tongues are meant for a [supernatural] sign, not for believers but for unbelievers [on the point of believing], while prophecy (inspired preaching and teaching, interpreting the divine will and purpose) is not for unbelievers [on the point of believing] but for believers.
23 Therefore, if the whole church assembles and all of you speak in [unknown] tongues, and the ungifted and uninitiated or unbelievers come in, will they not say that you are demented?" (AMPC, 1 Cor. 14:22-23).

If you do not understand that there are different types of tongues, you might think that Paul completely contradicted himself when he wrote this. First he said, "Tongues are a sign for the unbeliever." Then, in the very next verse, we read, "If you speak with tongues, unbelievers will think you are demented" (which means crazy, insane; mad). With a better understanding of the four distinct tongues, we can see that Paul is writing about two different types of tongues.

The first type of tongue Paul mentions (tongues for a sign) is the type that draws unbelievers because it serves as a sign to them. The second type of tongue (tongues for interpretation) is only meant for the church's edification; these tongues are not signs to the unbeliever. In fact, Paul states that without interpretation, the act of believers speaking in the second kind of tongues would actually cause unbelievers to think we are crazy. Paul was instructing the church not to create an environment of confusion by misusing tongues for interpretation. Earlier, in the same chapter, Paul makes it clear that tongues are not to breed confusion, but rather to bring understanding and revelation.

"I thank God that I speak in [strange] tongues (languages) more than any of you or all of you put together;
19 Nevertheless, in public worship, I would rather say five words with my understanding and intelligently in order to instruct others, than ten thousand words in a [strange] tongue (language)," (AMPC, 1 Cor. 14:18-19).

It is pretty simple: if a public tongue is used, it must be interpreted for the benefit of those present. Otherwise, it would be better to simply communicate in a known language.

The function of tongues for public exhortation, the church, is a valuable part of worship:

There is more on the function of "tongues"— public exhortation. First Corinthians 14 bases the gifts of the Spirit on the one sure foundation of love (1 Cor. 14:1). We must recognize that it can be a vital and valuable part of worship when placed in its proper setting for the edification of the body (1 Cor. 14:12-13).

Prophecy and tongues with interpretation minister to the entire congregation, being understood by all. This understanding serves to affirm the fact of and distinguish the application of the two distinct ways "tongues" may be manifested—in private or public, in personal devotion or in corporate gatherings. Tongues exercised in a church meeting must therefore be interpreted.

In 1 Corinthians 14:1, Paul states here that noting love as our primary pursuit, prophecy is to be welcomed for the "edification and exhortation and comfort" of the congregation, corporately and individually (v 3). Such encouragement of each other is "prophecy", not "words" in the sense of the Bible, which uses the very words of God, but in the sense of human words the Holy Spirit uniquely brings to mind. The practice of the gift of prophecy is one purpose of Holy Spirit fullness (Acts 2:17).

The operation of the gift of prophecy is encouraged by Peter (1 Pet. 4:11), and Paul says that it is within the potential of every believer (1 Cor. 14:31). It is intended as a means of broad participation among the congregation, mutually benefiting each other with anointed, loving words of upbuilding, insight, and affirmation. Such prophecy may provide such insight that hearts are humbled in and during **worship** of God suddenly made aware of His Spirit's knowledge of their need and readiness to answer it (1 Cor. 14:24-25). Prophecy of this order is also a means by which vision and expectation are prompted and provided and without which people may become passive or neglectful (1 Sam. 3:1; Prov. 29:18; Acts 2:17). There are specific guidelines for the operation of the gift, as with all gifts of the Holy Spirit, to ensure that one gift does not replace the exercise of others or take over the authority of spiritual leadership. All such prophecy is subject to the plumb-line of God's eternal Word, the Bible—the standard by which all prophetic utterance in the church is to be judged (1 Cor. 14:26-33).

The *sincere,* Spirit-filled believer will not be preoccupied with this gift alone, for he sees it as only one of many gifts given for the "wholeness" of the church; they gather to worship God and to be thoroughly equipped for every good work through the teaching of His Word (2 Tim. 3:16-17). Therefore, the scripturally sensitive believer recognizes the following New Testament direction regarding spiritual gifts.

1. Speaking in "tongues" only edifies public worship when it is interpreted; thus, the worshiper is to pray for the interpretation, and if it is withheld, he keeps silent, unless someone who functions in the gift of interpretation (office-gift of the prophet) is known to be present (1 Cor. 14:5, 28).

2. The Spirit works only to edify; thus, whenever He is truly present, all things are in order and devoid of embarrassment or uneasiness (1 Cor. 14:26, 40).

3. *"The spirits of the prophets are subject to the prophets," (New King James Version, 1 Cor. 14:32).* That is, each truly Spirit-filled person ***can*** exercise ***self-control***; thus, confusion can and should be avoided so that decency with unity may prevail (1 Cor. 14:40).

4. The basis of all gifts is love. *Love*, not the experience of a gift, is the qualifying factor for those who would exercise spiritual gifts. So, in the administration of spiritual authority in the local congregation, the Word demands that we "judge" (1 Cor. 14:29) to confirm that those who exercise gifts actually do "pursue love and desire spiritual *gifts*" (1 Cor. 13:1-13; 14:1).

5. The Author and Dispenser of the gifts is the Holy Spirit, who divides them as He wills; thus, no gift becomes the exclusive possession of any believer for his personal edification and pride. Rather, the gifts are placed in the church to be exercised by the body for the mutual edification of the believers (1 Cor. 12:1-11) and as a means for expanded ministry.

6. The exercise of tongues is to be limited to sequences of two or three at the most (1 Cor. 14:27). While many hold this to be a rigid number, others understand it to be a guideline to keep the worship service in balance. In actuality, the Holy Spirit rarely moves beyond these limitations; however, on occasion, for special reasons to meet special needs, there may be more than one sequence of two or three appropriately spaced apart in a given service. The overarching guideline is, *"Let all things be done decently and in order," (NKJV, 1 Cor. 14:40).*

The Spirit-filled experience is more than just "speaking in tongues." In reality, it is coming into the fullness of the gifts and fruit of the Spirit as outlined in **Chapter 13** and is outlined in the New Testament (1 Cor. 12:7-11; Gal. 5:22-23). It also encompasses the broader scope of exercising God's gifts of spiritual enablement described in Romans 12:3-8 and Ephesians 4:7-12.

(Information on The Four Type of Tongues & Clarification about Private Tongues -"The Holy Spirit" Author John Bevere)

NOTES:

Chapter 12

The Three Baptisms

BAPTISM

is

FAITH IN ACTION

Anyone who believes and is baptized will be saved. But anyone who refuses to believe will be condemned.

Mark 16:16

Chapter 12

The Three Baptisms

Many Christians are unfamiliar with the baptism in the Holy Spirit. In fact, most believers only know about water baptism. We can easily deal with this baptism because the Bible talks about it clearly. Take John the Baptist's activity in the Jordan River, for example. When you attend church, water baptism is something that you see with your own eyes.

However, the Bible mentions two baptisms you can't see with your physical eyes; you can only see the after-effects of them in a person's life. Let's explore all three to understand three differences.

1. Baptism ***of*** the Holy Spirit

You probably already know about this baptism since it is in the previous chapters. However, you might know it by a different name: Salvation.

> *"For by one Spirit we are all baptized into one body—whether Jews or Greeks, whether slaves or free—and have all been made to drink into one Spirit," (NKJV, I Cor. 12:13).*

Who is doing the baptizing in this verse? The Holy Spirit. When you and I experienced salvation, we were both baptized into the same body—the body of Christ. The Holy Spirit is the agent who did the baptizing.

The baptism or infilling *of* the Holy Spirit is an experience subsequent to Christian conversion whereby the believer is placed into the body of Christ by faith in His redeeming work on the cross (1 Cor. 12:13). This is the baptism *of* the Holy Spirit, but it's not the baptism ***in*** the Holy Spirit. We will talk about this at number 3.

2. Water Baptism

Water baptism, by immersion is a prescribed procedure commanded by Jesus Christ to be practiced in the Church. Let's look at Matthew 28:18-20.

> *"And Jesus came and spoke to them, saying, 'All authority has been given to Me in heaven and on earth. Go therefore and make disciples of all the nations, baptizing them in the name of the Father and of the Son and of the Holy Spirit, teaching them to observe all things that I have commanded you; and lo, I am with you always, even to the end of the age.' Amen," (NKJV, Matt. 28:18-20).*

> *"And He said to them, 'Go into all the world and preach the gospel to every creature. He who believes and is baptized will be saved; but he who does not believe will be condemned,' " (NKJV, Mk. 16:15-16).*

It is essentially an action of obedient response to Christ's Lordship, following repentance and faith (Acts 2:38-39). The importance of this practice should never be minimized in the light of Christ's command. This is an outward indication of an inner change which has already occurred in the believer's life. It serves as a public testimony. The believer submits to it because Jesus commanded that this be done and He gave us the example by being baptized Himself. So, baptism is an act of obedience, commitment, and proclamation (Matt. 28:18-20; Mk. 16:15, 16).

Many Christians find a dynamic view on the power built in the Holy Spirit's presence at water baptism. While repentance and faith must precede the moment, and new birth has been experienced, water baptism by immersion is seen as a moment:

(1) at which a breaking of past bonds to sin may be severed, as the believer's death (and burial) to sin and resurrection to new life (1 Cor. 10:2) as well as the death and resurrection of Christ (2) when a commitment to separate from the past life of carnal indulgence is made, as circumcision symbolized (Col 2:11-15) and (3) when the fullness or overflowing of the Holy Spirit's power may be added to enhance the believer's power for witness and ministering (Acts 2:38, 39). This position sees baptism as both a witness and as an encounter. It is symbolic (burial to the past – Rom. 6:3-4) but is also releasing and empowering for the future.

My Slate
is
Clean!

Many Christians feel that their slate is clean from water baptism, which is a powerful tool in repentance of sins and knowing the past is behind them, dead and gone. Water baptism is a death-and-life experience. That is, it signifies both the death of our old self, and the new life we have received in Christ. To be submerged beneath the water signifies the death of all that we used to be without Christ; the old life built around myself and what I wanted is dead and buried.

> *"Therefore we were buried with Him through baptism into death, that just as Christ was raised from the dead by the glory of the Father, even so we also should walk in newness of life," (NKJV, Rom. 6:4).*

When we submit to this immersion, we let go of our old life, together with all the sin that entangled it, recognizing that it is worthy of death and must be left behind.

But thank God that baptism does not end there. After death comes resurrection.

> *"For if we have been united together in the likeness of His death, certainly we also shall be in the likeness of His resurrection," (NKJV, Rom. 6:5).*

To be raised up from the water signifies the birth of our new life in Christ. We leave behind the old life in order to take up the new. From now on we are dead to sin, but alive to God (Rom. 6:11). Through baptism, we identify with Christ, declaring our faith in His death and resurrection, and our experience of these things in our own lives.

3. Baptism ***in*** the Holy Spirit.

In Matthew 3:11, John the Baptist refers to Jesus, saying:

> *"I indeed baptize you with water unto repentance, but He who is coming after me is mightier that I, whose sandals I am not worthy to carry. He will baptize you with the Holy Spirit and fire," (NKJV, Matt. 3:11).*

John's statement here is one of just a handful of statements or accounts present in all four gospels. You can find the three versions of this verse in Mark 1:8, Lk. 3:16, and John 1:33. You'll also find accounts of the death and resurrection of Jesus in all four Gospels, as these events are obviously central to the Gospel story and explain vital truths believers need to understand.

Scripture clearly shows us *Jesus is the one who performs this baptism, immersing us* **in** *the Holy Spirit.* (Matt. 3:11; Lk. 3:16; 24:49; Jn. 1:33; 7:37-39; 15:16-17; 15:26; Acts 1:4-8; 11:16).

The difference between a filling and a baptism of the Spirit by measure and without measure may be illustrated by a glass and a pitcher of water. To the extent the water is poured into the glass, it is filled but not baptized. By burying the glass in the fulness of the water, it is both filled and baptized. By taking the glass out of the fullness of the water, it is no longer baptized. So, it is with believers to the extent one is filled with the Spirit, he has that measure of power and can do things according to the degree of anointing he has. If he is merely filled and has the Spirit by measure, he is limited in spiritual power. If he has the Spirit in all fullness, there is no limitation. He can do the works of Christ and the apostles (Matt. 17:20; 21:22; Mk. 9:23; 11:22-24; 16:17-18; Jn. 14:12; Acts 2:43; 3:6; 5:16; Rom. 15:18-19, 29).

A filling does not always come with a baptism, but a baptism always come with a filling. At Pentecost, they were both filled and baptized (Acts 1:1-8; 2:4) and many fillings kept coming to them to replenish the Spirit and power they had received (Acts 4:8, 31; 13:52). One must continue to **live** and **walk** in the Spirit and **be filled** with all the fullness of God in order to maintain the baptismal fullness (Eph. 3:16-20; 5:18; Gal. 5:16-26).

"What shall we do?"

How does Peter respond? Acts 2:37-39. Then Peter said to them, *"Repent, and let everyone of you be baptized in the name of Jesus Christ for the remission of sins; and you shall receive the gift of the Holy Spirit. For the promise is to you and to your children, and to all who are afar off, as many as the Lord our God will call," (NKJV).*

1. Repent. This is the vital primary step in the baptism of salvation.
2. Be baptized. Peter urges his listeners to follow Jesus' example by submitting themselves to water baptism.
3. Receive the gift of the Holy Spirit. This is the third baptism. As Peter indicates here, the Holy Spirit will not force Himself upon anyone. He must be "received".

From here on out, the third baptism continually follows the first two as an essential, critical part of the Christian life.

FOR FURTHER STUDY READ THE BOOK OF ACTS

Notes:

Chapter 13

Embrace The Gifts of the Trinity

"It is important
to seek these gifts
with the
Spirit of
Excellence."

"No sloppy agape."

Chapter 13

Embrace the Gifts of the Trinity

As mentioned a few chapters before in regards to moving beyond one's fullness in the Holy Spirit, it is important to understand the impact of the Spirit's full operation of gifts in and through the life and witness of the Church.

The Spirit-filled experience is more than just "speaking in tongues". In reality, it is coming into the fullness of the gifts and fruit of the Spirit as outlined in the New Testament (1 Cor. 12:7-11; Gal. 5:22-23). There is a broader scope of exercising God's gifts of spiritual enablement described in Romans 12:3-8 and Ephesians 4:7-12.

The Greek word '*charisma*' (singular) or '*charismata*' (plural) is used to designate spiritual gifts, and in the most technical sense, it means "gifts of holy grace". In Ephesians 4:11-13, the words '*dorea*' and '*doma*' are also used to designate "gifts", referring to these gifts as "enablers" or "equippers" for personal service in the Kingdom of God. Also, the word '*pneumatika*' engaged in 1 Corinthians 12:1 is used to describe the gifts as "things belonging to the Spirit". The point is that each of these words gives a contemporary meaning to the supernatural work of the Spirit in our lives as He prepares us for kingdom service and growth in grace. For this to happen, we are called upon to "earnestly desire the best gifts."

> *"But earnestly desire and zealously cultivate the greatest and best gifts and graces (the higher gifts and the choicest graces). And yet I will show you a still more excellent way [one that is better by far and the highest of them all–love]," (Amplified Classic Edition, 1 Cor. 12:31).*

We need to actively and zealously seek to understand the operation of and the appropriate response to all spiritual gifts. The gifts are placed in the church as resources to be utilized at the point of need for ministry in the body. This means that not every believer will have the same gifts as every other believer. Rather, the Holy Spirit is the Author and Dispenser of the gifts to bring about integrity in worship and kingdom expression. It is important to seek these gifts with the "Spirit of Excellence". No sloppy agape. ['Agape' in Greek means "the highest form of love".]

The Gifts of the Godhead

For many, clarification of the distinct role each member of the Godhead plays in giving gifts to mankind is helpful.

1. Our existence—human life— is given by the Father (Gen. 2:7; Heb. 12:9), who also gave His only begotten Son as the Redeemer for mankind (John 3:16).
2. Redemptively, Jesus is the giver of eternal life (Jn. 5:38-40; 10:27-28): He gave His life and shed His blood to gain that privilege (Jn. 10:17-18; Eph. 5:25-27).
3. The Father and Son have jointly sent the Holy Spirit to advance the work of redemption through the Church's ministry of worship, growth, and evangelism.

> "17 *And it shall come to pass in the last days, God declares, that I will pour out of My Spirit upon all mankind, and your sons and your daughters shall prophesy [telling forth the divine counsels] and your young men shall see visions (divinely granted appearances), and your old men shall dream [divinely suggested] dreams.*
> *33 Being therefore lifted high by and to the right hand of God, and having received from the Father the promised [blessing which is the] Holy Spirit, He has made this outpouring which you yourselves both see and hear," (AMPC, Acts 2:17, 33).*

First, you will find in Romans 12:3-8 the description of gifts given by God as Father. They seem to characterize basic "motivations," that is, inherent tendencies that characterize each different person by reason of the Creator's unique workmanship in their initial gifting. Only seven categories are listed. Few people are fully described by only one. More commonly, a mix is found with different traits of each gift present to some degree, while usually one will be the dominant trait of that person. It would be a mistake to suppose that an individual's learning to respond to the Creator's gifting of them in one or more of these categories fulfills the Bible's call to "earnestly desire the best gifts" (1 Cor. 12:31). These gifts of our place in God's created order are foundational.

Second, in 1 Corinthians 12:7-11, the nine gifts of the Holy Spirit are listed. Their purpose is specific—to "profit" the body of the Church. ("Profit", Greek *sumphero,* means "to bring together, to benefit, to be advantageous", which is experienced as the body is strengthened in its life together and expanded through its ministry of evangelism.). These nine gifts are specifically available to every believer as the Holy Spirit distributes them (1 Cor. 12:11). **They are not to be merely acknowledged in a passive way, but rather are to be "<u>actively welcomed and expected"</u>** (1 Cor. 13:1; 14:1). Seriously, why would you come to church and not expect a move of God in the gifts to benefit you, to actively welcome the Holy Spirit for a miracle in your life or for someone else?

> *"IF I [can] speak in the tongues of men and [even] of angels, but have not love (that reasoning, intentional, spiritual devotion such as is inspired by God's love for and in us), I am only a noisy gong or a clanging cymbal," (AMPC, I Cor. 13:1).*

> *"EAGERLY PURSUE and seek to acquire [this] love [make it your aim, your great quest]; and earnestly desire and cultivate the spiritual endowments (gifts), especially that you may prophesy (interpret the divine will and purpose in inspired preaching and teaching)," (AMPC, I Cor. 14:1).*

Third, the gifts which the Son of God has given are critical in assuring that the first two categories of gifts are applied in the body of the church. Ephesians 4:7-16 indicates the "office gifts" Christ has placed in the church along with their purpose. The ministry of these leaders is to "equip" the body by assisting each person: (1) to perceive the *place* the Creator has made him to fill by His creative workmanship in him and the possibilities that salvation now opens to his realization of what he was made to be and (2) to receive the *power of* the Holy Spirit and begin to respond to His gifts, which are given to expand each believer's capabilities *beyond* the created order and toward the redemptive dimension of ministry, for edifying the church and evangelizing the world.

In view of this, examine these designated categories of gifting clearly: The Father's (Rom. 12:6-8), the Son's (Eph. 4:11), and the Holy Spirit's (1 Cor. 12:8-10). The study so expands beyond those listings and beyond the above outlined structure of the gifts of the Godhead. This general outline will help in two ways. (1) It assists us by noting the distinct interest and work of each member of the Trinity in providing for our unique purpose and fulfillment. (2) It prevents us from confusing our foundational motivation in life and service for God with our purposeful quest for and openness to His Holy Spirit's full resources and power for service and ministry.

Gifts of the Father

Romans 12:3-8 (Basic Life Purpose and Motivation)

1. PROPHECY
   a. To speak with forthrightness and insight, especially when enabled by the Spirit of God (Joel 2:28).
   b. To demonstrate moral boldness and uncompromising commitment to worthy values.
   c. To influence others in one's arena of influence with a positive spirit of social or spiritual righteousness.

NOTE: Because all three categories of gifts involve some expression of "prophecy", it is helpful to understand in this category (Rom. 12) the focus is *general,* characterized by that level of the prophetic gift which would belong to every believer—"all flesh". The Holy Spirit's "gift of prophecy" (1 Cor. 12) refers to supernatural prompting, so much so that tongues with interpretation is equated with its operation (1 Cor. 14:5). The office-gift of the prophet, which Christ gives to His Church through individual ministries, is yet another expression of prophecy; those holding this office must meet *both* the Old Testament requirements of a prophet's accuracy in his message and the New Testament standards of life and character required of spiritual leadership.

2. MINISTRY
   a. To minister and render loving, general service to meet the needs of others.
   b. Illustrated in the work and office of the deacon (Matt. 20:26).

3. TEACHING
   a. The supernatural ability to explain and apply the truths received from God for the Church.
   b. Presupposes study and the Spirit's illumination providing the ability to make divine truth clear to the people of God.
   c. Considered distinct from the work of the prophet who speaks as the direct mouthpiece of God.

4. EXHORTATION
   a. Literally means to call aside for the purpose of making an appeal.
   b. In a broader sense, it means to entreat, comfort, or instruct (Acts 4:36; Heb. 10:25).

5. GIVING
    a. The essential meaning is to give out of a point of generosity.
    b. In a more technical sense, it refers to those with resources aiding those without such resources (2 Cor. 8:2; 9:11-13).
    c. This gift is to be exercised without outward show or pride and with generosity (2 Cor. 1:12; 8:2; 9:11-13).

6. LEADERSHIP
    a. Refers to the one "standing in front".
    b. Involves the exercise of the Holy Spirit in modeling, overseeing, and developing the body of Christ.
    c. Leadership is to be exercised with diligence.

7. MERCY
    a. To feel sympathy with the misery of another.
    b. To relate to others in understanding, appreciation, compassion, respect, and honesty.
    c. To be effective, this gift is to be exercised with kindness and cheerfulness—not as a matter of duty.

Gifts of the Holy Spirit

The Holy Spirit gives different gifts to believers to be used to build up the Church. The gifts include both ministry gifts and manifestation gifts. Let's look at them below.

> *"8 To one is given in and through the [Holy] Spirit [the power to speak] a message of wisdom, and to another [the power to express] a word of knowledge and understanding according to the same [Holy] Spirit;*
> *9 To another [wonder-working] faith by the same [Holy] Spirit, to another the extraordinary powers of healing by the one Spirit;*
> *10 To another the working of miracles, to another prophetic insight (the gift of interpreting the divine will and purpose); to another the ability to discern and distinguish between [the utterances of true] spirits [and false ones], to another various kinds of [unknown] tongues, to another the ability to interpret [such] tongues," (AMPC, I Cor. 12:8-10).*

> *"So God has appointed some in the church [for His own use]: first apostles (special messengers); second prophets (inspired preachers and expounders); third teachers; then wonder-workers; then those with ability to heal the sick; helpers; administrators; [speakers in] different (unknown) tongues," (AMPC, I Cor. 12:28).*

Classification and Definition of Gifts (1 Cor. 12:8-10).

Gifts Fall Into 3 Natural Divisions:

(1) Gifts of revelation—the mind gifts

1. *WORD OF WISDOM*

a. Supernatural perspective to ascertain the divine means for accomplishing God's will in given situations.
b. Divinely-given power to appropriate spiritual intuition in problem-solving.
c. Sense of divine direction
d. Being led by the Holy Spirit to act appropriately in a given set of circumstances.
e. Knowledge rightly applied: wisdom works interactively with knowledge and discernment.

The word of wisdom is supernatural revelation, or insight into the divine will and purpose, showing how to solve any problem or situation that may arise that cannot be solved by man's ideas. (1 Kings 3:16-28; Matt. 2:20; Lk. 22:10-12; Jn. 2:22-24; 4:16-19; Acts 26:16; 27: 21-25; 1 Cor. 5).

2. *WORD OF KNOWLEDGE*

a. Supernatural revelation of the divine will and plan.
b. Supernatural insight or understanding of circumstances or a body of facts by revelation, that is, without assistance of any human resource but solely by divine aid.
c. Implies a deeper and more advanced understanding of the communicated acts of God.
d. Involves moral wisdom for right living and relationships.
e. Requires objective understanding concerning divine things in human duties
f. May also refer to acknowledgment of God or of the things that belong to God as related in the Gospel.

The word of knowledge is supernatural revelation of divine knowledge or insight in the divine mind, will, or plan and also the plans of others that man could not know of himself. Perhaps it could be concerning someone in need or some future event. The Holy Spirit will sometimes reveal information that could not have been known by man. (Gen. 1:1-2:25; 1 Sam. 3:7-15; 2 Kings 6:8-12; Acts 9:11-12; Matt. 16:16; Jn. 1:1-3; Acts 5:3-4; 21:11; Eph. 3)

3. *DISCERNING OF SPIRITS*
    a. Supernatural power to detect the realm of the spirits and their activities.
    b. Implies the power of spiritual insight—supernatural revelation of plans and purposes of the enemy and his forces.
    c. To tell the difference between God's work and demonic counterfeit.

Discerning of spirits is supernatural revelation, or insight into the realm of spirits to detect them and their plans and to read the minds of men. He also provided a way for us to tell the difference between God's work and demonic counterfeit. Not all that is supernatural is from God, so we need discernment to protect us from false prophecy and occult fakery. We also need this gift to set people free from demonic bondage. (Matt. 9:12; Lk. 13:16; Jn. 2:25; Acts 13:9-10; 16:16; 1 Tim. 4:1-4; 1 Jn. 4:1-6).

(2) Gifts of inspiration—vocal gifts

4. *PROPHECY*
    a. Divinely inspired and anointed utterance.
    b. Supernatural proclamation in the known language (1 Cor. 14:3).
    c. Manifestation of the Spirit of God, not of intellect (1 Cor. 12:7).
    d. May be possessed and operated by all who have the infilling of the Holy Spirit (1 Cor. 14:31).
    e. Intellect, faith, and will are operative in this gift, but its exercise is not intellectually based. It is calling forth words from the Spirit of God.

Prophecy. This is supernatural utterance in the native tongue (1 Cor. 14:3). It is a miracle of divine utterance, not conceived by human thought or reasoning. It includes speaking for edification, exhortation, and comfort. This is a special gift because God loves to speak to His people. He wants to use us to relay His message. I consider the gift of prophecy "supernatural encouragement" because it always edifies the person who receives a word from the Lord, even if it is **correction**. Will you allow God to use you to speak His direct message to others? (Acts 3:21; 11:28; 21:11; 2 Pet. 1:21; 1 Cor. 14:23-32 and 1 Cor. 14:3).

5. *DIFFERENT KINDS OF TONGUES*
   a. Supernatural utterance in languages not known to the speaker: these languages may be existent in the world, revived from some past culture, or "unknown" in the sense that they are a means of communication inspired by the Holy Spirit.
   b. Serve as an evidence and sign of the indwelling and working of the Holy Spirit.

Different kinds of tongues is supernatural utterance in other languages which are not known to the speaker. There are "various kinds of tongues" mentioned in 1 Corinthians 12:10. Believers can have their own private prayer language, but some people are also gifted to speak in tongues in a church meeting. I know of situations where Christians received a special ability to speak in a foreign language so they could communicate the Gospel. (Isa. 28:11; Mk. 16:17; Acts 2:4; 10:44-48; 19:1-7; 1 Cor. 12:10; 28-31; 13:1-3; 14:2; 22, 26, 27-32).

6. *INTERPRETATION OF TONGUES*
   a. Supernatural power to reveal the meaning of tongues.
   b. Functions not as an operation of the mind of man but as the mind of the Spirit.
   c. Does not serve as a translation (interpreter never understands the tongue he is interpreting), but rather is a declaration of meaning.
   d. Is exercised as a miraculous and supernatural phenomenon as are the gifts of speaking in tongues and the gift of prophecy.

The *interpretation of tongues* is the supernatural ability to interpret in the native tongue which is uttered in other languages not known by the one who interprets by the Spirit. Similar to prophecy, this gift can relay a message from God that was spoken in a foreign or angelic tongue. (1 Co. 12:10; 14:5, 13-15, 27-28).

(3) Gifts of power—working gifts

7. *FAITH*
   a. Supernatural ability to believe God without doubt.
   b. Supernatural ability to combat unbelief.
   c. Supernatural ability to meet adverse circumstances with trust in God's messages and words.

d. Inner conviction impelled by an urgent and higher calling.

This *Faith* is supernatural ability to believe God without human doubt, unbelief, and reasoning. This is not the normal kind of faith we need daily. The gift of faith is a special ability to believe for big things. A person operating in supernatural faith will motivate others to pray until the answer comes. (Rom. 4:17; James 1:5-8; Matt. 17:20; 21:22; Mk. 9:23; 11: 22-34; Heb. 11:6; 12:1-3).

8. *GIFTS OF HEALING*
   a. Refers to supernatural healing without human aid.
   b. May include divinely assisted application of human instrumentation and medical means of treatment.
   c. Does not discount the use of God's creative gifts.

The *gift of healing* is supernatural power to heal all manner of sickness and cures of various diseases without human aid or medicine. (Mk. 16:18; Jn. 14:12; 1 Cor. 12:9).

9. *WORKING OF MIRACLES*
   a. Supernatural power to intervene and counteract earthly and evil forces.
   b. Literally means a display of power giving the ability to go beyond the natural.
   c. Operates closely with the gifts of faith and healings to bring authority over sin, Satan, sickness, and the binding forces of this age.

The *working of miracles* is supernatural power to intervene in the ordinary course of nature and to counteract natural laws if necessary. The book of Acts is a series of miracles, so why would we ever assume God pulled the plug on the power? He still opens prison doors, breaks chains, releases angels, opens blind eyes, changes weather patterns, and delivers people of demons. He is still a Miracle Worker! (1 Cor. 12:10; 27-31; Heb. 2:3-4; Psa. 107; Exod. 7:10-25; 14:21; 2 Kings 4:1-44; 6:1-7; Matt. 17:20; Mk. 9:23; 11:22-24; Jn. 14:12).

Gifts of the Son

Ephesians 4:11 also 1 Corinthians 12:28
(To Facilitate and Equip the Body of the Church)

Let's take a look at these two scriptures.

> *"His gifts were [varied; He Himself appointed and gave men to us] some to be apostles (special messengers), some prophets (inspired preachers and expounders), some evangelists (preachers of the Gospel, traveling missionaries), some pastors (shepherds of His flock) and teachers," (AMPC, Eph. 4:11).*

> *"So God has appointed some in the church [for His own use]: first apostles (special messengers); second prophets (inspired preachers and expounders); third teachers; then wonder-workers; then those with ability to heal the sick; helpers; administrators; [speakers in] different (unknown) tongues," (AMPC, I Cor. 12:28).*

1. APOSTLES

a. In apostolic days, this referred to a select group chosen to carry out directly the ministry of Christ; it included the assigned task given to a few to complete the sacred canon of the Holy Scriptures.
b. Implies the exercise of a distinct representative role of broader leadership given by Christ.
c. Functions as a messenger or spokesman of God.
d. In contemporary times, refers to those who have the spirit of apostleship in remarkably extending the work of the Church, opening fields to the Gospel, and overseeing larger sections of the body of Jesus Christ.

2. PROPHET

a. A spiritually mature spokesman/proclaimer with a special, divinely focused message to the Church or the world.
b. A person uniquely gifted at times with insight into future events.

3. EVANGELIST

a. Refers primarily to a special gift of preaching or witnessing in a way that brings unbelievers into the experience of salvation.
c. Functionally, the gift of evangelism operates for the establishment of new works, while pastors and teachers follow up to organize and sustain.
d. Essentially, the gift of evangelism operates to establish converts and to gather them spiritually and literally into the body of Christ.

4. PASTOR / TEACHER
    a. The word 'pastor' comes from a root meaning "to protect" from which we get the word "shepherd".
    b. Implies the function of a shepherd/leader to nurture, teach, and care for the spiritual needs of the body.

5. MISSIONARY [some see "apostle" or "evangelist" in this light]
    a. Implies the unfolding of a plan for making the Gospel known to all the world (Rom. 1:16).
    b. Illustrates an attitude of humility necessary for receiving a call to remote areas and unknown situations (Isa. 6:1-13).
    c. Signify an inner compulsion to lead the whole world to an understanding of Jesus Christ (2 Cor. 5:14-20).

Special Graces

1. HOSPITALITY
    a. Literally means to love, to do, or to do with pleasure.
    b. Illustrates Peter's notion of one of the two categories of gifts:

(1) teaching, and

(2) practical service. Look at 1 Peter chapter 4.

"As each of you has received a gift (a particular spiritual talent, a gracious divine endowment), employ it for one another as [befits] good trustees of God's many-sided grace [faithful stewards of the extremely diverse powers and gifts granted to Christians by unmerited favor].
11 Whoever speaks, [let him do it as one who utters] oracles of God; whoever renders service, [let him do it] as with the strength which God furnishes abundantly, so that in all things God may be glorified through Jesus Christ (the Messiah). To Him be the glory and dominion forever and ever (through endless ages). Amen (so be it)," (AMPC, 1 Pet. 4:10-11).

    c. Was utilized in caring for believers and workers who visited to worship, work, and become involved in the body of Christ.
    d. Illustrated in the teaching of Jesus concerning judgment (Matt. 25:35, 40).

2. CELIBACY (Matt. 19:10; 1 Cor. 7:7-9, 27; 1 Tim. 4:3; Rev. 14:4)
   a. The Bible considers marriage to be honorable, ordained of God, and a need for every person.
   b. Implies a special gift of celibacy, which frees the individual from the duties, pressures, and preoccupations of family life, allowing undivided attention to the Lord's work.

3. MARTYRDOM (1 Pet. 4:12-13)
   a. Illustrated in the spirit of Stephen (Acts 7:59-60).
   b. Fulfilled in the attitude of Paul (2 Tim. 4:6-8).

This may be only a partial list; there may be more different kinds of manifestation gifts. Romans 12:6-8 reads:

> *"Having gifts (faculties, talents, qualities) that differ according to the grace given us, let us use them: [He whose gift is] prophecy, [let him prophesy] <u>according to the proportion of his faith;</u>*
> *7 [He whose gift is] practical service, let him give himself to serving; he who teaches, to his teaching;*
> *8 He who exhorts (encourages), to his exhortation; he who contributes, let him do it in simplicity and liberality; he who gives aid and superintends, with zeal and singleness of mind; he who does acts of mercy, with genuine cheerfulness and joyful eagerness," (AMPC, Rom. 12:6-8).*

It is important to understand, though, that manifestation gifts are temporary. Once the manifestation is over, the gift is no longer the possession of the individual. Individuals do not possess manifestation gifts. They are simply channels through which these manifestations operate. Some of these gifts may be given to an individual on particular occasions and rarely or never be repeated. It is the Spirit's prerogative to give as he chooses. <u>Each individual, however, is responsible for the way his spiritual gifts are used in the Church.</u>

Ministry gifts, on the other hand, may be given on a long-term basis to be exercised continually in an individual's ministry. The term 'ministry gift' includes both equipping ministry gifts and body ministry gifts. The equipping ministry gifts are actually gifted individuals God has given to the Church to equip believers for the work of ministry (Eph. 4:11-16).

Each believer also has a role to play in the functioning of the body. This role is determined by the body ministry gifts of that individual. Certain activities are essential in a church—worship, teaching, evangelizing, etc. The form that these functions take in any church should be determined to some extent by the spiritual gifts of the equippers and the people they are equipping.

There are several important things to remember about the gifts of the Spirit:

1. The gifts are given for the building up of the church, not for the exaltation of any individual (1 Cor. 12:7).
2. The gifts are not a sign of holiness or spiritual maturity (1 Cor. 1:7; 3:1).
3. The exercise of the gifts is under the control of the individual, who is responsible to use them in obedience to the will of God (1 Cor. 14:32-33). We are not infallible, and we can misuse the gifts, so our exercise of them is subject to the judgment of those in authority (1 Cor. 14:29).
4. The gifts are always to be exercised in love (1 Cor. 13:1-2).

What are the Fruits of the Spirit?

What is good fruit?

Jesus explains it here:

> *"For there is no good (healthy) tree that bears decayed (worthless, stale) fruit, nor on the other hand does a decayed (worthless, sickly) tree bear good fruit.*
> *44 For each tree is known and identified by its own fruit; for figs are not gathered from thornbushes, nor is a cluster of grapes picked from a bramblebush.*
> *45 The upright (honorable, intrinsically good) man out of the good treasure [stored] in his heart produces what is upright (honorable and intrinsically good), and the evil man out of the evil storehouse brings forth that which is depraved (wicked and intrinsically evil); for out of the abundance (overflow) of the heart his mouth speaks," (AMPC, Lk. 6:43-45).*

You can also find more descriptions of what good fruit is in Psalm 1:1-3, Isaiah 32:17, and in Matthew 12:33.

What is bad fruit? *Acts of the sinful nature.* (Gal. 5:19-21; Col. 3:5-9)

- Sexual immorality
- Debauchery
- Drunkenness
- Filthy language
- Selfish ambition

- Impurity
- Factions
- Jealousy
- Witchcraft
- Orgies

- Idolatry
- Hatred
- Lust
- Envy
- Greed

The most important ministry of the Holy Spirit is the planting of Christ's character in His people. The Holy Spirit's presence in our lives is seen most clearly by the fruit that comes forth in our attitudes and actions. The Holy Spirit is the Spirit of Christ, and a Spirit-filled Christian is a Christlike Christian. Let's take a look at Galatians 5:22-26.

> *"But the fruit of the Spirit is love, joy, peace, longsuffering, kindness, goodness, faithfulness,*
> *23 gentleness, self-control. Against such there is no law.*
> *24 And those who are Christ's have crucified the flesh with its passions and desires.*
> *25 If we live in the Spirit, let us also walk in the Spirit.*
> *26 Let us not become conceited, provoking one another, envying one another,"*
> *(New King James Version, Gal. 5:22-26).*

Unlike the gifts of the Spirit, which vary from believer to believer, all of these qualities are meant to be **found in every Christian**. May the Lord fill us with His Spirit, in order that Christ may be formed and exalted in us!

Let's take a look at "The 9-fold Fruit of the Spirit".

1. **Love**: divine love; a strong, ardent, tender, compassionate devotion to the wellbeing of someone (v 22; 1 Cor. 13:4 a).
2. **Joy:** emotional excitement, gladness, and delight over blessings received or expected for oneself and others.

3. **Peace:** the state of quietness, rest repose, harmony, order and security in the midst of turmoil, strife, and temptations (Isa. 45:7a).
4. **Long-suffering/Patience:** patient endurance with the frailties, offenses, injuries, and provocation of others, without complaint or resentment (1 Cor. 13:4-7; 2 Cor. 6:4-6; Eph. 4:1-2; Col. 1:11; 3:12-13; 1 Tim. 1:16; 2 Tim. 3:10; 4:2).
5. **Kindness:** a disposition to be gentle, soft-spoken, even-tempered, cultured, and refined in character and conduct (2 Tim. 2:24-26; Titus 3:1-2; Jas. 3:17).
6. **Goodness:** the state of being kind, virtuous, benevolent, generous, and God-like in life and conduct (Ex. 33:19; 34:6; Psa. 23:6; 31:19; 33:5; 107:9; Rom. 2:4; Eph. 5:9; Matt. 5:44-48; Lk. 6:27-32).
7. **Faithfulness:** the living divinely implanted, acquired, and created principle of inward and wholehearted confidence, assurance, trust, and reliance in God and all that He says.
8. **Gentleness:** the disposition to be kind, indulgent, even balanced in tempers and passions, and patient in suffering injuries without feeling a spirit of revenge (v 23; Psa. 25:9a).
9. **Self-control:** a moderation in the indulgence of the appetites and passion (Prov. 23:1-3; 25:16; Dan. 1:8-16; Rom. 13:14; 1 Cor. 9:25-27; Phil. 4:5; 1 Thess. 5:6-8; Titus 2:2-3; 11-12; 2 Pet. 1:5-10).

Jesus said that you cannot bear fruit unless you remain in me.

> *"I am the true vine, and My Father is the vinedresser.*
> *2 Every branch in Me that does not bear fruit He takes away; and every branch that bears fruit He prunes, that it may bear more fruit.*
> *3 You are already clean because of the word which I have spoken to you.*
> *4 Abide in Me, and I in you. As the branch cannot bear fruit of itself, unless it abides in the vine, neither can you, unless you abide in Me.*
> *5 "I am the vine, you are the branches. He who abides in Me, and I in him, bears much fruit; for without Me you can do nothing," (NKJV, Jn. 15:1-5).*

Bearing Fruit

The fruit that the heavenly Vinedresser looks for in His people is Christlikeness (see Gal. 5:22,23). In order to be productive, a branch must submit to pruning, that is, to the beneficent discipline of the Father (v 2) and must maintain an abiding union with the vine (vv 4,5). If you continue to read beyond a few more scriptures in John 15:6-11, there you will find what He does with the fruitless branches. The fruitless branch, which does not abide in the vine (v 6), is destroyed. When we abide in Christ, our prayers are effective (v 7), we glorify God in our fruit bearing (v 8), we demonstrate our discipleship (vv 8-10), and our joy becomes full through experiencing Christ's own joy within us (v 11).

> *"Blessed is the man who trusts in the Lord, And whose hope is the Lord.*
> *8 For he shall be like a tree planted by the waters, Which spreads out its roots by the river, And will not fear when heat comes; But its leaf will be green, And will not be anxious in the year of drought, Nor will cease from yielding fruit," (Amplified Classic Edition, Jer. 17:7-8).*

Gifts of the Godhead are from *Hayford's Bible Handbook, The Complete Companion for Spirit-Filled Bible Study* by author Jack W. Hayford. The List of the Fruit of the Spirit from The Dakes Annotated Reference Bible NKJV

Notes:

Chapter 14

The Word of God for Me – The Bible

"The Word of God
Is alive and powerful!
It will set you Free,
Comfort you,
Heal you, Feed your
soul.... And bring
you peace.

Chapter 14

The Word of God for Me - The Bible

A Tribute to the Bible

The Bible is not an amulet, charm, or a book that will work wonders by its very presence. It is a book that will work wonders in every life, here and hereafter, if acted upon and obeyed in faith and sincerity. It is God's inspired revelation of the origin and destiny of all things, written in the simplest human language possible so that the most unlearned can understand and obey its teachings. It is self-interpreting and covers every subject of human knowledge and need, now and forever.

As a literary composition, the Bible is the most remarkable book ever made. It is a divine library of 66 books, some of considerable size, and others no larger than a tract. These books include various forms of literature—history, biography, poetry, proverbial sayings, hymns, letters, directions for elaborate ritualistic worship, laws, parables, riddles, allegories, prophecy, drama and others. They embrace all manner of literary styles in human expression.

It is the book that reveals the mind of God, the state of man, the way of salvation, the doom of sinners, and the happiness of believers. Its doctrines are holy, its precepts binding, its histories true, and its decisions immutable.

Read it to be wise, believe it to be safe, and practice it to be holy. The Bible contains light to direct you, food to support you, and comfort to cheer you. It is the traveler's map, the pilgrim's staff, the pilot's compass, the soldier's sword, and the Christian's charter. Here, Heaven is opened, and the gates of Hell disclosed. Christ is its grand subject, our good is its design and the glory of God its end. It should fill your memory, rule your heart, and guide your feet in true righteousness and true holiness.

Read it slowly, frequently, prayerfully, meditatively, searchingly, devotionally, and study it constantly, perseveringly, and industriously. Read it through and through until it becomes a part of your being and generates faith that will move mountains.

What are the other names of the Bible?

1. The Scripture (Mk. 15:28; Jn. 7:38)
2. The Scriptures (Lk. 24:27; Jn. 5:39)
3. The Promises (Rom. 9:4-5; 15:8)
4. The Oracles of God (Rom. 3:2; Heb. 5:12; 1 Pet. 4:11)
5. The Living Oracles (Acts 7:38)
6. The Law of Moses, the Prophets, and the Psalms (Lk. 24:25, 44)
7. The Law of the Lord (Psa. 1:2)
8. The Law and the Prophets (Matt. 5:17; 11:13; Acts 13:15)
9. The Book of the Lord (Isa. 34:16)
10. The Word of God (Mk. 7:13; Rom. 10:17)
11. The Sword of the Spirit (Eph. 6:17)
12. The Old and New Covenant (2 Cor. 3:6-15)
13. The First and Second Covenant (Heb. 8:7)
14. The Word of Christ (Col. 3:16)
15. The Word of Life (Phil. 2:16)
16. The Scripture of Truth (Dan. 10:21)
17. The Word of Truth (2 Tim. 2:15)
18. The Gospel of Christ (Rom. 1:16)
19. The Word of Faith (Rom. 10:8)
20. The Word of the Lord (2 Thess. 3:1)
21. The Word of Righteousness (Heb. 5:13)

How was the Bible given?

Except for the tablets of stone given to Moses on Mount Sinai (see Exod. 34:28; Deut. 10:4), God did not write the Bible directly. We are told that *"holy men of God spoke as they were moved by the Holy Spirit," (New King James Version, 2 Pet. 1:21).* God used men to write His words to us.

The Bible was written by some 40 different men over a period of about 1600 years, and yet the 66 books fit together to present one complete and consistent revelation of God. The Scriptures are said to be *"God-breathed," (Amplified Classic Edition, 2 Tim. 3:16),* meaning that through the Holy Spirit, God directed men to write what He wanted written. He allowed the writers to say what they wanted to say, to express themselves in their own words and writing styles.

The Bible was given *"at various times and in various ways," (New King James Version, Heb. 1:1), "precept upon precept, line upon line, here a little, there a little," (King James Version, Isa. 28:10).* There is only one plan of God for man. All the prophets gave perfect and harmonious testimony that Jesus Christ was the Son of God and Savior of the world (Acts 10:43).

The sovereignty of God over these men whom He created and whose lives He directed, together with the inspiration of His Spirit within them, ensured that what they wrote were the very words of God.

Nine Ways the Bible Was Given — Through:

1. Audible voice of God (Exod. 19:19; Deut. 5; Matt. 3:16-17; Jn. 12:28)
2. Angels (Acts 7:38; Heb. 2:2)
3. Prophets (Acts 3:21; Heb. 1:1)
4. Jesus Christ (Heb. 1:1; Rev. 1)
5. Apostles (Acts 1:2; Eph. 4)
6. Visions (Isa. 6: Dan. 7-8; Ezek. 1)
7. Dreams (Dan. 2; Matt. 1:20; 2:12)
8. Revelation (1 Cor. 1:7c; Gal. 2:2a; Revelation)
9. Inspiration (2 Tim. 3:15-17)

What are the languages of the Bible?

1. The Old Testament, with the exception of Ezra 4:8-6:18 and 7:12-26, Jeremiah 10:11, and Daniel 2:4-7:28, was written in Hebrew. These passages were written in Aramaic (the so-called Chaldee), a dialect related to Hebrew which gradually took its place as the spoken language after the exile.
2. The language of the New Testament was the common *Koine* Greek, the commercial language spoken throughout the Roman Empire at the time of Christ. This was also the language spoken by the Hellenistic Jews, who introduced many Hebrew dialects into the Greek language which became well-known among them through the influence of the Septuagint and Jewish businessmen who traveled everywhere. *Koine* Greek was the language most adapted to express Christian doctrine.
3. The Bible is now printed in over 1,100 languages and dialects.

How do we know the Bible is the Word of God?

We have many good reasons for believing in the authority and inspiration of Scripture:

1. Scripture claims for itself divine authority. Time after time, the prophets whose words are recorded claimed to be delivering the "Word of the Lord", and often they paid for this privilege with their lives.
2. The apostles of Christ bore witness to the authority and inspiration of Scripture (Rom. 15:4; 2 Tim. 3:16; 2 Pet. 1:21).
3. Jesus Christ, the Son of God, testified to the infallibility and eternal truth of the scriptures as the written Word of God (Jn. 10:35; Matt. 5:17-18; Matt. 4:4; Jn. 17:17).
4. Scores of predictive prophecies recorded in the scriptures have come to pass, thus testifying to their divine authorship.
5. Archaeological discoveries continue to confirm the Bible's descriptions of ancient life and history.
6. The Church throughout its history has always affirmed that the Bible is the inspired Word of God, and the saints through the ages have based their lives upon it.
7. The unified message, enduring wisdom, and the sublime beauty of Scripture point to a Source beyond the diverse, and often unlettered, men who authored it.
8. The Bible proves itself to be the Word of God in our own experience when we read it and find it revealing the secrets of our hearts as only God can and when we obey it and find that God keeps the promises recorded therein.

How did we come to have the English Bible we use today?

Our English Bible is the result of 1200 years of work by all kinds of learned men. Portions were translated from the Latin Vulgate beginning as far back as A.D. 700 when Aldhelm translated the Psalms in Saxon. Egbert translated the four Gospels some time later. In A.D. 735, Bede translated parts of the scriptures into Saxon. King Alfred undertook a translation of the Psalms but died in A.D. 900 before it was finished. Elfric translated the Pentateuch and some of the historical books in the 10th century.

Nothing else was done about translation from then to the time of John Wycliffe, who made the first complete English Bible from the Vulgate in A.D. 1380. The next was a New Testament by William Tyndale in 1535 and the Pentateuch in 1530. In 1535, Miles Coverdale made the first complete printed English Bible. Then came the Geneva Bible in 1560, followed by the Bishop's

Bible in 1563 and revised in 1568. The Roman Church came out with the Douay Version of the New Testament in 1582, and the whole Bible in 1609 which has been used by the Church up until now. In 1604, King James authorized 47 men to make a complete translation of the Bible from the original languages. It was finished in 1611 after 7-8 years of diligent work. It has been the most popular and accepted version of the English speaking world from that day until now. There have been several revised versions since then, and a number of Bibles in modern English, but none have been as well accepted and as lasting as the King James Version and perhaps never will be.

What are the parts of the Bible?

The Old Testament contains 39 books and 5 divisions:

1. Books of Law: The first 5 books of the Bible called the *Pentateuch*, telling the story of early mankind and the story of the nation of Israel, God's "chosen" people and revealing God's laws. (Genesis through Deuteronomy).

2. The 12 Books of History: Joshua, Judges, Ruth, 1 & 2 Samuel, 1 & 2 Kings, 1 & 2 Chronicles, Ezra, Nehemiah, and Esther.

3. The 5 Books of Poetry and Wisdom: Job, Psalms, Proverbs, Ecclesiastes, and Song of Songs.

4. The 5 Books of Major Prophets: Isaiah, Jeremiah, Lamentations, Ezekiel, and Daniel.

5. The 12 Books of Minor Prophets: Hosea, Joel, Amos, Obadiah, Jonah, Micah, Nahum, Habakkuk, Zephaniah, Haggai, Zechariah, and Malachi.

The New Testament contains 27 Books and 5 divisions:

1. The 4 Gospels: The life of Jesus Christ: Matthew, Mark, Luke, and John.

2. One Book of History: Acts of the Holy Spirit and the apostles. This is the formation and growth of the early Church. Acts is the fifth book. Acts recounts the early history of Christianity. After the death and resurrection of Jesus Christ, the twelve apostles began to preach and minister in a variety of locations. Acts relates some of their stories and depicts the growth of the Christian religion. The second half of Acts focuses on Paul, an anti-Christian who later converts and becomes a missionary.

3. The 14 Pauline epistles: Paul's epistles and Hebrews: Books 6 to 18 are letters called "epistles" written by Paul. Paul's epistles are addressed to various communities and deal with philosophical and social issues facing new Christians. These 14 Books are Romans, 1 & 2 Corinthians, Galatians, Ephesians, Philippians, Colossians, 1 & 2 Thessalonians, 1 & 2 Timothy, Titus, Philemon, and Hebrews.

4. The 7 General Epistles: James, 1 & 2 Peter, 1 John through 3 John, and Jude are ascribed to various authors and are addressed to a general Christian audience, rather than the specific communities addressed in Paul's epistles.

5. The One Book of prophecy: Revelation – the 27th and final book of the New Testament is called the Book of Revelation. It is one final vision given to the apostle John concerning the future victory of Christ and His people over Satan and all other enemies.

Bible Chronology

The length of certain periods is definitely stated in Scripture which give a total of 6,220 years between the creation of Adam and 2019, according to The Dake Annotated Reference Bible as follows:

Adam to flood of Noah (Gen. 5)..............................1,656

Flood to call of Abraham at

75 yrs. age (Gen. 11:10–12:5)....................................427

Abraham to Exodus (Exod. 12:40;

Gal 3:17; Gen. 15:15,a)..430

Exodus to Christ's ministry 1,718

From Christ's ministry

(about A.D. 30) to 1962 1,932

From 1962 to 2019 .... + 57

Total — Adam to 2019.. **6220**

What is the message of the Bible?

The Bible deals with the most important questions that confront us today. It addresses many basic issues of life and death, of the present and the future. One of the main messages of the Bible is the wonderful presentation of salvation, and this is extremely important, but it is only part of the much greater message—the Revelation of God's plan and purpose for the universe. The Bible is about God—God who created all things, a God who has eternally existed before creation, and who made all things for His glory.

The message of the Bible is God's Word about Himself, about the world He created, about man, about Christ, and about salvation. We are told everything we need to know concerning our relationship to God and our life with Him. The Bible is the written Word of God, so Jesus Christ is the living Word (John 1). From Genesis to Revelation, the central theme of the Bible is Christ (Luke 24:27). He is the link that connects all the very different books, the key to understanding everything that is contained in them.

The Old Testament points forward to Christ, predicting His coming, describing His Kingdom, and picturing the salvation He brings. The New Testament, in turn, completes the Old, revealing Jesus Christ as the fulfillment of all God's purposes.

Why should I study the interpretation of the Bible?

Correct Bible study interpretation should answer the question, "How do I understand what this particular passage means?" The question of how to interpret the Bible is not a minor issue. If Satan has a list of what he does not want us to do, Bible study is at the top, along with prayer and worship. Through study of Scripture, we learn who Jesus is and are enabled to become like Him. How can we become like Him if we do not know what He is like? Devotional studies are important, but they must result from a serious study of Scripture. The apostle Paul prayed that the Colossians might be *"filled with the knowledge of His will in all wisdom and spiritual understanding," (NKJV, Col. 1:9).* How could you possibly know the will of God for your life if you don't read the Bible.

Knowing Scripture and obeying it are the two foundations of a godly life. A Holy Spirit-filled life produces the further desire to study God's Word. Bible study and the application of its meaning takes you from study to application, back to study, and on to further application, in a relationship toward God in devotion, in service and witness. Satan's attempt is to take away our desire to study Scripture. He doesn't want you to know your authority in Christ Jesus. His plan is to actually keep you ignorant of who you are in Christ. He doesn't want you to have any power, spiritual growth, and stability.

What are the basic principles of Bible study? How do I start?

Here are four basic principles at the heart of a sound method of biblical interpretation.

Because Scripture is a divine Book, prayer is an absolute necessity as we study the Bible. Paul teaches that the non-Christian and the spiritually immature Christian are limited in their ability to know Christian things. Take a look at 1 Corinthians starting in chapter 2.

> *"14 But the natural, nonspiritual man does not accept or welcome or admit into his heart the gifts and teachings and revelations of the Spirit of God, for they are folly (meaningless nonsense) to him; and he is incapable of knowing them [of progressively recognizing, understanding, and becoming better acquainted with them] because they are spiritually discerned and estimated and appreciated.*
> *15 But the spiritual man tries all things [he examines, investigates, inquires into, questions, and discerns all things], yet is himself to be put on trial and judged by no one [he can read the meaning of everything, but no one can properly discern or appraise or get an insight into him].*
> *16 For who has known or understood the mind (the counsels and purposes) of the Lord so as to guide and instruct Him and give Him knowledge? But we have the mind of Christ (the Messiah) and do hold the thoughts (feelings and purposes) of His heart.*
>
> *1 HOWEVER, BRETHREN, I could not talk to you as to spiritual [men], but as to nonspiritual [men of the flesh, in whom the carnal nature predominates], as to mere infants [in the new life] in Christ [unable to talk yet!]*
> *2 I fed you with milk, not solid food, for you were not yet strong enough [to be ready for it]; but even yet you are not strong enough [to be ready for it],*
> *3 For you are still [unspiritual, having the nature] of the flesh [under the control of ordinary impulses]. For as long as [there are] envying and jealousy and wrangling and factions among you, are you not unspiritual and of the flesh, behaving yourselves after a human standard and like mere (unchanged) men?" (Amplified Classic Edition, 1 Cor. 2:14-3:3).*

For this reason, we must pray that God will bridge the gap that separates us from understanding spiritual things, by having the Holy Spirit teach us (Jn. 14:26; 16:13). Without this illumination or insight from God's Spirit, we cannot learn. This need for insight was the concept Paul referred to when he told Timothy to:

> *"Think over these things I am saying [understand them and grasp their application], for the Lord will grant you full insight and understanding in everything," (AMPC, 2 Tim. 2:7).*

The Bible is also a human book and, to a degree, must be interpreted like any other book. This brings us to the principle of common sense. For example, the grammatical historical method of studying the Bible instructs us to look at the passage carefully to see what it says literally and to understand a biblical statement in light of its historical background. We understand a historical statement as a straightforward statement and do not change its literal, grammatical sense. This is "common sense". Using the common sense principle, under the control of the Holy Spirit, is a valid principle of interpreting the Bible.

The primary rule of biblical interpretation is "context". The context refers to (1) the setting of the verse or passage, the surrounding verses and their subject matter, and (2) the historical or social setting in which the event happened or the words which were spoken. When allowed to speak for itself within the context of the paragraph, chapter, or book, the Bible itself will prevent the majority of all possible errors in interpretation. But to interpret the Bible correctly is to humbly seek the Lord and listen to what the Holy Spirit Himself has breathed into the text—to find what the text itself is saying and then draw the meaning *out of* the passage. If we allow a passage to be basically defined by what it and the surrounding verses say, then we have taken a large step toward interpreting the Bible properly.

Four key words—*observation, interpretation, evaluation,* and *application*—these are the heart of all approaches to finding out what the Bible means. They provide the structure of what questions you ask of the text and when.

1. *Observation:* Do I understand the basic facts of the passage such as the meaning of all the words?
2. *Interpretation:* What did the author mean in his own historical setting?
3. *Evaluation:* What does this passage mean in today's culture?
4. *Application:* How can I apply what I have learned to how I live my life?

It is important to remember that just as a biblical passage can be set in its culture, so the interpreter is likewise controlled to some extent by his own culture. We must be careful about allowing our own culture to influence our view of Scripture.

Above all, humility and an openness to the Holy Spirit are fundamental to "hearing the Word of God" when you read and study it. Rules of interpretation are *not* to inhibit this but to help us avoid the mistakes of those who, through history, have used the Bible recklessly unto their own shipwreck of faith and holy living or to guard against any who would mishandle and or misuse the Word and submit themselves to error. This is why it is very important to study the Bible so you are NOT misled, and you are able to judge what the person is doing or saying and see if it lines up with the Word of God.

In studying and interpreting the Bible, we must remember from Whom it comes. We are handling the Lord's message, given by the Holy Spirit for our illumination. This calls for an attitude of gratitude, humble respect and for our willingness to subject ourselves to its truth, its authority, and its call to holiness, forgiveness, and love.

There are many different ways to study the Bible. One good way is to take a particular subject, such as love or grace and, with the aid of a concordance or references, study what the Bible has to say on the subject. Another is to study the lives of various individuals such as David or Paul.

The best Bible study method for beginners is to study a complete book at a time so as to follow what the author is saying from start to finish. The important thing is to get started and to form a consistent habit of Bible study.

Remember to put into practice what you read; it is the *"doers of the Word"* who really understand it and experience its blessings (James 1:22).

How to Start

- Daily Bible Study is best. I read first thing in the morning. I call it my "First Fruits" for the day. I pray and ask the Lord to bless me with wisdom, knowledge, and understanding of His Word, His message for me today. I ask Him to place it deep within my spirit and in my heart. I want it to be illuminated.

- Ask the Holy Spirit to give you insight into His Word. We are blessed to have the Author of the Scriptures, the Spirit of God Himself, present with us to help us to understand them; don't neglect to ask for His help. It won't be long before you will come to see that life itself is to be found in *"every word that proceeds from the mouth of God," (New King James Version, Matt. 4:4).*

- It is best to read slowly, carefully, and prayerfully, alert to what God may be wanting to teach you. Read the commentary too if there is one at the bottom of each page. This will give you a better understanding of the Scripture. In some Bibles, there will be a middle column on a page that you are reading. It will have a verse number in bold print with extra Scripture references for further information in your study.

- Write down questions you may have or lessons you learned or want to learn.

- Memorize verses that have special meaning or importance so they will become a part of your life.

- Study systematically with a view to covering the whole Bible.

- Study both alone and together with others. This can benefit you greatly.

- Do not be surprised or discouraged when you come across something you don't understand. You can't expect to understand everything in the Bible right away, or even after many years; but your comprehension will increase as you study more and more. There will be plenty that you can understand right away. The rule is to never let something you don't understand obscure something that is clear.

What is a Rhema and Logos word?

The Bible describes itself in Hebrews 4:11-13 (NKJV): *"The Word of God is living and powerful."* The term for 'word' here is the Greek word ***logos***, which commonly indicates the expression of a complete idea and is used in referring to the Holy Scriptures. It contrasts with ***rhema*** which generally refers to "a word spoken or given". This recommends our understanding the difference between all of the Bible and the single promise or promises the Holy Spirit may bring to our minds from the Word of God. When facing a situation of need, trial, or difficulty, the promises of God may become a ***rhema*** to you, that is, a weapon of the Spirit, *"the Word of God," (NKJV, Eph. 6:17).* The Spirit's voice in our hearts is one example of ***rhema***. Another example of ***rhema*** is when verses leap off the pages of Scripture and into our hearts as this is the Holy Spirit speaking to us, applying the verse directly to our lives. Its authority is that this "word" comes from the Bible—God's Word—the completed ***logos***. Its immediate significance is that He has "spoken" it to your soul by His Spirit and is calling forth faith. Faith's confession receives God's "words" (***rhema***) and stands firm upon these promises. However, faith's confession is strong, not in human willpower but in the divine will revealed in the whole of the scriptures, the Holy Bible, the ***logos*** (completed Word) from which the ***rhema*** (present "word of promise") has been received. ***Logos*** is "the entire communication process". One example of logos is the Bible, the Word of God. We are to prayerfully meditate on the Bible, which allows God to speak to us through scriptures, which, in turn, ignites our hearts (Lk. 24:32). The Bible also tells us to treasure or hide Scripture in our hearts so we do not sin against God (Psa. 119:11).

What does the word 'Selah' mean?

Selah—the word *selah* is found in two books of the Bible, but is most prevalent in the Psalms, where it appears 71 times. It also appears three times in the third chapter of the minor prophet Habakkuk. The short answer is that no one really knows. However, many commentators think that Selah meant "to pause" or "to reflect".

Selah is also thought to be rendered from two Hebrew words: *s_lah*, "to praise"; and *s_lal*, "to lift up". Another commentator believes it comes from *salah*, "to pause". From *salah* comes the belief that *selah* is a musical notation signifying a rest to the singers and/or instrumentalists who performed the psalms. If this is true, then each time *selah* appears in a psalm, the musicians paused, possibly to take a breath, to sing a cappella, or to let the instruments play alone. It could be they were pausing to praise the One about whom the song was speaking, perhaps even lifting their hands in worship. This theory would encompass all these meanings—"praise", "lift up", and "pause". When we consider the three verses in Habakkuk, we also see how *selah* could mean "to pause and praise". Habakkuk's prayer in chapter 3 inspires the reader to pause and praise God for His mercy, power, sustaining grace, and sufficiency.

The best way to think of *selah* is a combination of all these meanings. The Amplified Bible adds "**pause and calmly think about that**" to each verse where *selah* appears. When we see the word '*selah'* in a psalm or in Habakkuk 3, we should pause to carefully weigh the meaning of what we have just read or heard, lifting up our hearts in praise to God for His great truths. (Psa. 66:4 AMPC)

> *"All the earth shall bow down to You and sing [praises] to You; they shall praise Your name in song. Selah [pause, and calmly think of that]!" (Amplified Classic Edition, Psa. 66:4).*

What does 'Anointed' mean?

In the Old Testament, the anointed person belonged to God in a special sense. The phrases, "the Lord's anointed", "God's anointed", "My anointed", "Your anointed", or "His anointed" are used of Saul (1 Sam. 26:9, 11), David (2 Sam. 22:51), and Solomon (2 Chron. 6:42). In the New Testament, all who are Christ's disciples are said to be anointed; they are God's very own, set apart, and commissioned for service (2 Cor. 1:21).

Priest, kings, and prophets were anointed. Oil was poured on the head of the person being anointed (Exod. 29:7). Kings were set apart through the ritual of anointing, which was performed by a prophet who acted in God's power and authority (1 Sam. 15:1). The Old Testament also records two instances of the anointing of a prophet (1 Kings 19:16; Isa. 61:1).

Jesus is described as "anointed" which is the meaning of the Hebrew-based word 'Messiah' or the Greek-based word 'Christ'.

Anointing for healing

In the New Testament, anointing was frequently used in connection with healing. The Holy Spirit's activities in a believer's life are pictured in terms associated with anointing. Jesus' disciples anointed the sick (Mk. 6:13), and James instructed the elders of the church to anoint the sick with oil (James 5:14). This anointing was for the purpose of healing.

What does "There was a real anointing present" mean?

Anointing in the New Testament also refers to the anointing of the Holy Spirit, which brings understanding and truth (1 Jn. 2:20, 27 NKJV).

"20 But you have an anointing from the Holy One, and you know all things.
27 But the anointing which you have received from Him abides in you, and you do not need that anyone teach you; but as the same anointing teaches you concerning all things, and is true, and is not a lie, and just as it has taught you, you will abide in Him," (New King James Version, I Jn. 2:20,27).

The anointing is unique. It is the unction from the Lord. It is the energy and the very life of God that is released through the laying on of hands and prayer, and it can bring deliverance and healing to those oppressed by the devil in Acts 10:38.

This anointing is not only for kings, priests, and prophets, it is for everyone who believes in the Lord Jesus Christ. The anointing occurs physically with a substance such as oil, myrrh, or balsam. But this is also a spiritual anointing as the Holy Spirit anoints a person's heart and mind with the love and truth of God.

When there is a special sense of Christ's presence or the Holy Spirit's working, people will often say, "There was a real anointing present." These words are not technically biblical, but convey the idea of Christ's presence "with power" as in Mark 5:30, Luke 5:17, and Acts 4:33, 6:8, and 8:6-8.

Anointed (Isa. 61:1) *mashach* (mah-shahch); Strong's #4886:

To anoint, to rub with oil, especially in order to consecrate someone or something. Appearing almost seventy times, *mashach* refers to the custom of rubbing or smearing with sacred oil to consecrate holy persons or holy things. Priests (Lev. 8:12; 16:32) and kings (2 Sam. 2:4; 5:3; 1 Kings 1:39) in particular were installed in their offices by anointing. In Exodus 40:9-14, the tabernacle was to be anointed, as well as the altar, the laver, and the high priest's sons. The most important derivative of *mashach* is *mashiyach* (Messiah), 'anointed one". As Jesus was and is the promised Anointed One, His title came to be "Jesus the Messiah". Messiah was translated into Greek as *Christos*, thus His designation, "Jesus Christ".

What does it mean to Bind and Loose in Matthew 18:18?

"Assuredly, I say to you, whatever you bind on earth will be bound in heaven, and whatever you loose on earth will be loosed in heaven," (NKJV, Matt. 18:18).

You have the authority to bind and loose.

Bind: Webster's dictionary defines the word ***bind*** as, "to make secure by tying; to confine, restrain or restrict as if with bonds … to constrain with legal authority … to exert a restraining or compelling effect. (2) It also means to arrest, apprehend, handcuff, lead captive, take charge of, lock up, restrain, check, or put a stop to. Binding is done by legal authority. We have legal authority in the name of Jesus to bind the works of darkness, [the devil, the enemy, Satan] which encompass sin, iniquity, perversion, sickness, disease, infirmity, death, destruction, curses, witchcraft, sorcery, divination, poverty, lack, strife, lust, pride, rebellion, fear, torment, and confusion. We have legal authority to put a stop to these things in our lives and in the lives of those we minister to.

Loose means to untie, to free from restraint, to detach, to disjoin, divorce, separate, unhitch, get free, get loose, escape, break away, unbind, unchain, unfetter, free, release, unlock, liberate, disconnect, and forgive. People need to be loosed from curses, evil inheritance, familiar spirits, sin, guilt, shame, condemnation, control, domination, manipulation, intimidation, mind control, religious control, sickness, disease, deception, false teaching, sin, habits, worldliness, carnality, demons, tradition, ungodly soul ties, ungodly pledges, ungodly vows and spoken words, hexes, vexes, jinxes, trauma, and cults. We have legal authority in the name of Jesus to loose ourselves and others to whom we minister from these destroying influences.

Bible devotionals are a very important part of your everyday life. You can either purchase a daily devotional at a Christian book store or you can download Bible reading plans of your choice for free www.biblereadingproject.com. Print it out and keep it in your Bible.

To purchase: www.liferesources.cc look under "Life Journal".

"The Bible is a mine of wealth,
the source of health,
and a world of pleasure.
It is given to you in this life,
will be opened at the judgment,
and will stand forever.
It involves the highest responsibility,
will reward the least to the greatest of labor,
and will condemn all who trifle
with its sacred contents."

—Author Unknown

Notes:

Chapter 15

I Can Talk to God – Prayer

To be a **Christian**
without **prayer**
is no more possible
than to be alive
without
breathing.

Chapter 15

I can talk to God - Prayer

What is prayer?

Prayer is communication with God. God is personal, all people can offer prayers. And yet, at the same time, nothing could be simpler than prayer, for praying is just talking and listening, things we do every day.

God is a God who speaks. He is not a silent deity; it is His nature to communicate. God knows our innermost thoughts and feelings even without our putting them into words; even so, God desires the kind of communal relationship that comes only with our active participation. God wants us to talk with Him. He actually listens to the words we say!

Prayer is not just talking to God; it is also listening to Him. Although God doesn't often speak in an audible voice, He does often speak directly from His Spirit to ours. **God's voice may come to us in the form of thoughts implanted in our minds, a leading toward some course of action, or simply light which causes us to see things we hadn't seen before. Hearing the voice of God requires concentration on our part, a conscious turning of our attention to Him, a quieting of our soul before Him.**

For an example: just as one person may dominate a conversation with another, not allowing the other a chance to be heard. We can so fill our prayers with our own thoughts and desires that we don't hear what God is trying to say to us. It requires disciplined effort on our part to make room for God to speak. We must *want* to hear Him. If we do listen, we can be confident that God will speak, for it is His desire to communicate with us. That is what makes prayer possible.

The most meaningful prayer comes from a heart that places its trust in God. God speaks to us through the Bible and we, in turn, speak to Him in trustful, believing prayer. Be assured by the scriptures that God is personal, living, active, all-knowing, all-wise, and all-powerful. We know that God can hear and help us. A confident prayer life is built on the cornerstone of Christ's work and words as shown by the prophets and apostles in the Spirit-inspired writings of the Bible. With this awareness of God's holiness, it leads to an awareness of our own sinfulness. We must confess our sins. If we don't, our prayers go nowhere. We should confess our sins immediately so we are in right standing before God.

> *"Woe is me! For I am undone and ruined, because I am a man of unclean lips, and I dwell in the midst of a people of unclean lips; for my eyes have seen the King, the Lord of hosts!" (Amplified Classic Edition, Isa. 6:5).*

Our Father promises to forgive us of all our unrighteousness (1Jn. 1:9). As we know that God is love, He has demonstrated His love in the gift of His Son. Our love should be expressed, as His has been expressed, in both deeds and words. Some people find it difficult to say to others and to God, "I love You." However, when love for God fills our lives, we will express our love in prayer to the One who is ultimately responsible for all that we are. We praise Him for His *"mighty acts … according to His excellent greatness!" (New King James Version, Psa. 150:2),* and for his *"righteous judgments," (NKJV, Psa. 119:164).* For God Himself, for His works, and for His words, His people give sincere praise.

> To be a Christian without prayer is no more possible than to be alive without breathing.

Thankfulness will flow ceaselessly from the understanding soul. God has forgiven our sins, granted us acceptance as His people, and given us His righteous standing and a new heart and life. So many reasons there are to thank Him! While ingratitude marks the ungodly (Rom. 1:21), the believer lives thankfully, seeing God at work on his or her behalf in countless ways. So, in everything we give thanks (Col. 3:17; 1 Thess. 5:18).

This study seeks to help people to practical applicable-to-life patterns of prayer as well as unveiling prayer secrets that help for habits by igniting understanding which prompts believers into dynamic prayer patterns rather than merely issuing rules. The result is prayer that builds blessing and fruitfulness in your life.

Different Kinds of Prayer

Petition

Asking God for something, this is called *petition.* It is not the only kind of prayer, but it is an important one. Father God encourages you to bring your needs to Him, including the basic necessities of life (Matt. 6:11).

The Bible is full of examples of people who asked God for things and received them. Jesus tells us plainly to *"ask and you will receive, that your joy may be full," (NKJV, Jn. 16:24).* It is God's pleasure to give to His children. Just like any earthly parent, God sometimes has good reason to refuse the requests His children make. He knows what is best for you, and He also takes note of the motives behind your requests (James 4:3). However, we should never hesitate to bring our needs and desires to our Father, for it is His delight to give.

Praise

Praise is giving glory to God with your voice, telling Him of your love for Him and giving thanks for all He has done for you. *Praise* exalts God and lifts up our own souls as well. God's people are a people of praise.

It is commanded by Him: (Psa. 148) "*Praise* to the Lord from Creation", (Psa. 149) "*Praise* to God for His Salvation and Judgment", (Psa. 150) "Let All Thing *Praise* the Lord". Giving *praise* to God also silences the devil (Psa. 8:2).

Confession

Confession means allowing the Spirit of God to convict us of our sins and responding in regret and repentance. This requires humbling ourselves before God and being willing to face up to what we have done wrong. Sin will wreck our relationship with God, but *"If we confess our sins, He is faithful and just to forgive us our sins and to cleanse us from all unrighteousness," (NKJV, 1 Jn. 1:9).*

Intercession

Intercession means praying to God on behalf of others. *Intercession* is an extremely important ministry which is open to any child of God. Our Father is pleased when we are unselfish enough to pray for someone else. There is nothing greater that we can do for another person than to intercede for him before God.

Communion

Finally, there is what we might call communion in which like a child with his father, we open our hearts to God and share with Him our feelings, our thoughts, and our dreams. Such times of prayer develop and enrich our relationship with God and draw us closer to Him (Jn. 15:7).

How should I pray?

You don't have to speak in some special formal or flowery language when you talk with God. He is interested in sincerity of heart, not eloquence of speech. If we have trouble putting our thoughts into words, it can be helpful to use the prayers in the Scripture as a model. That is the purpose of what is known as the Lord's Prayer (Matt. 6:5-13). You can also pray in your prayer language which you received from the baptism ***in*** the Holy Spirit.

There is no set pattern or posture which you must follow in prayer. We are given freedom to pray any way or place. We can pray silently or aloud, eyes open or closed. The important thing is to pray with reverence which is a feeling or attitude of deep respect and sincerity.

Here is something to consider. Jesus said this in Matthew chapter 6.

> *"5 And when you pray, you shall not be like the hypocrites. For they love to pray standing in the synagogues and on the corners of the streets, that they may be seen by men. Assuredly, I say to you, they have their reward.*
> *6 But you, when you pray, go into your room, and when you have shut your door, pray to your Father who is in the secret place; and your Father who sees in secret will reward you openly.*
> *7 And when you pray, do not use vain repetitions as the heathen do. For they think that they will be heard for their many words.*
> *8 "Therefore do not be like them. For your Father knows the things you have need of before you ask Him," (NKJV, Matt. 6:5-8).*

When should I pray?

A Christian's prayer life should include all of the following:

- *Daily prayer time.* A specific time should be set aside for prayer each day, perhaps 10 or 15 minutes to begin with or longer as we become more proficient. Many Christians follow the pattern of Jesus in praying first thing in the morning so as to begin the day by drawing close to God. Choose a time that fits your schedule and stick with it. The important thing is to develop a habit of daily prayer.

- *Group prayer.* Our prayers gain strength when united with those of others (Matt. 18:19-20). We should participate in regular prayer meetings and join with others who come together to pray for revival or other special needs.

- *Spontaneous prayer.* A given situation may call for immediate prayer. This could be anything from prayer for the sick or some other emergency to an expression of thanksgiving for a beautiful day. We should be ready to pray anytime, anywhere.

- *Continual prayer.* The Scripture tells us to "pray continually" (1 Thess. 5:17). This involves learning to maintain a continual awareness of God's presence, a heart that seeks him, and an ear open to His voice.

Why should I pray?

- God commands us to pray (Isa. 55:6; Matt .6:9; Lk. 18:1; 1 Thess. 5:17.)

- Prayer is necessary for our spiritual health. It increases and enriches our knowledge of God and our relationship with Him and is a source of power for witnessing and holy living.

- The Scripture is full of promises for those who seek the Lord in prayer (Jer. 33:3; Matt. 7:7-11). The blessings of Heaven are open to those who pray.

- God loves you and wants to spend time with you, and your love should cause you to seek out and spend time with Him.

How can I pray effectively?

As with everything else, practice makes perfect. The more you pray, the more you will learn about prayer. It is also helpful to study the prayers recorded in Scripture to see how Christ, the apostles, or the prophets prayed. The Psalms can be especially instructive, as many of them are prayers that capture perfectly the desires or concerns of the heart. Above all, the Holy Spirit is there to help us to pray and to pray for us and through us (Romans 8: 26-27).

You can also learn how to pray from other Christians in a group prayer setting.

Helps to Prayer

- *Faith* (Matt. 21:21-22) — Our prayers are more effective when we see God for who He is and become confident in our Father's love and power. Our faith is increased, not by trying to make ourselves believe but by meditating on God, who He is, and what He has done.

- *Sincerity* (Heb. 4:13) — It is essential that we be **totally open** and **honest** with God. It does no good to pretend with Him and only prevents Him from meeting our real need.

- *Righteousness* (James 5:16) — You cannot live your life any way you please, neglecting God and His commands/laws and then expect Him to respond when you want something from Him.

- *Humility* (Psa. 131:1-2) — God hears those who realize their need for Him.

- *Persistence* (Lk. 11:5-10) — Don't give up! The promise is there for those who persevere. Jesus teaches a persistence in prayer, along with a sense of urgency and boldness.

Hindrances to prayer

- *Unbelief* (Matt. 13:58) — Unbelief causes us to continue worrying and keeps us from leaving the problem with God. It can prevent us from being receptive to the answer or even seeing it when it comes.

- *Hypocrisy* (Matt. 6:5-8) — Prayer that seeks only to appear "spiritual" will accomplish nothing beyond that.

- *Pride* (Lk. 18:9-14) — Prayer that is focused on ourselves is not in a position to receive anything from God.

- *Sin* (Psa. 66:18) — Unconfessed sin or an unrepentant heart builds a barrier that blocks the path of prayer. (Also see Isaiah 59:2 in the Amplified Classic Edition, *"Your iniquities have made a separation between you and your God, and your sins have hidden His face from you, so that He will not hear."*)

- *Selfishness* (James 4:3) — What are the motives behind our prayers?

- *Unforgiveness* — (Mk. 11:25) — Unforgiveness is sin, and unconfessed sin creates "static" in a believer's relationship with God. So it's important to forgive others before prayer or worship (Matt. 5:23-24). Unforgiveness produces bitterness that will pollute all your fruit. When the Holy Spirit is grieved, our thinking can become distorted. Refusal to forgive means God steps back and lets you cope with your own problem in your own strength.

- *Being Inconsiderate*—In the New International Version, 1 Peter 3:7 states, *"Husbands, in the same way be considerate as you live with your wives, and treat them with respect as the weaker partner and as heirs with you of the gracious gift of life, so that nothing will hinder your prayers."*

The importance of prayer cannot be overemphasized. Let Jesus be our example; if He needed to spend much time in prayer, how much more do we? Nothing can be done without prayer; with prayer, anything is possible!

The Lord's Prayer.

"9 Our Father in heaven,
Hallowed be Your name.
10 Your kingdom come.
Your will be done
On earth as it is in heaven.
11 Give us this day our daily bread.
12 And forgive us our debts,
As we forgive our debtors.
13 And do not lead us into temptation,
But deliver us from the evil one.
For Yours is the kingdom and the power and the glory forever.
Amen," (NKJV, Matt. 6:9-13).

The Lord's Prayer is a prayer outline:
With seven major topics, each representing a basic human need:

1. The Paternal Need: "Our Father" (v 9). When you pray, all needs are met by the benevolence of a loving Father.

2. God's Presence: "Hallowed be Your name" (v 9). Enter His presence through praise Psa. 100:4), and call Him "Father" because of Christ's atoning blood (Heb. 10:19-22; Gal. 4:4-6).

3. God's Priorities: "Your kingdom come" (v 10). Declare that His Kingdom priorities (Rom. 14:17) shall be established in yourself, your loved ones, your church, and your nation.

4. God's Provision: "Give us" (v 11). Jesus, the Need Meeter, told us to pray daily, asking Him to supply all our needs.

5. God's Forgiveness: "And forgive us" (v 12). You need God's forgiveness, and you need to forgive others. Daily set your will to walk in love and forgiveness.

6. Power Over Satan: "And do not lead us … deliver us from the evil one" (v 13). Pray a hedge of protection about yourself and your loved ones (Job 1:9, 10; Psa. 91), and verbally put on the armor of God (Eph. 6:14-18).

7. Divine Partnership: "For Yours is the kingdom" (v 13). Praise God for sharing His Kingdom, power, and glory with you (2 Tim. 4:18; Lk. 10:19; Jn. 17:22). This is the prayer that teaches you how to pray.

If you have no prayer life, you have no relationship with God. Start one today. You will see a difference in your life right away.

Reference: Hayford Bible Hand book. *First Things First* by author Russell Board. Spirit Filled Life Bible NKJV

Notes:

Chapter 16

My Family, The Church

Church is not a place.
It's a body –
A family with
blood ties through
Jesus Christ.

Chapter 16

My Family, the Church

What is the Church? (Acts 8:1) *ecclesia*; Strong's #1577

You might have heard of the Greek word spoken '*ecclesia'* which means an assembly, or congregation, actually the whole body of professing Christians throughout the world, without respect to locality or time. It is an ancient Greek term for the people of a kingdom who are called to take their role as responsible citizens. This word is used 115 times in the New Testament, mostly in the Book of Acts and the writings of the apostle Paul and the general epistles. At least 92 times this word refers to a local congregation. The New Testament uses the word in the former sense in Acts 19:32, 39, and 41, and in the latter sense in Acts 7:38 and Hebrews 2:12. The dominant use in the New Testament is to describe an assembly or company of Christians in the following ways:

1. The whole body of Christians
2. A local church constituting a company of Christians gathering for worship, sharing, and teaching
3. Churches in a district.

Other related terms are: "spiritual house", "chosen race", and "God's people". (Compare "ecclesiastic" and "ecclesiastical"). The survival of the Christian Church against all its opponents is assured in Jesus' words, *"On this rock I will build My church, and the gates of Hades shall not prevail against it," (NKJV, Matt. 16:18).*

The Church is a local assembly of believers as well as the redeemed of all the ages who follow Jesus Christ as Savior and Lord. The assembly of all the redeemed in one place will become a reality only after the return of Christ (Heb. 12:23; Rev. 21:22). Most of the New Testament emphasis on the church is on the idea of the local church or congregation, the visible operation of the church in a given time, place, or community.

The Church did not begin until the Day of Pentecost after the ascension of Christ (Acts 1:14). The Church began on the Day of Pentecost and may be demonstrated in various ways:

1. Christ Himself declared the Church to be yet future.
2. It was founded upon the death, resurrection, and ascension of Christ, and such an accomplished fact was not possible until Pentecost (Gal. 3:23-25).
3. There could be no Church until it was fully purchased with Christ's blood (Eph. 1:20).

The Church is God's Family and My Family

Church is not a place.
It's a body –
A family with blood ties through Jesus Christ.

Those who God has called out from the world become His children, His family. Whenever anyone puts his faith in Christ for salvation, he becomes a member of the family of God. The Church is made up of all God's children all over the world, in every nation, of every race and language (Rev. 7:9). As children of God our Father, all Christians are brothers and sisters. We are united by our faith in Christ, and the same Holy Spirit dwells within each of us (Eph. 4:4-6). As members of the same family, it is natural for Christians to love one another, and this love proves we belong to Christ (Jn. 13:35).

The people of Israel built a temple for God because they wanted His presence with them, even though it was not possible for God to live in such a house of wood and stone (1 Kings 8:27). We sometimes refer to the building in which we worship as "the church", but this is not really correct. ***The church is made up of people, not bricks and mortar. We are all "living stones" (1 Pet. 2:5) being built together to form God's house with Jesus Christ as the cornerstone.*** What a glorious calling, to be part of a temple where God lives!

The Church is the Body of Christ (1 Corinthians 12:12-13)

Christ's place is the Head of the Church, which is His body. [You can find this in Col. 1:18-24 and Eph. 4:4-12]. When the Son of God became a man, He walked the earth in a physical body just like the rest of us. When He ascended into Heaven after His resurrection, He sent His Holy Spirit here so that His presence would remain here on the earth. But He also maintained a physical presence here: the Church is now Christ's body on the earth, indwelt by His Holy Spirit. Just as our physical bodies are made up of many different parts with many different functions, so also Christ's body on Earth is composed of many different people with many different roles and abilities (1 Cor. 12:14-20). As members of the Church, we have different jobs according to the place God assigns us in the body, but we all work together. Each member has its place; all are needed, and none are left out. It is only together that we can fulfill our role as the body of Christ, carrying out His will on the earth.

The Church is the Bride of Christ

Christ is the bridegroom (Jn. 3:29), and the Church is His bride (Eph. 5:25-33). When Jesus lived and ministered on the earth, He never took a wife, but He shed His blood and sacrificed His life in order to cleanse and sanctify a people who would become His bride. The Church is called "The Bride of Christ" because He loves us and wants to be united with us in an intimate relationship that will bear fruit for Him.

John the Baptist called Jesus the "bridegroom" (Jn. 3:29). Jesus referred to Himself as the "bridegroom" (Matt. 9:15). Jesus' bride, of course, is the Church—those who are spiritually united with Him by faith. As Christ's Bride, the Church is called to be pure and holy. We are to remain faithful to Him, never allowing our affections to be stolen by the things of this world. As Christ has loved us supremely and sacrificially, we give Him our love in return, and faithfully await the day when He returns to take us to Himself (Rev. 19:7).

What does the church do?

1. <u>The church ministers to God</u>. The church is called to *worship*. We were redeemed in order to praise and glorify our Father and Redeemer (1 Pet. 2:9). God's people are a people of praise for they have tasted the goodness of the Lord and know His marvelous love and grace. As a church, we gather together to unite our voices in songs of praise, and we testify to what the Lord has done for us. We lift our hands and our hearts up to the Lord, offering ourselves individually and corporately as sacrifices unto Him (Rom. 12:1). God is worthy of our worship, and it is our privilege and our delight to give our best in honor and praise to Him.

2. <u>The church ministers to believers in Christ</u>. The church is called to *edification*. The members of the body are to use their gifts to serve and build up one another, so that the whole body will grow into what it is meant to be in Christ (Eph. 4:11-13). This growth takes place through several kinds of ministry (Acts 2:42).

Worship — (Psa. 99:5) *shachah* Strongs #7812. Worship is an act of submission or reverence; to worship; to bow down when paying homage to God. The primary meaning is "to make oneself low." In the present reference, *shachah* is used in contrast to exaltation: exalt the Lord (Lift Him up high) and worship (bow yourselves down low before Him) at the place of His feet. Worship was characterized by a joy and thanksgiving because of God's gracious redemption in Christ, as early church worship focused on the presence of God. True worship was defined as that which occurred under the inspiration and animation (full of vigor and life) of the Holy Spirit (Jn. 4:23-24; Phil. 3:3).

"Happy moments,
PRAISE GOD.
Difficult moments,
SEEK GOD.
Quiet moments,
WORSHIP GOD.
Painful moments,
TRUST GOD.
Every moment,
THANK GOD."

Praise — Either by individuals or in hymns sung in common, praise reflects the frequent use of psalms in the church. Such a walk of praise-filled openness to Him will cultivate deep devotion, faithful obedience, and constant joy. Our daily approach to God in that communion is to be paved with praise.

> *"Enter into His gates with thanksgiving and a thank offering and into His courts with praise! Be thankful and say so to Him, bless and affectionately praise His name," (Amplified Classic Edition, Psa. 100:4).*

Prayer — The members of the church come together to pray, interceding for one another's needs and finding strength in united prayer.

Preaching — The church gathers to hear the Word of God proclaimed and explained, allowing its truth to penetrate and transform their hearts.

Fellowship —The church partakes together of the Lord's Supper, proclaiming their unity in Christ, and showing it by their practice of encouraging one another, bearing each other's burdens, sharing with those in need, and simply loving each other.

3. <u>The church ministers to the world.</u> The church is called to *witness*. It is the responsibility of the church to proclaim the message of Christ, both in the local community and to the world at large (Acts 1:8). We must evangelize at home and also send missionaries to other lands (Matt. 28:19-20). We bear witness to Christ through word and deed, both explaining and demonstrating the truth of the Gospel. The way we live our lives and the love and unity we demonstrate as Christians are powerful testimonies to the reality of Christ among us (Jn. 17:23). Above all, we are called as a church to follow in the footsteps of Christ, for we are His body on the earth (Jn. 17:18). We are to pattern our ministry after His, speaking His words, doing His works, loving with His love. We are to continue the life and ministry He began, and this we shall do for His Spirit lives within us (Jn. 14:12).

Why should I belong to a local church?

"Why should I join and belong to a local church when I can just church-hop, church-shop, podcast, or live-stream from my living room? What's the point of being a member?" You might have asked that question if you're a young adult and are not a committed church member. You're not alone. Millennials are notoriously disconnected consumers in this area. Some older adults have a different set of ideas too. All I can actually say is, you ARE alone and in a way that really matters since you're missing out on one of God's greatest gifts to you.

You need the local church. The local church provides growth, encouragement when we are struggling, instruction in the truth, and protection from the enemy. As brothers and sisters in Christ, we pray together, laugh together, cry together (1 Cor. 12:26). We are all members of the body of Christ, but no member can function on their own. Separated from the rest of the body, it is dead and useless. We can never achieve God's purpose for our lives alone, for we are made to fit into our place in the body. God has gifted all of us to work for Him, but none of us is gifted to work alone. Besides, it is not healthy to do life alone.

You want to be really careful with whom you surround yourself. You need to *choose your friends carefully*, because the wrong ones will lead you astray. *Spend time with wise people* because harm is coming your way if you spend it with fools. Surround yourself with God's people by joining a church that puts a priority on living in authentic biblical community.

It is very important to submit yourself to godly leadership. We're all led by somebody, so who are you following? God has set up the local church as the place where every Christian should be able to follow godly leaders. Hebrews 13:17, which is written to a local church, tells them to obey their leaders and submit to them because the leaders are accountable for keeping watch over their souls. Being a part of a local church defines which leaders you need to be listening to and which ones are watching over you. If someone is keeping watch over your soul and over your children, wouldn't you want them to do a good job? Acts 20:28 tells church elders to pay careful attention to themselves and to those God has entrusted to their care. ***The role of an elder*** is no small thing, and you want to be under the leadership of people who take it seriously.

Submit yourself to godly leadership by joining a church whose elders are committed to knowing and following God's Word.

The local church needs you.

The local church needs your ministry. The church is not complete without you. The gifts God has given you are meant to be used to help your fellow Christians (1 Cor. 14:26). You may think there is nothing you can do, but God knows better; He has no useless members in His body (1 Cor. 12: 27).

The local church needs your prayers. The church leadership and the rest of your fellow believers need your prayer support. You need to pray for them and to pray with them as well.

The local church needs your financial support. The tasks God has called His church to do require the resources of His people. If the local church is to do its part in worshiping the Lord, ministering to believers, and evangelizing the lost at home and abroad, you must contribute your share. The Lord urges us to commit ourselves to the local church (Heb. 10:25). Our faithfulness to His body is faithfulness to the Lord.

Notes:

Chapter 17

I Will Worship

One of the most significant
and important points to understand
about worship is that it's the
point of the church's being,
not just a part.
If worship is true to God's purpose and plan,
it will serve as the
"front line" of Christ's
power to change and restore human lives.
Healing through the presence of God –
"The power of the Lord was present to heal them,"
(NKJV, Luke 5:17).
Praise and Worship is there
to invite God's presence in so
that people will get healed.

Chapter 17

I Will Worship

I will worship because I *want to* worship Him. My experience with worship is that I go to church "expecting" a move of God. An encounter with God during worship changes you. It makes you thankful from where you came from and hungry for more of Him. Surrender yourself under His care; you will not be disappointed.

Who should worship God?

Everyone! All living creatures were made by Him and receive their life from Him, and all owe Him their worship (Psa. 150:6). Christians especially should worship the Lord (Psa. 107:1-3). Christians have greater knowledge of who God is and of what He has done. He has not only created us but also redeemed us; He has given us not only life on Earth but life in Heaven as well. Therefore, we of all people should worship God.

Worship goes on continually in Heaven (Rev. 4:8), and one day all creatures will bow before the Lord and acknowledge Him (Phil. 2:10-11).

When should we worship God?

Always! There is no time when worship is not appropriate (Psa. 34:1).

Our worship doesn't depend upon the circumstances. We praise God when things are going well and when they are not (Hab. 3:17-18). God is always in control and always worthy of our worship.

Our worship doesn't depend upon our feelings. We do not praise God only when we feel like it. He does not change with our feelings and neither should our worship. Moreover, worship can be therapeutic; when we choose to offer the **"sacrifice of praise"** in spite of how we feel (Heb. 13:15), we often find that our feelings change for the better.

In the work place, do your job as if you are working for the Lord. He gave it to you.

Worship should be an every-day thing, not just a Sunday-only activity, making it a ritual. Worship begins in our own private prayer time when we come aside from the cares and burdens of life to meet with our Father. It is there that we set the tone for the day and for our lives. A daily time of devotion leads to life of praise and worship.

Where should we worship God?

Everywhere! Worship isn't only something we do in a church building; it is a way of life, an attitude of praise that we carry wherever we go. Worship flows from our hearts at home, at work, driving in the car, shopping in the store, anywhere. The whole world is God's sanctuary, a place where He is to be worshipped.

Corporate Worship

Having said that, we must still recognize that there is something special about gathering together with God's people for corporate worship. From the time of the ancient Israelites in the Old Testament on through the time of the early Church and the centuries that followed, the people of God have made it a habit to meet regularly to worship together. This should be our practice as well (Heb. 10:25). Individual worship is good, but corporate worship is better still. God's purpose is to make of believers a temple in which He can dwell (Eph. 2:21); thus, when we join together in worship, the presence of the Lord is displayed in a special way. Alone we are just single stones; together we form a sanctuary which can contain a greater measure of the glory of God.

The Lord is especially pleased to see the hearts of His people united in worship and to hear their voices join in exclaiming His praise. We ourselves find a foretaste of Heaven when we come together with our brothers and sisters in Christ, rejoicing in our God and what He has done for us. **Worship** is celebration, and a celebration is always better when lots of people are involved.

An encounter with
God
during worship
changes YOU…
It makes you
Thankful from where
you came from and
Hungry for more of
Him

During Worship, it is **not a time to go visit a friend in the congregation. It is **rude** to interrupt their worship time with the Lord.

Those in church who worship and trust the Lord Almighty can rise high above what they are because He is their God and Source of unlimited strength. They ***surrender*** to the One who saved them, to the One whom they are so grateful for deliverance, for healing, for being set free, for a new life. Those who consciously choose to worship God gradually conform to His image, becoming increasingly like Him.

"Whatever may be your task, work at it heartily (from the soul), as [something done] for the Lord and not for men, Knowing [with all certainty] that it is from the Lord [and not from men] that you will receive the inheritance which is your [real] reward. [The One Whom] you are actually serving [is] the Lord Christ (the Messiah)," (AMPC, Col. 3:23-24).

Our service to God is primarily one of conforming to Him and His Son, Jesus Christ. Worshipping Him is a major factor in this process. In so doing, we become as the Scripture states below.

"God's [own] handiwork (His workmanship), recreated in Christ Jesus, [born anew] that we may do those good works which God predestined (planned beforehand) for us [taking paths which He prepared ahead of time], that we should walk in them [living the good life which He prearranged and made ready for us to live]," (AMPC, Eph. 2:10)

We worship Him because He commands it. We worship Him because He alone deserves it, knowing what He is and what He does. We worship Him because without so doing, we cannot rise to the measure of the stature of the fullness of Christ.

Why should we worship God?

1. God commands us to worship Him (Psa. 150).

2. God is worthy of our worship (Rev. 4:11). We should praise Him for who He is, the supreme Creator and holy Sovereign of the universe and for what He has done, His marvelous works of creation and redemption.

3. Worship has profound and beneficial effects on us:

- In worship, we draw nearer to God and have a greater sense of His presence (Psa. 100:4).
- Through worship, we see God more clearly and gain a better understanding of who He is (Psa. 48:1).
- In worshiping God, our own problems fade into the background, and we see just how inconsequential they are (Acts 4:23-31).
- As we praise God, our faith is strengthened because we become aware of His greatness (Psa. 56:10-11).
- We can find freedom in praise, looking at God rather than ourselves and letting go of things that bind us (Psa. 34:1-4).
- The Holy Spirit fills us when we praise and glorify God (Eph. 5:18-20).
- As we look to Christ in praise and worship, the Holy Spirit works to transform us into His likeness (2 Cor. 3:18).

How should we worship God?

You can praise the Lord through singing, dancing, crying, praying, shouting, drama, and all kinds of music (Psa. 150:3-5). The way you choose to worship at a given time will depend upon where you are, your particular tastes and talents, and what is in your heart. You can even worship the Lord in total silence, bowing before Him in quiet and reverent humility (Psa. 46:10). The most important thing is that we worship God *"in spirit and in truth," (King James Version, Jn. 4:24).* What does that mean?

1. WE MUST WORSHIP GOD IN SPIRIT.

This means, first of all, that worship is a matter of the heart. The inward reality is much more important than the outward expression. True worship originates deep within our spirit and then comes forth in words or actions. To worship God in spirit also means to let our worship be directed by the Holy Spirit. As the Holy Spirit is to be our Guide in all things (Jn. 16:13), even so, He will guide us in worship. The Holy Spirit helps us in our weakness (Rom. 8:26), and since the goal of His ministry is to exalt and glorify Christ, this means that He will inspire and direct our worship.

On an individual level, the Holy Spirit reveals within your heart the reality of who God is and what He has done for you (1 Cor. 2:9-10), calling forth praise and thanksgiving in response.

The Spirit helps to give expression to the praise in our hearts. He may lead us to shout, to sing, to laugh, to cry or to dance. He may also give us words in an unknown tongue with which to praise God, words that go beyond the limits or our understanding to more clearly express what is in our hearts (1 Cor. 14:15).

On a corporate level, Pentecostal worship (singing in your prayer language, singing in the spirit … mentioned in the Scripture above) seeks to allow the Holy Spirit to direct the praise of the whole congregation. We can think of the congregation as an orchestra, with the individual members as the musicians. The Holy Spirit inspires each musician to play a melody of praise, but the Spirit also seeks to orchestrate the individual strains into a combined symphony of praise to God. When we allow the Holy Spirit to conduct our worship, the result is a beautiful, harmonic unity of worship itself.

Pentecostal worshipers are not spectators but participants in worship. Some lift their hands as a sign of surrendering all to the Lord. Worship leaders seek the input of the Holy Spirit in everything from song selection, to order of service, to taking the offering. They allow room for individuals to contribute to the service in song, prophecy, testimony, or giving and interpreting messages in tongues (1 Cor. 14:26). At the same time, individuals must submit to the leadership who are responsible for maintaining an orderly flow in the service (1 Cor. 14:32-33, 40). There must be a balance between freedom and order for everything is to be done for the good of the church and the glory of God (1 Cor. 14:26).

2. WE MUST WORSHIP GOD IN TRUTH

This means first of all that our worship must be sincere, without hypocrisy, that what comes forth from our lips is matched by what is in our hearts. We must open our hearts to God, not concealing anything or pretending to be something we are not, but coming to Him just as we are. To worship God in truth also means to worship Him as He has revealed Himself in the Bible. We must worship God in true knowledge of who He is, not in some false idea of Him that comes from our own imagination.

Finally, to worship Father God in truth means to come to Him through Jesus Christ, who is the Truth and the only way to the Father (Jn. 14:6). We have access to Father God only through Christ; our prayers, our songs, our praise. Everything we offer to God must be offered in His name.

What is worship?

You can think of worship as a three-step process:

1. Worship begins when we recognize who God is and what He has done for us.

2. This brings forth a response of thanksgiving and praise, and we begin to glorify God for His greatness and goodness to us.

3. Worship culminates in consecration as we offer unto God not only our praise but also ourselves. Worship begins in our hearts but is not complete until we go on to offer our whole lives unto God as living sacrifices (Rom. 12:1-2).

Our lives are to be given unto God for Him to transform and use for His purposes. God wants what has begun in the sanctuary to continue until all areas of our lives, everything we are and everything we do, become an offering of praise unto Him (Col. 3:17). For God's people, worship is a way of life.

When you surrender yourself to worship, I've come to some conclusions in the last few years. The first is that God uses people who are desperate for His grace to lead others in worship. Vocal precision and perfection fade next to the posture of a worshiper's heart. Secondly, worship is much more than singing, dancing, reading, or any other physical manifestation. Worship is an offering of ourselves—our bodies, minds, souls, and spirits—to God. Giving Him the first fruits of our attention and affection is more valuable than anything we could ever put in the offering plate on Sunday. One of the most significant and important points to understand about worship is that it's the point of the church's being, not just a part. If worship is true to God's purpose and plan, it will serve as the "front line" of Christ's power to change and restore human lives. There is healing through the presence of God (Luke 5:17); *"The power of the Lord was present to heal them."*

Praise and worship is there to invite God's presence in so that people will get healed. It is not a warm-up to the message.

Reference: *First Things First* I will Celebrate Chapter 9 by author Russell A Board-

Chapter 18

I Will Praise the Lord!

When You Enter
His Presence
With Praise,
He Enters Your
CIRCUMSTANCES
With POWER!

Chapter 18

I will praise the Lord!

What is the difference between praise and worship?

Praise is ***about*** God. Worship is ***to*** God. Praise is opening up. Worship is entering in. Praise is boldly declaring. Worship is humbly bowing in the presence of a Holy God. Praise applauds what God ***has done.*** Worship is honoring God for who He ***is***.

Praise is something that we can do by ourselves or with others. Worship is something that we do alone in our innermost being.

Praise has to do with our telling God and others how wonderful He is. Praise has to do with the shouting forth of His marvelous character, compassion, and marvelous creation, just to name a few of His powerful attributes.

Praise usually precedes worship.

> *"Enter His gates with thanksgiving, and into His courts with praise." Be thankful to Him, and bless His name," (New King James Version, Psa. 100:4).*

When David danced before the Lord, he did so with all his might, (2 Sam. 6:14-16, 1 Chron. 15:29). It was in a public setting. It was boisterous, energetic with shouting and wild movements with his feet, leaping and whirling, rejoicing, and probably to a fast song. So, was he worshiping or praising? It seems clear it was both!

God highly values His people's devotion in worship. David's humility in worship, along with Michal's criticism regarding worship, have much to teach us. Worship and praise must be our very highest priority. **Learn to praise God** for all victories and spiritual gains. **Understand** that this will increase your chances for

> Praise is about God.
> Worship is to God.
> Praise is opening up.
> Worship is entering in.
> Praise is boldly declaring.
> Worship is humbly bowing in the presence of a Holy God.
> Praise applauds what God has done.
> Worship is honoring God for who He is.

further victories. **Worship** the Lord with your whole being as an appropriate response to His presence.

Be careful not to criticize forms of worship unfamiliar to you. To do so may cause future unfruitfulness (2 Sam. 6:16, 23). Read what Dr. Jack W. Hayford wrote about it.

> "With all the people watching, David celebrated God's presence by "leaping and dancing before the Lord" (2 Samuel 6:16). David's wife, Michal, became infuriated at his spectacle, even though his dance honored God. But as Michal watched, "she despised him in her heart." When David arrived at home, she unloaded on him. As a result of her rejection, Michal had to face another kind of music – barrenness (2 Samuel 6:23). Barren, childless, fruitless, and unproductive are all adjectives that not only describe Michal, but also describe worship that's neither pleasing to God nor obedient to His Word.
>
> "Michal continued to live her life, but it was a cardboard existence. She existed without all the joys that might have been hers. Congregations who fail to understand the purpose and true meaning of worship and who fail to worship according to God's Word are subject to the same existence."
> – Dr. Jack W. Hayford.
> www.renewingworshipnc.org Quotes on Worship

The Pathway of Praise

Daily living calls us to prayer and the Word for fellowship and wisdom in living. Our daily approach to God in that communion is to be paved with praise: *"Enter into His gates with thanksgiving, and into His courts with praise."* Such a walk of praise-filled openness to Him will cultivate deep devotion, faithful obedience, and constant joy. The intention of this study is to show believers how praise can bring steadfastness in godly living while teaching a praise walk that is neither boring, thoughtless, or reduced to a mere ritual, but one of life-delivering power available to each believer.

- **Praise Cures "Dry Times"** (read Num. 21:16-17). Praise is the cure for the "dry times" that come to every believer. The praise of God caused waters to flow from a well. Note four truths: (1) God's *instruction – "Gather the people together."* There is unity and power in corporate gathering. (2) God's *promise – "I will give them water [life]."* 3) The people's *responsibility* –They sang, *"Spring up, O well! All of you sing to it."* (4). Our *lesson* – In times of pressure, anxiety, or depression, do not stay alone. Gather with God's people, especially a praising people. Regardless of your personal feelings, join in audible praise, and sing to your well—the living God. Let your song be one of thanksgiving for past blessings and a song of faith in God's promises for the present and the future!

- **Power in Unity of Praise** (read 2 Chron. 5:13). This Scripture demonstrates the power in unity of praise, thanksgiving, and music: (1) The trumpeters and singers were as one (2) to make one sound in praise and thanksgiving to the Lord, saying, *"For He is good, for His mercy endures [lasts] forever."* (3) The house [temple] was filled with a cloud (the glory of God's presence.) Remember, even in praise, thanksgiving, and worship, *"God is not the author of confusion"* (1 Cor. 14:33). Anything said or done that draws attention to the praiser/worshiper and away from God, Jesus, and the Holy Spirit needs to be reconsidered.

- **Powerful Praise Births Victory** (read 2 Chron. 20:15-22). Here is a great lesson on the power of *praise*. Judah was confronted by mortal enemies, Moab and Ammon. The people sought God in prayer and with faith in His Word (20:1-14). Then came the word of the prophet: *"Do not be afraid ... for the battle is not yours, but God's," (NKJV, 2 Chron. 20:15).* The victory came in a strange but powerful manner. The Levites stood and praised *"the LORD God of Israel with voices loud and high," (NKJV, 2 Chron. 20:19).* Then some were actually appointed to sing to the Lord and praise Him in the beauty of holiness. These went before the army, saying: *"Praise the LORD, for His mercy endures [lasts] forever," (NKJV, 2 Chron. 20:21).* The result of this powerful praise was total victory!

- **Praise Stops the Advancement of Wickedness** (Psa. 7:14-17). This short passage contains two truths about praise. First, praise is the answer when wickedness and iniquity come against the believer. Temptation to sin and living wickedly will soon disappear in the face of sincere, powerful, and audible praise. This will bring the glorious presence of Jesus driving out the desire to identify with the sinful act and/or thought. Second, the writer declares, "*I will praise the LORD,*" *(NKJV, Psa. 7:17).* Praise is an act of the will. It is not merely an exuberance overflowing with words, but a self-induced declaration of thanksgiving—a sacrifice. The praiser *chooses* to praise. Learn this about praise: (1). Do not wait until all conditions and circumstances are favorable, but (2) offer a thanksgiving of praise *because* God is *worthy* and it is *right*. (See also Isa. 12:1-3 and Jer. 33:11)

- **Praise Spotlights God** (Psa. 18:3). Here is the most basic reason for our praise to God: He is "worthy to be praised" [Hebrew *halal*, "praise with a loud voice"]. The most primitive meaning of *halal* is "to cause to shine". So, with our praise, we are throwing the spotlight on our God, who is worthy and deserves to be praised and glorified. The more we put the spotlight on Him, the more he causes us to shine. Modern medicine attests to the value of bringing a depressed person into a brightly lighted room, acknowledging that the light greatly helps to heal their depression. How much more will praise introduce the light of God and bring us into the joy of the Lord.

- **Praise, the Pathway to God's Presence** (Psa. 22:3-4). Unquestionably, one of the most remarkable and exciting things about honest and sincere praise is taught here: *Praise will bring the presence of God.* Although God is everywhere present, there is a distinct manifestation of His rule which enters the environment of praise. Here is the remedy for times when you feel alone, deserted, or depressed. Praise! However simply, compose your song and testimony of God's goodness in your life. **The result:** God enters! His presence will live (take up residence) in our lives. The word 'inhabit' (Hebrew *yawshab*) means "to sit down, to remain, to settle, or marry". In other words, God does not merely visit us when we praise Him, but His presence abides with us and we partner with Him in a growing relationship. Let this truth create faith and trust and lead to deliverance from satanic harassment, torment, or bondage. Notice how this text ties three words together: "praised," "trusted," and "delivered"!

- **Sing Praises With Understanding** (Psa. 47:7). The word 'understanding' (Hebrew *sakal*, "prudent or cautious, and hence, intelligent") is linked to wisdom and prosperity. Proverbs 21 provides contrast to such understanding: *"A man who wanders from the way of understanding will rest in the assembly of the dead," (NKJV, Prov. 21:16).* But when we "sing praises with understanding," we are giving testimony to God's love for us and our love for Him. Life results instead of death. Others listening to us praise God hear testimony of our salvation and our joyful relationship with Him, which often leads to their own salvation.

- **Praise—the Road to Success** (Psa. 50:22-23). This whole chapter relates God's power, majesty, and glory, and is summed up in these closing verses, which apply to us as well as to the people of Israel. If we leave God out of our lives and live in rebellion, destruction follows. In contrast, the simple road to success is set forth. (1) Offer praise, and we glorify God. The focus of praise is directed toward God, but in His wisdom, we are the ultimate beneficiaries. (2) We receive power to order our conduct so that our lifestyle comes into obedience to God.

(3) *Result*: We receive a revelation (understanding)—this is, insight into God's salvation. Our praise becomes a vehicle for God to come to us and to minister through us.

- **Praise Releases Blessings and Satisfaction** (Psa. 63:1-5). This classic passage teaches how *expressed* praise releases the blessings of praise. Notice, this is not a silent prayer: *"My mouth shall praise You with joyful lips."* And look at the fruit: (1) *"O God, You are my God"* (affirmed relationship); (2) *"Early will I seek You"* (clear priorities); (3) *"My soul thirsts ... My flesh longs for You"* (deep intensity); (4) *"I have looked for You in the sanctuary, to see Your power and glory"* (desire for corporate involvement); (5) *Because Your lovingkindness is better than life, my lips shall praise You"* (appropriate gratitude); (6) *Result: "My soul* [the real me] *shall be satisfied as with marrow and fatness"* (personal needs met).

If we don't teach our children to follow Christ, the world will teach them not to.

- **Creative Praise Stays Lively** (Psa. 71:14). In this Scripture, the psalmist makes a commitment: *"I ... will praise You* [God] *yet more and more."* The idea expressed is beautiful, saying, "I will find fresh and new ways to express my praise toward God." This does not mean to abandon the old ways but to become as creative in our praises to God as God is creative in meeting our needs. Therefore, we will not fall prey to careless praise, which becomes dull and boring and ends in merely mouthing phrases. God wants us to be creative.

- **Teach Your Children Praise** (Psa. 145:4). This verse emphasizes the importance of passing on the praise of God from one generation to another. Praise is to be taught to our children. The Bible instructs us to raise a "generation of praisers." We must not merely "suppose" that children will grow up and desire God. We must be careful. Whatever we possess of God's blessing and revelation can be lost in one generation. We must consistently praise Him, and we must also teach (by example, as well as by words), so our children and our children's children will do the same.

- **A Mighty Appeal to Praise** (Psa. 150:1-6). The Psalms conclude with a mighty appeal to praise the Lord. Some Psalms are desperate cries, some filled with thanksgiving, and some have theologically or historically-based instruction to "praise the LORD" for His own Person, holiness, power, or goodness. But the important point is, **it is a command** to praise the Lord. We are to praise God (1) *in His sanctuary*—that is, His earthly temple and throughout His created universe and (2) *for His mighty acts* and according to *His excellent greatness*. Then a list of instruments and ways to praise follows. This list is not exhaustive but demonstrates how creative our praise is to be. Finally, in case even one person feels less than inclined to praise Him, the instruction is clear: If *you* have God's gift of life breath, you should praise Him. Hallelujah!

- **The Glorious Garment of Praise** (Isa. 61:3). The Hebrew root for "garment" (*'atah*) shows praise as more than a piece of clothing casually thrown over our shoulders. It literally teaches us "to wrap" or "cover" ourselves, that the garment of praise is to leave no openings through which hostile elements can penetrate. This garment of praise repels and replaces the heavy spirit. This special message of instruction and hope is for those oppressed by fear or doubt. "Put on" this garment. A warm coat from our closet only resists the cold wind when it is put on. When distressed, be dressed with praise! Act according to God's Word! In Isaiah 61:3, he talks about the oil of joy for mourning and the garment of *praise* for the spirit of heaviness.

- **Perfected Praise Produces Power** (Matt. 21:16). In response to the criticism leveled against the verbal praise, which was powerful, vocal, and strong, Jesus quotes Psalm 8:2 and reminds us of a great secret. Perfected praise will produce strength! It is powerful! At the very moment Jesus is being rejected by the leaders, these young people are captivated by the full meaning of who Jesus is. Capturing this revelation about Him causes loud and powerful praise to come forth. How heartening this must have been to Jesus as He marched toward the cross!

- **Praise Springs Open Prison Doors** (Acts 16:25-26). We need to study this example of the power of praise, even in difficult circumstances. Beaten and imprisoned, Paul and Silas respond by singing a hymn of praise—a song sung directly from the heart of God. The relationship between their song of praise and their supernatural deliverance through the earthquake cannot be overlooked. Praise directed toward God can shake open prison doors! A man was converted, his household saved, and satanic captivity overthrown in Philippi. Today, as well, praise will cause every chain of bondage to drop away. When you are serving God and things do not go the way you planned, learn from this text. Praise triumphs gloriously!

- **Encouraging One Another in Praise** (Eph. 5:18-19). This Scripture instructs interaction in our praise. Paul tells the Ephesians to be *"speaking to one another,"* using psalms and hymns and spiritual songs. Entering a gathering of believers, even with a small offering of praise, our worship begins to be magnified as we join with others. Their voices encourage us, and we inspire them. Separation from the local assembly deprives a person of this relationship and its strength. Let us assemble often and praise much, encouraging one another in praise.

- **Praise Releases the Spirit of Prophecy** (Heb. 2:11-12). This Scripture quotes the messianic prophecy in Psalm 22:22, showing how the Spirit of the Christ fills the New Testament Church and how Christ identifies Himself so closely with His people when they sing praises. As they do, two important things happen: (1) He joins in the song Himself, and (2) this praise releases the spirit of prophecy. The latter is in the words, *"I will declare Your name to My brethren."* As we joyfully sing praise to our God, Christ comes to flood our minds with the glory of the Father's character ("name"). There is no doubt about it, the praises of the people in the church service release the spirit of prophetic revelation, the magnifying of God through Jesus Christ. Thus, praise introduces edification, exhortation, and comfort to bless the whole body.

Prayer:
Father, help me to offer a sacrifice of praise to You in good times and in bad.

- **The Sacrifice of Praise** (Heb. 13:10-15). Why is praising God a sacrifice? The word "sacrifice" (Greek *thusia*) comes from the root *thuo*, a verb meaning "to kill or slaughter for a purpose". Praise often requires that we "kill" our pride, fear, or sloth—anything that threatens to diminish or interfere with our worship of the Lord. We also discover here the basis of all our praise: the sacrifice of our Lord Jesus Christ. It is by Him, in Him, with Him, to Him, and for Him that we offer our sacrifice of praise to God. Praise will never be successfully hindered when we keep its focus on Him—the Founder and Completer of our salvation. His Cross, His blood—His love gift of life and forgiveness to us—keep praise as a *living sacrifice!*

- **Worshipful Walk with God** (1 Pet. 2:9). This Scripture not only appoints praise, but represents *a basic revelation of the Bible*: God wants a people who will walk with Him in prayer, march with Him in praise, and thank and worship Him. Note the progression in Peter's description of the people of the New Covenant: (1) *We are a chosen generation*—a people begun with Jesus' choice of the Twelve, who became 120, to whom were added thousands at Pentecost. We are a part of this continually expanding generation, "chosen" when we receive Christ. (2) *We are a royal priesthood.* Under the Old Covenant, the priesthood and royalty were separated. We are now, in the Person of our Lord, all *"kings and priests to His God," (NKJV, Rev. 1:6)*, a worshiping host and a kingly band, prepared for walking with Him in the light or warring beside Him against the hosts of darkness. (3) *We are a holy nation,* composed of Jews and Gentiles—of one blood, from every nation under Heaven. (4) *We are His own special people.* God's intention from the time of Abraham has been to call forth a people with a special mission, to proclaim His praise and to propagate His blessing throughout the earth.

Notes:

Chapter 19

Stewardship

Stewardship is defined as:
"The responsibility that Christians have in maintaining and using wisely the gifts that God has bestowed."

Stewardship is managing everything God brings into the believer's life in a manner that honors God and impacts eternity.

Stewardship begins and ends with the understanding that God has ownership of all.

Chapter 19

Stewardship

What is stewardship?

"The [whole] Earth is the Lords, and everything that is in it,"
(Amplified Classic Edition, 1 Cor. 10:26).

This includes you and me and everything we possess. It is the management of another person's property, finances, or household affairs. The believer's stewardship embraces accountability for the way in which he or she manages life's affairs as given as a personal oversight (Matt. 25:14-30). The care of the matters of one's "house" (Heb. 3:2) includes all the affairs of (1) personal responsibility to private duties, (2) attention to one's family and its obligations, (3) pursuit of vocational tasks and scope of influence, (4) service of God by serving human need and use of appropriate opportunities to extend the Kingdom. These include the stewardship of one's monies, time, abilities, and influence.

The Bible gives us clear guidelines for the wise and careful use of the many gifts God has bestowed upon us. This study focuses on just a few of the many passages that address the importance of being disciplined with regard to our time, material wealth, minds, and bodies.

1. **Time is Short – Use it Well** (Psa. 90:1-17) – This is a heart-moving prayer from Moses, the man of God. It centers on the shortness of life and the stewardship of time. When you pause and think about that, Moses compares life to grass that withers (vv 5-6). But God Himself, on the other hand, is from everlasting to everlasting (v 2). Because of sin (vv 7-9), God has shortened man's time at least twice. The early days of man averaged hundreds of years (Gen. 5:5). Seth, for example, lived 912 years (Gen. 5:8); Cainan, 910 years (Gen. 5:14); and Methuselah 969 years (Gen. 5:27). After the flood, however, God shortened man's time to 120 years (Gen. 6:3). When we reach the time represented in Psalm 90, man's years have been cut to seventy or eighty years. The final word recorded in James 4:13-16 is that man's life is a vapor with no guarantee as to the number of his years. Therefore, it is critical that we allow God to teach us wisdom to manage well the brief time we are here (v 12).

2. **Take Time to Be Holy** (Gen. 2:2-3) – God designated the law of the Sabbath to teach man stewardship of time. God Himself labored six days in the creation, but He rested on the seventh day as seen in this passage. From the Hebrew word '*Sabat'*, 'sabbath' means "rest". This "rest" can mean any day of the week. Take one day to rest and do nothing which is fairly difficult for most of us. According to Genesis 3:17-19 and 2 Thessalonians 3:10, we learn that God commanded man to work, but in Exodus 20:8-11, we read that He also commanded man to rest. God emphasized this point when He provided the Israelites with manna in the wilderness (Exod. 6:21-30). The manna was to be gathered every morning, only gathering enough for a two-day supply on the day before the Sabbath. God's law of the Sabbath commanded to the children of Israel was to be obeyed forever. Therefore, as Christians and followers of Jesus Christ, we have accepted our role as stewards of time.

   We show ourselves to be good stewards by using the Sabbath for worshiping our Lord and Savior and gaining refreshing in His presence. Because of Jesus' resurrection on the first day of the week (Matt. 28:1-6; Mk. 16:1-6; Lk. 24:1-3), His disciples began meeting on the first day of the week. The Holy Spirit came upon the church on the Day of Pentecost, which was the first day of the week. [More on Why we go to church on Sunday in Chapter 24]. The word 'Pentecost' means "fiftieth," and it was that day called *"the morrow after the seventh Sabbath," (King James Version, Lev. 23:16).* The early Church met twice each day as evidenced in the New Testament, once in the temple and again at a person's house (Acts 2:46), so one day out of seven is the minimum time that Christians are to dedicate to refreshing and renewal in corporate worship and service.

3. **Redeem the Time** (Eph. 5:15-16) – In the Old Testament, there is plenty of scriptures that speak a lot about idleness in a person's life, and we are warned against being an idle person. However, Paul expressed in these verses that he considered it foolish to waste time. [Look how much time is wasted on video gaming]. The fact is he advocated "redeeming", or buying back, every precious wasted minute because evil days were near at hand. When you think about it, money can be restored. Property can be restored, broken-down cars, old furniture, old houses. Relationships can be restored. But one thing that can never be restored is time. Time flies and it does not return. Years pass and we never get them back. Paul understood that God has made us stewards over our most irreplaceable possession—time.

   We are to be good stewards of our time, using it wisely, constructively, and in the worship and service of our Lord. For me, it was eye opening, thinking of the time I have wasted by being depressed over something out of my control. The past problems can be very painful. I realized one day that Satan stole that day from me and I can't get it back. Yet, God promises the impossible: *"I will restore to you the years that the swarming locust has eaten" (New King James Version, Joel 2:25).* The immediate meaning of this promise is clear. Lost years, lost days of our lives—what do "lost years" look like for us? Lost years (or locust years) are years that you can't get back, and they come in many different ways. But the Good News is that our sins, our grief, our sorrows, were laid on Him. Our judgment fell on Him. Our locusts swarmed all over Him. He offers Himself to us, and He says what no one else can ever say: *"I will restore the years that the locusts have eaten."* Jesus Christ can restore lost years by deepening your fellowship with Him.

4. **Tithing: Managing Material Wealth** (Gen. 14:17-24) – Tithing, giving ten percent of our income, is the physical manifestation of Christian stewardship. Although we are no longer bound by the Mosaic law which commands tithing, there are nevertheless abundant reasons for us to continue this practice. Tithing is important because it is the recognition of God as the sole possessor of Heaven and Earth (v 22). Jesus reinforced the practice of tithing as an "ought to do" and so we should (Matt. 23:23). King David, one of God's most admired servants, also gave recognition to God as being the only divine king when he accumulated wealth to build the temple. David says, *"All that is in heaven and in earth is Yours," (NKJV, 1 Chron. 29:11).* Verse 12 in the same passage says, *"Both riches and honor come from You,"* and verse 14 says, *"for all things come from You, and of Your own we have given You."* Finally, in verse 16, he says, *"O Lord our God, all this abundance that we have prepared to build You a house for Your holy name is from Your hand, and is all Your own."* Giving of ourselves and of what we've been given by God can be an act of worship and gratitude to Him. Being motivated by God's love for us should bring us to a place where we feel compelled to give and help others after all Christ has done for us. Giving is the fruit of a relationship with God. Tithing and free-will giving are both meant to bring us into relationship with Jesus and, in the end, point us (and others) toward Him. Tithing and giving are for our own good when we do it in a spirit of love and grace.

Read what Paul says.

> *"Let each one [give] as he has made up his own mind and purposed in his heart, not reluctantly or sorrowfully or under compulsion, for God loves (He takes pleasure in, prizes above other things, and is unwilling to abandon or to do without) a cheerful (joyous, "prompt to do it") giver [whose heart is in his giving]," (Amplified Classic Edition, 2 Cor. 9:7).*

Giving is a natural byproduct of a changed life and helps us to overcome the power of greed and a love of money. Giving helps us to be less selfish people, and helps us to be an example to others. I think we can all agree that giving is something that all Christians are called to do. We must first follow Christ as our Savior. Once we have made a decision to follow Him, as a natural extension of our repentance before Him, we give of ourselves, our time, and our money as a way to express our gratitude and our desire to share his saving grace with others.

The Scripture mentions two areas of ministry in particular to which every Christian (and church) ought to give:

(1) *Missions* – Christ commissioned His Church to take His Word into every nation (Matt. 28:19), and those who do not go have an obligation to support those who do (Rom. 10:14-15). The task of world missions is the responsibility of every Christian. What better use of our money than in spreading the gospel?

(2) *The Poor* – Time and again the Bible admonishes those who have to share with those who have not (Lev. 19:10; 1 Jn. 3:17). God promises to repay those who give to the poor (Prov. 19:17) for He sees what we give to the poor as gifts unto Him (Matt, 25:40). We must never forget our responsibility to the poor, for it is only by God's grace that we do not find ourselves among them.

5. **Good Stewards of God's Gifts** (Hag. 1:8) – The same principle of stewardship King David emphasized in accumulating the wealth to build the original temple (1Chron. 29:14) was also emphasized in its restoration in Haggai 1:8. After seventy years of captivity in Babylon, the children of Judah returned to Jerusalem and rushed to the task of rebuilding their own houses. They took the position that the proper time had not come for the Lord's house to be built (Hag. 1:2). The prophet's response was, *"Is it time for you yourselves to dwell in your paneled houses, and this temple to lie in ruins?" (New King James Version, Hag. 1:4).* As verse 5 goes on to point out, we must always consider our ways when we seek to use the Lord's money for our purposes and neglect His house and the ministries that seek to accomplish His mission. The children of Judah were made to understand that their lack of material goods was directly related to their unfair and unjust stewardship: *"You have sown much, and bring in little; you eat, but do not have enough; you drink, but you are not filled with drink; you clothe yourselves, but no one is warm; and he who earns wages, earns wages to put into a bag with holes," (NKJV, Hag. 1:6).* Stewardship in all of life rests on the knowledge that all we are and all we have has been given to us by God through Christ and

belongs to God. We are therefore under His Lordship. Laziness and selfishness are acts of ingratitude and betrayal toward God, and they portray a lack of trust in the very God who has given us all things pertaining to life and godliness. Stewardship is MORE than money. Stewardship in its full sense is about being a caretaker, a steward, representing God with everything He has blessed you with: your church, your home, your car, your yard and, yes, even cleaning your home. As God's child, as a created being of God, we have each been given a gift from God to be used to His glory. In essence, we must be stewards of God's gift. Stewardship is glorifying God with all that He has given us, caring for it, cultivating it, and using it to reflect His glory back to Him.

6. **Our Lifestyle and Body** (Rom 12:1) – Apostle Paul reminds Christians that we are but stewards over our physical bodies. Many Christians live defeated lives by yielding to the flesh, which seemingly has a will of its own. Paul was keenly aware of this fact and dealt with it in passages such as Romans 8:1-13. Paul also instructed the believer to *"put on the Lord Jesus Christ, and make no provision for the flesh, to fulfill its lusts," (NKJV, Rom. 13:14).* Paul tells us in Romans 12 that a Christian lifestyle is possible when (1) Christians present both spirit and body to Christ; (2) Christians recognize that the Christian life is sacrificial; and (3) Christians recognize that the Christian lifestyle is holy, not worldly, but God-conscious and God-centered. Nothing else is acceptable to God. Our bodies are not ours to defile with willful acts of sins.

   Paul further adds in verse 2 that Christians must be nonconformists to the systems of this world. Christians are not to be conformed to the world, but rather are to be transformed by a renewed mind. The worldly conform to the fads and customs of the times as seen and passed on with mass communication. The believer's mind is to be renewed by adherence to God's Word. There is something we should fear and that is being desensitized by the sins of this world. When it doesn't bother you anymore or stir your spirit, something is definitely wrong with you. When we become *desensitized* to the world and its sins and to God's truth we will surely be *lost*!

7. **Our Bodies Belong to God** (2 Tim. 2:22) – Paul was concerned that Timothy, as a young man, should live the life of a Christian in such an honorable manner that he did not bring reproach upon the Church. Earlier, Paul admonished Timothy to live his life in such a way as to not be despised as a Christian youth, but rather be an example of purity (1 Tim. 4:12).

Paul's message was clearly "Total Abstinence" from sexual pleasures until marriage. Today's youth and young adults should hear this same message. It is a message of stewardship over the body. Many of our youth are dying from sexually transmitted diseases while parents, teachers, and even some ministers are teaching safe sex before marriage. The Christian youth must be made to understand that his or her body belongs to God and, therefore, he or she has no right to do anything with it that is not approved by God. Paul's word is "flee", run away from fornication (1 Cor. 6:18). Run also from youthful lusts (2 Tim. 2:22), for *"the body is not for sexual immorality, but for the Lord, and the Lord for the body,"* (1 Cor. 6:13).

8. **The Temple of the Holy Ghost** (NKJV, 1 Cor. 6:13-20) – Paul, in an effort to bring the church at Corinth into a right relationship with God, emphasizes the stewardship of the believer over his or her body. *"The body is ... for the Lord,"* (v 13). *"Do you not know that your bodies are members of Christ?"* (v 15). He says the believer's body is not autonomous, self-governing, and self-sustaining but is a member of Christ; Christ is the believer's life. Jesus said, *"I am the vine, you are the branches," (NKJV, Jn. 15:5).* With these facts in mind, He declares that the believer cannot take the body, which is a member of Christ, and join Christ's body to a harlot (1 Cor. 6:15-17). Paul moves this stewardship of the body into a divine state in verse 19. The believer's body is a temple, the temple of the Holy Ghost. Since the Holy Ghost lives in the believer's body, the believer cannot call the body his or her own. In verse 20, Paul gives another reason why the believer should not think of the body as his or her own: *"You were bought at a price."* God purchased the believer's body and spirit with the precious shed blood of Jesus Christ.

9. **Judgment on Poor Stewardship of the Body** (Rom. 1:18-32) – In this passage of Scripture, the apostle Paul tells the fate of those in the past who failed to recognize their position of stewardship over their bodies. They were judged, given over and given up. They knew God but did not glorify Him; their imagination was unwholesome; through foolishness, their hearts were darkened. They departed from Christianity religion, principles, and stewardship in character and of the body. Once God gave them up, women went against nature to lie with women, and men rejected women to lie with men. This insistence upon doing their own things with their bodies led to a long list of sinful acts, which greatly displeased God. In the verses below, Romans 1:21-32 will be broken down of the "sins" for which God gave men up to defile the body.

They knew God by experience (v 21). They made God a mystery and gave the people images of all kinds (v 23). "Their thoughts"—reasoning within themselves (v 21c). They substituted foolish concepts of God, and fooled themselves. When they formed their gods in human shape, they endowed them with passions and represented them as slaves to disgraceful sexual perversions and as possessing unlimited powers of sexual gratification.

> *"21 Because when they knew and recognized Him as God, they did not honor and glorify Him as God or give Him thanks. But instead they became futile and godless in their thinking [with vain imaginings, foolish reasoning, and stupid speculations] and their senseless minds were darkened.*
> *22 Claiming to be wise, they became fools [professing to be smart, they made simpletons of themselves].*
> *23 And by them the glory and majesty and excellence of the immortal God were exchanged for and represented by images, resembling mortal man and birds and beasts and reptiles," (Amplified Classic Edition, Rom. 1:21-23).*

Result of the apostasy: sexual uncleanness or perversion. God permitted them to give themselves over to homosexual sins and similar perversions.

> *"24 Therefore God gave them up in the lusts of their [own] hearts to sexual impurity, to the dishonoring of their bodies among themselves [abandoning them to the degrading power of sin]," (AMPC, Rom. 1:24).*

There were two sins for which God gave men up to defile their souls. They established idolatry for the true worship, a lie for the truth, and worshiped creatures more than the Creator.

> *"25 Because they exchanged the truth of God for a lie and worshiped and served the creature rather than the Creator, Who is blessed forever! Amen (so be it)," (AMPC, Rom. 1:25). [See also Jer. 2:11.]*

Result of apostasy: homosexuality, lesbianism, sodomy, and wickedness; vile, shame and dishonor; passions and lust. Vile passions are those of infamy and shame. This is lesbianism—unnatural sexual relations between women (homosexuality). In verse 27, this is sodomy, pederasty [pederasty means sexual relations between man and a boy, a minor], or homosexuality. They were inflamed, indecent, receiving back in full, crror—wrong action and wickedness. Here, both men and women by unnatural prostitution, drained and weakened their bodies so that they received in themselves the penalties of their wickedness.

> *"26 For this reason God gave them over and abandoned them to vile affections and degrading passions. For their women exchanged their natural function for an unnatural and abnormal one,*
> *27 And the men also turned from natural relations with women and were set ablaze (burning out, consumed) with lust for one another–men committing shameful acts with men and suffering in their own bodies and personalities the inevitable consequences and penalty of their wrong-doing and going astray, which was [their] fitting retribution," (AMPC, Rom. 1:26-27).*

Three sins to which God gave men up: (1) dishonor of their bodies (v 24); (2) vile passions in their souls (v 26); (3) debased minds (v 28).

Debased—adokimos—Greek [Strong's Concordance] = failing to pass the test, unapproved, counterfeit.

Disqualified (1 Cor. 9:27; 2 Cor. 13:5-7; Titus 1:16); Disapproved (2 Tim. 3:8); and rejected (Heb. 6:8). Christ is not in such.

> *"28 And so, since they did not see fit to acknowledge God or approve of Him or consider Him worth the knowing, God gave them over to a base and condemned mind to do things not proper or decent but loathsome," (AMPC, Rom. 1:28).*

Result of apostasy: 23 sins that will damn the soul.
(Mk. 7:21-23; 1 Cor. 6:9; Gal. 5:19; Col. 3:5) They filled up with every vice contrary to justice and righteousness. Unlawful sex sins of single and married people (evil nature; criminal, intense lust for gain). The envy was a pain felt and malignity conceived at the sight of the blessing of another. There is murder, strife, heated and bitter disagreements over fundamental issues and discord. It is not the same as disputing for truth as in Acts 9:29; 15:2, 7; 17:17; 19:8-9. Their lying, falsity are included. They are producing evil habits. It means malignity [disease] of the mind, which leads its victim to put the worst construction on every action; ascribing the best deeds the worst motives. Also in this list is a backbiter, she-devil [enemy], secret detractors, those who pretend secrecy, and carry our accusations against men, whether true or false, blasting their reputation by fraudulent gossip.

> *"29 Until they were filled (permeated and saturated) with every kind of unrighteousness, iniquity, grasping and covetous greed, and malice. [They were] full of envy and jealousy, murder, strife, deceit and treachery, ill will and cruel ways. [They were] secret backbiters and gossipers," (AMPC, Rom. 1:29).*

They are evil speakers, false accusers, slanderers of absent men. They are hateful to God, atheists, condemners of sacred things, despisers of providence, scorners of good. They are boisterous, abusing the characters and persons of those under them, scornful, hateful. They indulge in pride or self-gratulation, being exalted, elated, glorying in self. They display or strut self before others. They have an undue sense of superiority, unnatural self-esteem, arrogance, wishing all men to receive their sayings as oracles. They are self-exalted, vain, and arrogant braggarts. They are originators of wicked, immoral, and sinful customs, rites and fashions. They are the beginners of the abominable religious orgies of Bacchus [the Greek god of wine and fertility], the horrors of the arena, the debasing cruelties of the cockpit, the degrading shows of the theater, the gambling tables, etc. They are rebellious against parents, indifferent to rule and order, showing a lack of respect, and are disrespectful.

> *"30 Slanderers, hateful to and hating God, full of insolence, arrogance, [and] boasting; inventors of new forms of evil, disobedient and undutiful to parents," (AMPC, Rom. 1:30).*

Final result of apostasy: God's judgment known but not feared by apostates. They are ignorant and destitute of capacity for spiritual things, stubborn. They are not morally bound to any agreement. They are not dependable. They are treacherous to covenants, faithless to promises, false to trusts. They are destitute of natural affection, that is, filled with desire for unnatural affection experiences with husband or wife or same sex partners in the homosexual and other sex deviation sins of verses 24-28. They are without libation (libation means "a pouring out of wine or other liquid in honor of a deity which accompanied a treaty"). Greeks used it to appease the angry gods and reconcile them to the contracting parties. A person who would not pour libation was a deadly enmity with the other one and showed the highest pitch of an unforgiving spirit. He could not be soothed, appeased, or pacified by God if he were a person who would not pour libation. They are without mercy or care, destitute of all benevolence to the needy, cruel, merciless, irreconcilable, severe, unappeasable, unforgiving, unyielding.

> *"31 [They were] without understanding, conscienceless and faithless, heartless and loveless [and] merciless.*
> *32 Though they are fully aware of God's righteous decree that those who do such things deserve to die, they not only do them themselves but approve and applaud others who practice them," (AMPC, Rom. 1:31-32).*

But the Good News Is – You can be set free from "the judgments of the poor stewardship of your body." This is God's plan for you. The Lord Jesus Christ wants to set you free. There are many who need deliverance from these demons and the other demons that accompany them. And sometimes the key to their deliverance is first yours. You can blaze a trail for deliverance, and your testimony will build others' faith for their own deliverance.

Judgment on Poor Stewardship of the Body. Break down of Scripture Dake Annotated Reference Bible Romans 1:21-32 pages 274-275

Notes:

Chapter 20

The Great Commission "GO"

The Great Commission

is enabled by

the power

of the

Holy Spirit.

Chapter 20

The Great Commission "GO!"

After Jesus was resurrected and before He ascended into Heaven, He gave this command to His disciples:

> *"And Jesus came and spoke to them, saying, 'All authority has been given to Me in heaven and on earth.*
> *19 Go therefore and make disciples of all the nations, baptizing them in the name of the Father and of the Son and of the Holy Spirit,*
> *20 teaching them to observe all things that I have commanded you; and lo, I am with you always, even to the end of the age.' Amen,"*
> *(New King James Version, Matt. 28:18-20).*

This is called "The Great Commission". With these words, Jesus Christ essentially outlines what He expected the apostles and those who followed them to do in His absence.

It is interesting that in the original Greek, the only direct command in Matthew 28:19-20 is "make disciples". The Great Commission instructs us to make disciples while we are going throughout the world. The instructions to "go", "baptize", and "teach" are indirect commands. How are we to make disciples? By baptizing them and teaching them all that Jesus commanded. "Make disciples" is the primary command of the Great Commission. "Going", "baptizing", and "teaching" are the means by which we fulfill the command to "make disciples" of those who would believe. The Church has taken these instructions as its marching orders ever since.

What is a Disciple?

A disciple is someone who receives instruction from another person; a Christian disciple is a baptized follower of Christ, one who believes the teaching of Christ. A disciple of Christ imitates Jesus' example, clings to His sacrifice, believes in His resurrection, possesses the Holy Spirit, and lives to do His work. The command in the Great Commission to "make disciples" means to teach or train people to follow and obey Christ.

Part of the Great Commission is Acts 1:8 as well:

> *"But you shall receive power when the Holy Spirit has come upon you; and you shall be my witnesses to Me in Jerusalem, and in all Judea and Samaria, and to the end of the earth," (NKJV, Acts 1:8).*

The Great Commission is enabled by the power of the Holy Spirit. We are to be Christ's witnesses, fulfilling the Great Commission in our cities (Jerusalem), in our states and countries (Judea and Samaria), and anywhere else God sends us (to the ends of the earth).

Throughout the book of Acts [*they went into action*], we see how the apostles began to fulfill the Great Commission as outlined in Acts 1:8. First, Jerusalem is evangelized; in Acts 1-7, then the Spirit expands the Church through Judea and Samaria in Acts 8-12; finally, the Gospel reaches into "the ends of the earth" in Acts 13-28. Today, we continue to act "as ambassadors for Christ", and we plead on Christ's behalf to be reconciled to God as stated in 2 Corinthians 5:20.

Who is supposed to carry out the Great Commission?

The Great Commission was given by Jesus to His eleven disciples. But obviously He didn't intend for these eleven men to take the gospel into the whole world. No, we are also His disciples, and the burden of evangelizing the lost rests upon us as well.

The word 'evangelize' means "to tell the good news". From the beginning of the Bible story of redemption, the redeemed are assigned to world evangelization. Believers are living this truth: (1) receiving God's grace and then (2) sending God's truth; in (1) being filled with the Spirit and then (2) going to the uttermost part of the earth. The Gospel is the good news of the coming of Christ, His death for us, His resurrection, and the forgiveness He offers. God has not written the message of salvation in huge letters across the sky nor has He given to angels the task of communicating it to a lost humanity. God has ordained that the message of salvation is to be spread by those who have experienced it. Evangelism can sound like a scary word. However, it can be as simple as sharing what God is doing in your life now or giving your testimony to someone. It can be very simple, even as easy as sharing something you have "overcome" can truly give hope to someone in need.

His Field—A Promise of Harvest

> *"37 He answered, He Who sows the good seed is the Son of Man.*
> *38 The field is the world, and the good seed means the children of the kingdom; the darnel is the children of the evil one," (Amplified Classic Edition, Matt. 13:37-38).*

To the farmer, the field is a promise of harvest. This area of land prompts his vision of a yielding crop. Having given the parables of the sower (vv 3-9) and the wheat and the tares (vv 24-30), Jesus interprets the parabolic picture: "The field is the world." Christ's own imagery points to the process of world evangelism: Go and sow. The field may or may not appear fertile; the field may be ravished by drought (spiritual need) or insect (spiritual opponents), but in either case, the field is itself the summons. Lift up your eyes (Prov. 29:18; Jn. 4:35-37).

The Gospel and "The End"

> *"And this good news of the kingdom (the Gospel) will be preached throughout the whole world as a testimony to all the nations, and then will come the end," (AMPC, Matt. 24:14).*

In these words, Jesus linked the worldwide witness of the Gospel to His Second Coming. The text contains: (1) an anticipation of ministry – "this Gospel … will be preached" involving the declaration of the Kingdom message of grace for forgiveness and power for deliverance; (2) an area of effort – "to all the nations" including every group of people; (3) a certainty of "signs" for a witness (see Mk. 16:15-20), ensuring "proof" of Christ's resurrection life and present power to save and heal. How pointedly Jesus' words speak of the Father's desire toward the nations of the world: God cares for **all people**; Jesus dies for **every person**; and the Word of God is for **every nation** – before "the end".

What is the scope of our responsibility?

> *"There is salvation in and through* ***no one else,*** *for there is* ***no other name*** *under heaven given among men by and in which we must be saved," (AMPC, Acts 4:12).*

The call to take the Gospel to the nations is founded in these basic assumptions: (1) that humankind without Christ is lost, whether the entire race or the individual is concerned; (2) that there is "no other name under Heaven given among men by which we must be saved" – that is, that no other authority, no other personality, no other system or philosophy, and no other religion can affect the rescue of the human soul.

Our responsibility includes three levels:

(1). *Those we know* – On an individual level, we are to bear witness to our family and friends, our co-workers and acquaintances. They can sometimes be difficult to talk to, but those who know us best are likely to be more influenced by who we are than by what we say.

(2). *Our Community* – As a part of the local church, we should be engaged in outreach to our community or city. Every local church should be a lighthouse beaming forth the Gospel message, shining with the glory of Christ in the midst of the surrounding darkness. The church should make a priority of multiplying believers, praying, and planning to reach the lost in the immediate area. We must join in and do our part, helping in any way we can with revivals, crusades, visitation, special programs, and in making our church a place where people can meet God, feel the love from other believers and "welcomed". If you don't show the "love" to visitors or show them that they are "welcomed", why would they want to make it their home church?

(3). *The World* – As stated above in this chapter, there is no race, nation, or tribe that doesn't need to hear the message of salvation. The Gospel of Christ is for everyone, and God intends for this Gospel to be preached in the whole world. Throughout the centuries, these missionaries have left their homes, endured hardships, even risked their lives to tell the world about Christ. However, missions is not just the responsibility of missionaries. The task is too large to leave with just a few. Taking the Gospel into the whole world is the responsibility of the whole Church, and every one of us has a part to play, a job to do.

> *"14 How then shall they call on Him in whom they have not believed? And how shall they believe in Him of whom they have not heard? And how shall they hear without a preacher?*
> *15 And how shall they preach unless they are sent? As it is written: 'How beautiful are the feet of those who preach the gospel of peace, Who bring glad tidings of good things!'*
> *16 But they have not all obeyed the gospel. For Isaiah says, 'LORD, who has believed our report?' " (New King James Version, Rom. 10:14-16).*

It is up to us to find out what role the Lord wants us to play: Does He want us to go? Does He want us to intercede in prayer for the lost and for those who go to minister to them? Does He want us to give of our finances so that others may go? Every Christian should be a witness for Christ. Every Christian should help his local church with the task of evangelizing the community. And every Christian should be involved in world missions. Little or much, we can all do something to help fulfill the Great Commission. What will you do?

NOTES:

Chapter 21

Jesus said, "I will be back for you!"

"You

also must be ready,

because the

Son of Man

will come at an hour when

you

do not expect

Him."

Luke 12:40

New International Version

Chapter 21

Jesus said, "I will be back for you!"

Just as Jesus came the first time about 2000 years ago, He will return again. His second coming is as certain as His first. He promised to return (Matt. 26:64). Many times, He spoke to His disciples about His return, urging them to be ready for the day (Matt. 24-25). The apostles taught that He would return (Acts 3:19-21), and angels reaffirmed His promise (Acts 1:11). The return of Christ is a prominent theme of the whole New Testament. It has been the Blessed Hope of believers from the first days of the Church to the present (Titus 2:13).

Confirmed: Jesus Will Return

Before Jesus left His disciples, He promised them that He would return.

> *"10 And while they looked steadfastly toward heaven as He went up, behold, two men stood by them in white apparel,*
> *11 who also said, 'Men of Galilee, why do you stand gazing up into heaven? This same Jesus, who was taken up from you into heaven, will so come in like manner as you saw Him go into heaven,' " (New King James Version, Acts 1:10-11).*

The second coming of Christ – Jesus will return boldly, not just in some spiritual or symbolic sense (Acts 1:11). He will come back to Earth, in the same glorified body in which He was resurrected and ascended into Heaven.

The second coming of Christ will be different from the first in several ways:

- Jesus came the first time to begin the process of redemption; He will come the second time to complete it (Rom. 8:23).

- Jesus came the first time to bring salvation; He will come the second time to bring judgment (Acts 17:31).

- Jesus came the first time as the silent Lamb, offering no resistance to His enemies; He will come the second time as the conquering Lion, destroying them with the breath of His mouth (2 Thess. 2:8).
- Jesus came the first time in humility and meekness, His glory hidden from view; He will come the second time, and then they will see the Son of Man coming in a cloud with power and great glory (Luke 21:27). The second coming is called in Scripture the "revelation" of Jesus Christ, for then He will be seen as He is (1 Jn. 3:2).

The Threefold Announcement of the Lord's Coming

> *"15 For this we declare to you by the Lord's [own] word, that we who are alive and remain until the coming of the Lord shall in no way precede [into His presence] or have any advantage at all over those who have previously fallen asleep [in Him in death].*
> *16 For the Lord Himself will descend from heaven with a loud cry of summons, with the shout of an archangel, and with the blast of the trumpet of God. And those who have departed this life in Christ will rise first.*
> *17 Then we, the living ones who remain [on the earth], shall simultaneously be caught up along with [the resurrected dead] in the clouds to meet the Lord in the air; and so always (through the eternity of the eternities) we shall be with the Lord!*
> *18 Therefore comfort and encourage one another with these words," (Amplified Classic Edition, 1 Thess. 4:15-18).*

This is one of the most loved passages about the Second Coming, and it is also one of the most detailed. We are told that there will be a threefold announcement of the Lord's coming: a shout, the voice of an archangel, and the trumpet of God (v 16). In addition, there is a threefold promise to believers: (1) the dead in Christ shall rise (2) we who are alive will be caught away with them and (3) we shall always be with the Lord (vv 16-17).

It is important to know that this is the key text where the idea of a rapture is taught. The word 'rapture' is not used in the Bible, but the idea of the saints being "caught up" and gathered together at the second coming of the Lord is clearly spoken of here and in Matthew 24:30-31.

Only the Father Knows When Christ Will Return

> *"**Watch** therefore, for you know neither the day nor the hour in which the Son of Man is coming," (New King James Version, Matt. 25:13).*

This is a critical verse to remember whenever one considers the second coming. Throughout history, believers have mistakenly tried to determine when the Lord will return, and an ignorance of the history and the lack of good sense has led some in every decade to presume to pinpoint the time of Jesus' coming. Foolish as it may be, we are told in Scripture from Jesus that only the Father knows the time of His return.

People have interpreted the expression "hour or day" to mean that we may discover the month or year, but this is incorrect. We cannot be sure that it will be in any particular year, decade, or even in our lifetime. All I can say is, "Run" from any person or religious sect who tries to lead you astray and wants you to sell everything you own. This is why it is very important to know your Scripture, read your Bible, judge all things, and know the truth so you are not led into a false religion or cult.

Jesus began His sentence with the command, "Watch." The challenge the Lord gives us is to be constantly and eagerly waiting for His return. Our duty is twofold: to prepare ourselves for His coming so the Lord will receive a **bride** without "spot or wrinkle" (Eph. 5:27), and to "do business" until He returns, so that the Kingdom of God is preserved and extended on the earth (Luke 19:11-27). Let us be about the Father's business, live in expectation of the Master's return, and be done with all idle speculation or superstitious date-setting regarding the time of His coming.

What will happen when Jesus Christ returns?

The Rapture of the Church – At the time of the end, Jesus Christ will come to take His bride, and the Church will be "caught up" (raptured) to be united with Him (1 Thess. 4:16-17). Christians who have died will be resurrected into new, glorified bodies, and the believers who are living will be transformed without seeing death. All this will happen in a split second of time as we are changed from mortal to immortal and pass from decay to glory (1 Corinthians 15: 51-53).

The Great Tribulation – At this time, God will cease restraining the lawlessness that even now wreaks so much destruction in this world. A strong leader will arise who will set himself up in the place of God and gather the forces of evil, both human and demonic, behind him (2 Thess. 2:3-12). They will persecute the people of God, and many will be martyred or lose their faith (Matt. 24:9-11). At this time, God will begin to pour out His wrath upon this rebellious world (Rev. 16:11).

Christ's Victory and Millennial Reign – Jesus will come to Earth together with His saints and the hosts of Heaven and will put an end to the rebellion of men and demons (Rev. 19:11-21). His enemies will be destroyed (Rev. 20:2). During this time, Christ will set up His Kingdom on Earth, reigning together with His saints in perfect righteousness (Revelation 20:4). Then we will see what life on Earth was meant to be, as there finally will be peace among men, nations, even animals (Isa. 11:9).

The Final Judgment – At the end of the 1000-year reign, Satan will be released to organize one final rebellion against Christ, but he and those who join him will be defeated and destroyed (Rev. 20:7-10). Then all the unbelieving dead will be raised to life to face judgment before the throne of God. All will be judged according to what they have done and will suffer the punishment they deserve in Hell (Rev. 20:11-15).

The New Heaven and Earth – Then God will create a new Heaven and a new Earth, as all pain, sorrow, and destruction caused by sin will be ended (Rev. 21:1-4). We will live forever with Christ, enjoying the glories of God's new creation, the fellowship of our brothers and sisters in Christ, and most of all, the presence of God in our midst (Rev. 22:3-5). We cannot even dream of what God has in store for us, but we will have all of eternity to find out (1 Cor. 2:9).

Who will be in the Bride of Christ?

The Bride is the Church of Christ.

The Church is made up of everyone who is on the way to becoming completely free from all sin. (2 Pet. 1:4). Some people may be farther along this way than others. Some people may have just begun. But everybody who walks this way is a member of the body of Christ. They are preparing themselves to be the bride of Christ. They are making themselves ready (also mentioned in Chapter 15).

The Bride is composed of the ones who love Jesus, His followers. They are those who ache with longing to be with their Lord and Master. They are those who have made a decision to serve Jesus with all of their heart, all of their soul, all of their being. The Bride consists of the ones who Jesus cleanses and purifies; they will be a glorious Church without spot or wrinkle—holy. (Eph. 5:25-27)

A bride is somebody comparable to her bridegroom. This is why it is written in 1 Peter 1:15, *"But as He who called you is holy, you also be holy in all your conduct," (NKJV).* The bride of Christ is made up of those who will shine with a brightness and a purity and a holiness just as He who called her is holy.

"And to her it was granted to be arrayed in fine linen, clean and bright, for the fine linen is the righteous acts of the saints," (NKJV, Rev. 19:8). The Bride of Christ makes herself ready for Him. Every second she has on this earth is used to prepare herself for her bridegroom. Her fine linen is not something given to her during the marriage feast but it is something she has made herself during her time on Earth by walking in righteousness.

"Many are called, but few are chosen," (NKJV, Matt. 22:14). The Bride of Christ is the same as the Church, but there are not many who are truly counted among this number. Many invitations are sent out, but not many choose to answer.

Make yourself ready!

Rightly understood, the Bride is not "the best, the first-class or the cream of the crop" of high-class, special Christians that only a few get to be a part of. The Bride will be few in number, but this is not because only a few invitations were sent out. It is because few people choose to answer. To be a part of the Bride of Christ, you need to answer that call and start following Jesus on the way He Himself has gone.

This time on Earth is a time of engagement for Jesus Christ and His Bride. They have an intense love for one another and long to be reunited. The Bride wants to be near Jesus, her heavenly bridegroom. She will do everything and anything, she will pay whatever it costs, in order to be worthy of Him and be with Him.

Jesus will call for His Bride as soon as she is ready. Time is short, but there is still a time of grace for the Bride to prepare herself, and it's still possible to heed the call.

Answering the call to be in the Bride is the first step. It's as simple as deciding, "I want to serve God with all my heart." The way to go after this is described in Colossians chapter 3.

> *"1 If then you have been raised with Christ [to a new life, thus sharing His resurrection from the dead], aim at and seek the [rich, eternal treasures] that are above, where Christ is, seated at the right hand of God. [Psa. 110:1.]*
> *2 And set your minds and keep them set on what is above (the higher things), not on the things that are on the earth.*
> *3 For [as far as this world is concerned] you have died, and your [new, real] life is hidden with Christ in God.*
> *4 When Christ, Who is our life, appears, then you also will appear with Him in [the splendor of His] glory.*
> *5 So kill (deaden, deprive of power) the evil desire lurking in your members [those animal impulses and all that is earthly in you that is employed in sin]: sexual vice, impurity, sensual appetites, unholy desires, and all greed and covetousness, for that is idolatry (the deifying of self and other created things instead of God).*
> *6 It is on account of these [very sins] that the [holy] anger of God is ever coming upon the sons of disobedience (those who are obstinately opposed to the divine will),*
> *7 Among whom you also once walked, when you were living in and addicted to [such practices].*
> *8 But now put away and rid yourselves [completely] of all these things: anger, rage, bad feeling toward others, curses and slander, and foulmouthed abuse and shameful utterances from your lips!*
> *9 Do not lie to one another, for you have stripped off the old (unregenerate) self with its evil practices,*
> *10 And have clothed yourselves with the new [spiritual self], which is [ever in the process of being] renewed and remolded into [fuller and more perfect knowledge upon] knowledge after the image (the likeness) of Him Who created it. [See also Gen. 1:26.]*
> *11 [In this new creation all distinctions vanish.] There is no room for and there can be neither Greek nor Jew, circumcised nor uncircumcised, [nor difference between nations whether alien] barbarians or Scythians [who are the most savage of all], nor slave or free man; but Christ is all and in all [everything and everywhere, to all men, without distinction of person].*

12 Clothe yourselves therefore, as God's own chosen ones (His own picked representatives), [who are] purified and holy and well-beloved [by God Himself, by putting on behavior marked by] tenderhearted pity and mercy, kind feeling, a lowly opinion of yourselves, gentle ways, [and] patience [which is tireless and long-suffering, and has the power to endure whatever comes, with good temper].
13 Be gentle and forbearing with one another and, if one has a difference (a grievance or complaint) against another, readily pardoning each other; even as the Lord has [freely] forgiven you, so must you also [forgive].
14 And above all these [put on] love and enfold yourselves with the bond of perfectness [which binds everything together completely in ideal harmony].
15 And let the peace (soul harmony which comes) from Christ rule (act as umpire continually) in your hearts [deciding and settling with finality all questions that arise in your minds, in that peaceful state] to which as [members of Christ's] one body you were also called [to live]. And be thankful (appreciative), [giving praise to God always].
16 Let the word [spoken by] Christ (the Messiah) have its home [in your hearts and minds] and dwell in you in [all its] richness, as you teach and admonish and train one another in all insight and intelligence and wisdom [in spiritual things, and as you sing] psalms and hymns and spiritual songs, making melody to God with [His] grace in your hearts.
17 And whatever you do [no matter what it is] in word or deed, do everything in the name of the Lord Jesus and in [dependence upon] His Person, giving praise to God the Father through Him," (Amplified Classic Edition, Col. 3:1-17).

The Bride of Christ sets her mind on things above. The Bride is patient, humble, long-suffering, and does everything in the name of the Lord Jesus. The only thing she wants is to hasten the day of His return.

> *"While you wait and earnestly long for (expect and hasten) the coming of the day of God by reason of which the flaming heavens will be dissolved, and the [material] elements [of the universe] will flare and melt with fire?" (AMPC, 2 Pet. 3:12). [See also Isa. 34:4.]*

The Bride of Christ is purified and cleansed as He is pure and will be transformed into divine nature like His.

"Beloved, we are [even here and] now God's children; it is not yet disclosed (made clear) what we shall be [hereafter], but we know that when He comes and is manifested, we shall [as God's children] resemble and be like Him, for we shall see Him just as He [really] is.
3 And everyone who has this hope [resting] on Him cleanses (purifies) himself just as He is pure (chaste, undefiled, guiltless)," (AMPC, I Jn. 3:2-3).

The Marriage of the Lamb

Nothing less than perfection is acceptable. So she becomes holy as He is holy. These are the righteous acts of the saints as described in Revelation 19.

"7 Let us rejoice and shout for joy [exulting and triumphant]! Let us celebrate and ascribe to Him glory and honor, for the marriage of the Lamb [at last] has come, and His bride has prepared herself. [Psa. 118:24.]
8 She has been permitted to dress in fine (radiant) linen, dazzling and white–for the fine linen is (signifies, represents) the righteousness (the upright, just, and godly living, deeds, and conduct, and right standing with God) of the saints (God's holy people).
9 Then [the angel] said to me, Write this down: Blessed (happy, to be envied) are those who are summoned (invited, called) to the marriage supper of the Lamb. And he said to me [further], These are the true words (the genuine and exact declarations) of God," (AMPC, Rev. 19:7-9).

They are standing there in Heaven, a throng of warriors and heroes dressed in pure white – an army that has paid the price and given everything to be cleansed and purified and transformed into Christ's image. They are shining brighter than the sun, shining with a purity equal to Christ Himself. They are holy. They are His.

The heroes of the Old Testament and the martyrs of the great tribulation, amongst others, are of course servants of God and have fellowship with Christ. But the Bride of Christ has a very special calling. She is seated beside Him; she is equal with Him. She has suffered the same sufferings as He has on Earth and now she has her reward. It is a reward far greater than any given to anybody else in Heaven or on Earth. She is set above angels, above cherubim, above all of God's creation, to be a partner and a helper to God's very Son Himself.

The Bride's job in eternity will always be beside the bridegroom.

> *"The [Holy] Spirit and the bride (the church, the true Christians) say, Come! And let him who is listening say, Come! And let everyone come who is thirsty [who is painfully conscious of his need of those things by which the soul is refreshed, supported, and strengthened]; and whoever [earnestly] desires to do it, let him come, take, appropriate, and drink the water of Life without cost," (AMPC, Rev. 22:17). [See also Isa. 55:1.]*

There is no greater reward than this. And there is no greater use of our time on Earth than to prepare for the day of His coming, in earnest expectation, to be so in love with Jesus Christ that the lives we live here on Earth are worthy of the bride He wants to marry.

NOTES:

Chapter 22

Sacraments Are for Me

We should examine
our hearts before
we eat and drink,
confessing our sins
unto
God
in order to receive
forgiveness and
cleansing.

Chapter 22

Sacraments Are for Me

The word sacrament is not used in most English versions of the Bible. It comes from the Latin '*sacramentum'* which was the word for a soldier's oath of allegiance. Baptism and the Lord's Supper are the essential sacraments based on the fact that these are the only two actions involving visible symbols (the water, the bread, and wine) that were clearly observed by Christ (Luke 22:14-20) and commanded by Him (Matt. 28:19-20). A number of Evangelicals and Pentecostals practice foot-washing, following the example and instruction of Jesus (Jn. 13:1-17). Some observe foot washing as a third ordinance.

Water Baptism [Refer back to Chapter 12]

Water baptism is the sacrament of entry into the Christian life. Unlike the Lord's Supper, which is repeated over and over again, baptism is a one-time ceremony that need never be repeated. It symbolizes our entrance into the Kingdom of God, our new birth into His family.

Water baptism, by immersion is a prescribed procedure commanded by Jesus Christ to be practiced in the church.

Why do we celebrate the Lord's Supper?

Also known as Communion, this is a biblical practice usually done during a worship service where Christians partake of bread and wine (or grape juice) with the purpose of remembering Christ, receiving strength and healing from Him, and being renewed to serve His cause. It is one of two sacraments instituted by Christ to be observed by His Church until He returns.

The Lord's Supper took place on the night before Jesus died, at a meal commonly known today as the Last Supper (Matt. 26:17-30; Mk. 14:12-26; Lk. 22:1-23; 1 Cor. 11:23-25).

Many of Jesus' actions and words at the Last Supper, such as the breaking and distributing of the bread, were part of the prescribed Passover meal, but then Jesus said, "This is My body" and "This is My blood" while distributing the bread and the cup. Jesus often used figurative language. What He probably meant was, "This bread represents My body" and "This wine represents My blood."

The bread and wine are to be understood symbolically. The bread and wine were only symbols of the sacrificed body and blood of Christ. The Lord's Supper is primarily a memorial ceremony of Christ's finished work. Christ is not physically present in the elements because His risen, glorified body is in Heaven (Heb. 10:12-13).

Biblical Teachings on Holy Communion

In 1 Corinthians 10:16, the Apostle Paul rebuked the Corinthians for their involvement with idolatry. He referred to the cup as "the communion of the blood of Christ" and the bread as "the communion of the body of Christ." The Greek word for communion has the meaning of "fellowship, participating, and sharing". From the context, it appears that Paul is saying that when Christians partake of the cup and the bread, they are participating in the benefits of Christ's death (referred to as His blood) and resurrection life (His glorified body). The most important of these benefits are the assurance of sins forgiven (through Christ's blood) and the assurance of Christ's presence and power (through His body).

The "one body" (the universal Church) in 1 Corinthians 10:17 connects with the "body of Christ" in verse 16 in the sense that the entire Church of Christ is organically related to the living, glorified human body of Christ now in Heaven. The "one [loaf of] bread" (v 17), representing Jesus the "bread of life" (John 6:35), is eaten by all believers at the supper symbolizing their unity and common participation in the one body of Christ. The great discourse of Jesus on the bread of life (Jn. 6:25-68), while not intended to be a direct theological explanation of the Lord's Supper, helps to explain how receiving the Holy Communion can be one way in which Christians "feed" on the Lord (Jn. 6:55-57). Other important ways are by prayer and the hearing of God's Word through the Scriptures.

In 1 Corinthians 11:17-34, Paul rebuked the Corinthians for their pride and greed during the meal that accompanied the Holy Communion (vv 17-22). Then (vv 23-25) he described the institution of the Lord's Supper and emphasized the need for Christians to partake in a worthy manner. Many of them who had not been doing so were weak and sick, and many had even died as a result of misappropriating or neglecting the purpose of the Table (vv 27-34).

Examine Yourself

> *"27 Therefore whoever eats this bread or drinks this cup of the Lord in an unworthy manner will be guilty of the body and blood of the Lord.*
> *28 But let a man examine himself, and so let him eat of the bread and drink of the cup.*
> *29 For he who eats and drinks in an unworthy manner eats and drinks judgment to himself, not discerning the Lord's body.*
> *30 For this reason many are weak and sick among you, and many sleep.*
> *31 For if we would judge ourselves, we would not be judged.*
> *32 But when we are judged, we are chastened by the Lord, that we may not be condemned with the world.*
> *33 Therefore, my brethren, when you come together to eat, wait for one another.*
> *34 But if anyone is hungry, let him eat at home, lest you come together for judgment. And the rest I will set in order when I come," (New King James Version, 1 Cor. 11:27-34).*

Why does Paul use such strong language when speaking of the abuse of the Lord's Supper? The Corinthians were not properly discerning or recognizing the Lord's body. The wealthy Corinthians who shamed their poorer Christian brothers and sisters by their selfish eating practices (vv 21-22) were not discerning the true nature of the Church as Christ's body in which all distinctions such as social class and race were blotted out (Gal. 3:28).

Christians who received the bread and the cup after behaving disgracefully were failing to discern that Christ would not automatically bless and empower those who received the sacrament in this manner. Such persons were guilty of sin against the body and blood of Jesus (v 27).

Holy Communion is so important for the Christian to observe and we need to know why it is such a serious offense to misuse it. This corresponds well with those Scriptures that speak of God's nourishing and empowering work in His people (Eph. 3:14-21; Col. 2:6-10, 19).

How should we receive the Lord's Supper?

When you partake of the Lord's Supper, we must always do so in a reverent manner, fully aware of the significance of what we are doing (1 Cor. 11:27-28). We must never treat lightly the elements that symbolize the blood and the body of our Lord. We should examine our hearts before we eat and drink, confessing our sins unto God in order to receive forgiveness and cleansing. In addition, we should recognize and affirm our unity with the body of Christ in the local church and around the world for we all share together in the life of Christ.

Whether we partake of one loaf or individual wafers, whether we drink from a single cup or from individual glasses, the particular elements we use are not as important as the **attitude** of our hearts. The elements are but physical symbols of a spiritual reality and they contain no magical power but, mixed with faith, they become more than symbols; they become a *means* by which God's grace comes to us. Taken in faith, they impart to us that which was in the body and blood of Christ: **His very life.**

When we ask how the Lord's Supper should be meaningful to the Christian today, three concepts relating to the past, present, and future can be helpful.

First: The Lord's Supper is a time of remembrance and Holy Communion. Jesus said, "Do this in remembrance of Me" (Lk. 22:19; 1 Cor. 11:24-25). This is not to be so much our dwelling on the agonies of the crucifixion as it is to be our remembering the marvelous life and ministry of our Savior. Holy Communion is to be an occasion for expressing our deepest praise and appreciation for all Jesus Christ has done for us.

The Jewish Passover was to proclaim the Hebrews' deliverance from Egyptian bondage (Exod. 12:26-27), so at the Lord's Supper, Christians proclaim their deliverance from sin and misery through the death of "Christ, our Passover" (1 Cor. 5:7; 11:26).

Second: The Lord's Supper is a time of refreshment and communion. As we participate in the benefits of Jesus' death and resurrection life (Rom. 5:10; 1 Cor. 10:16), we are actually being nourished and empowered from the risen Christ through the Spirit.

John Wesley knew of this strengthening. On the average, he received communion every four or five days throughout his long and fruitful ministerial career. It is not that God cannot empower us without the Lord's Supper but that He has instituted the Supper for us, even as He has designated prayer and the hearing of Scripture as means of communicating His grace. While the Bible does not tell us how often to observe the Holy Communion, Wesley's guideline—"as often as you can"—deserves our serious consideration.

Third: The Supper is a time of recommitment and anticipation. We are to examine (literally "prove" or "test") ourselves and partake in a worthy manner (1 Cor. 11:28-29). In so doing, we renew our dedication to Christ and His people, in hopeful anticipation "till He comes" (1 Cor. 11:26). After Christ's return, we shall partake with Him—in His physical presence—in the Kingdom (Matt. 26:29).

NOTES:

Chapter 23

Jesus Descended into Hell

Immediately after dying,
and because the price of
mankind's deliverance
from sin was now
"paid in full"
through
His blood and death,
Jesus descended to
"the lower parts of the earth"

Ephesians 4:9

Chapter 23

Jesus Descended into Hell

The gates of Hell shall not prevail against the Church in this age (Matt. 16:18), but they did prevail against Old Testament saints, for they all went down into the paradise compartment of Sheol and were held captive by Satan against their will (Heb. 2:14-15). Since the resurrection of Christ, saints do not go to *Sheol-Hades* as before. He conquered Hell and liberated the righteous souls from Satan, leading them captive to Heaven (Eph. 4:8-10; Heb. 2:14-15). Saints of this age now go to Heaven at death instead of Sheol (2 Cor. 5:8; Phil. 1:21-24; Heb. 12:23; Rev. 6:9-11).

The Bible does say, "He descended."

Ephesians 4:8-10 and 1 Peter 3:18-20 and 4:6 make clear reference to this fact. For the record, this is what the Word of God says He did do:

- First: Jesus confronted Hell's powers on the cross and completely broke the hold of sin, Satan, and death through the blood of His cross (Eph. 2:13-16; Col. 2:13-15).
- Immediately after dying, and because the price of mankind's deliverance from sin was now paid in full through His blood and death, Jesus descended to "the lower parts of the earth" (Eph. 4:9).
- There He "preached to the spirits in prison" (1 Pet. 3:19):
  (a) *declaring* the fulfillment of God's promise of redemption to those temporarily residing "in Abraham's bosom" (Luke 16:19-31 – the abode of those who died in faith under the Old Covenant, awaiting the Redeemer—Messiah); and
  (b) *confirming* the faithfulness and judgment of God to those "in torment"; verifying the truth of God's promise and the justice of their consignment to eternal loss.

- Then He finalized His confounding of the powers of darkness, who were completely stunned by the reversal of circumstances they suffered at the cross (1 Cor. 2:6-8). He freed the forgiven faithful whose salvation He had now accomplished, taking them to Paradise (Luke 23:42-43), then, stripping the keys of death and Hell from our adversary, the devil (Rev. 1:18), He concluded any hold which Satan had over human destiny.

These are the things Jesus didn't do in Hell according to the Word of God:

- He *didn't* suffer there. His suffering at Calvary accomplished His procuring of all the prophetic intent of Isaiah 53:5, including those provisions for our healing and our deliverance.
- He *didn't* add to our salvation there. His blood and death are the completely adequate, fully required, and entirely accomplished price of our forgiveness for all sin, our justification from sin's claim on us, and our release unto eternal life (Rom. 5:6-10).

The Bible calls what Jesus did for us on the cross "so great salvation" and it is exactly that! As surely as its greatness is due to One Man—Jesus Christ our Savior, the Son of God—so is its completeness derived from One Source—His blood and death as the Sinless Lamb.

NOTES:

Chapter 24

Why Do Christians Worship on Sunday Instead of the Sabbath?

In remembrance of
the resurrection,
the early Christian
church
changed the day of
worship from
Saturday to Sunday

Chapter 24

Why do Christians worship on Sunday instead of the Sabbath?

There are good reasons why millions of Christians gather on the first day of the week for worship. First, in remembrance of the resurrection, the early Christian Church changed the day of worship from Saturday to Sunday. Within weeks, thousands of Jews willingly gave up a theological tradition that had given them their national identity. God Himself had provided the early Church with a new pattern of worship through Christ's resurrection on the first day of the week as well as the Holy Spirit's descent on Pentecost Sunday.

"So let no one judge you in food or in drink, or regarding a festival or a new moon or ***sabbaths****, which are a shadow of things to come, but the substance is of Christ,"*
(NKJV, Col. 2:16-17)

10 Reasons Why Christians Keep Sunday

1. To commemorate the resurrection and the finished work of Christ in His victory over death, Hell, and the grave (Matt. 28:1; Mk. 16:9; Jn. 20:1).

2. The Lord's manifestations to His disciples were on Sunday (Matt. 28:1; Mk. 16:9; Jn. 20:1, 19, 26).

3. Christ ignored completely the old Jewish Sabbath. The first day is the prominent day after the Resurrection (Matt. 28:1; Mk. 16:9; Jn. 20:1, 19, 26).

4. The outpouring of the Holy Spirit came on Sunday. Pentecost was the first day after 7 Jewish Sabbaths (Acts 2:1; Lev. 23:15-21). Thus, both Christ and the Holy Spirit manifested themselves to the Church on this day, completely ignoring the Jewish Sabbath.

5. Neither Christ nor any apostle commanded to keep the old Jewish Sabbath, or any other day, but did command all men not to be bound by any particular day (Rom. 14:5-6;

Gal. 4:9-11; Col. 2:14-17). Sin is sin, whenever committed. It is transgression of the law that constitutes sin (1 Jn. 3:4), not the day on which it is done. Anything sinful on Saturday or Sunday is sinful on every other day. If it is not sinful on Monday, Tuesday, etc., it is not sinful on Sunday.

6. Although no set day is commanded to be the Sabbath in the New Covenant, as in the Old Covenant which was abolished, they did keep Sunday as their day of worship (Matt. 28:1; Mk. 16:9; Jn. 20:1; 19, 26; Acts 20:7; 1 Cor. 16:2; Rev. 1:10).

7. Typology (the study and interpretation of types and symbols, originally in the Bible) of the Old Covenant made Sunday a day of worship:

a. The Jewish Sabbath was not a fixed Sabbath. On the contrary, it changed every year at Pentecost to be one day later until each day of the week was observed every 7 years. Pentecost was the first day after the 7th Sabbath (see Lev. 23:15-21).

b. The Feast of Firstfruits came on Sunday, typifying the Resurrection (Lev. 23:9-14; Matt. 28:1; Jn. 20:1).

c. The Feast of Unleavened Bread and Tabernacles also were observed at least on Sunday and perhaps two, being 7 and 8 days long (Lev. 23:6-36).

8. God honored Sunday by giving the law on that day (Exod. 19:1, 3, 11 with Lev. 23:3-6; Exod. 12:2-18).

9. God again honored Sunday when giving the book of Revelation (Rev. 1:10).

10. Constantine and the Pope did not change the Sabbath, AD 321 and 364 (1 Cor.16:2).

It is clear that many religious services were held on Sundays as well as on Saturday and other days of the week. They came together to worship and take the Lord's Supper (1 Cor. 10:16). It was after midnight the Supper was taken here. (See Matt. 26:26-30; 1 Cor. 10:16-22, 11:17-34; Acts 2:42, 46, 20:7.)

Notes:

Chapter 25

Put On the Whole Armor of God
For Spiritual Warfare

The Christian Soldier
must live up to the rules if
he expects a crown and
eternal fruit.

Everything that occurs in my world is
connected to the wrestling
I'm waged in regarding
the invisible Spiritual world of
wickedness!
Stand in readiness
For Spiritual Combat....
Recognize your
Demonic Enemies!

Chapter 25

Put On the Whole Armor of God For Spiritual Warfare

Dressed For Spiritual Warfare

Paul earnestly advises us to put on the whole armor of God in order to stand against the forces of evil. It is clear that our warfare is not against physical forces but against invisible powers who have clearly defined levels of authority in a real, though invisible, sphere of activity. Paul not only warns us of a clearly defined structure in the invisible realm, he instructs us to take up the whole armor of God in order to maintain a "battle stance" against this unseen satanic structure.

The Book of Ephesians is a delicate mix between God's gifts and our responsibilities. The first three chapters speak to the identity and status given to all believers in Christ. However, in the fourth chapter, it shifts to the responsibility of the believer to act on.

The first three chapters are the *indicatives*— everything that's been accomplished for us in Christ Jesus. He has already won the victory! The *imperatives*—how we are supposed to use them and what I am to do in response—are of vital importance. They are very critical for long-term victory in our everyday life.

Believe and receive what you have been given.

Three illustrations of a Christian taken from two different Bible versions.

> *"3 You therefore must endure hardship as a* ***good soldier*** *of Jesus Christ.*
> *4 No one engaged in warfare entangles himself with the affairs of this life, that he may please him who enlisted him as a soldier.*
> *5 And also if anyone competes in* ***athletics****, he is not crowned unless he competes according to the rules.*
> *6 The hardworking* ***farmer*** *must be first to partake of the crops.*
> *7 Consider what I say, and may the Lord give you understanding in all things," (NKJV, 2 Tim. 2:3-7).*

*"3 Take your share of suffering as a **good soldier** of Jesus Christ, just as I do;*
4 and as Christ's soldier, do not let yourself become tied up in worldly affairs, for then you cannot satisfy the one who has enlisted you in his army.
*5 Follow the Lord's rules for doing His work, just as an **athlete** either follows the rules or is disqualified and wins no prize.*
*6 Work hard like a **farmer** who gets paid well if he raises a large crop.*
7 Think over these three illustrations, and may the Lord help you to understand how they apply to you," (The Living Bible, 2 Tim. 2:3-7).

Just as a good soldier lives up to certain standards, a winning athlete obeys the rules of the game, and as a farmer tills according to natural laws of agriculture if he gets a crop, so the Christian soldier must live up to the rules if he expects a crown and eternal fruit.

Seven Observations About Spiritual Warfare

1. Many people blame their personal failures on someone else because they do not want to face the truth. It's is a lot easier to blame someone else than to be responsible for their actions.
2. Most "attacks" are our own mistakes.
3. Spiritual warfare is NOT a momentary gust of emotion.
4. Spiritual warfare is a mental condition and a lifelong commitment; it is not so much an action as it is an attitude of the mind.

"3 For though we walk in the flesh, we do not war after the flesh.
4 (For the weapons of our warfare are not carnal but mighty through God to the pulling down of strongholds;)
*5 Casting down **imaginations**, and every high thing that exalteth itself against the knowledge of God, and bringing into captivity every thought to the obedience of Christ," (King James Version, 2 Cor. 10:3-5).*

5. People go after weird teaching because they offer simple solutions to difficult lifelong problems. The thought of an instant cure is very alluring to the uncommitted and spiritually immature who are looking for a QUICK FIX to change deeply-rooted, habitual, and often self-imposed problems.
6. Much of spiritual warfare is mental preparation. Mental preparation removes the element of surprise. This will always give you the upper hand.
7. As you make spiritual progress, you encounter real spiritual warfare.

REDEMPTION — The Reason Why We Can Walk In Authority.

1. Spiritual warfare is not a fight for freedom. We are already FREE. (Eph. 2:5-6; Col. 1:13-14; Col. 2:14-15)
2. We are redeemed of the Lord! (Psa. 107:2)

   "Let the redeemed of the LORD say so, whom He has redeemed from the hand of the enemy," (New King James Version).

Redeem 1. To recover ownership of by paying a specified sum. 2. To pay off (a promissory note, for example). 3. To turn in (coupons, for example) and receive something in exchange. 4. To fulfill (a pledge, for example). 5. To convert into cash. 6. To set free; rescue or ransom. 7. To save from a state of sinfulness and its consequences. 8. To make up for. 9. To restore the honor, worth, or reputation of.

3. Because we are **redeemed,** we have **authority** over the devil. We are equipped to beat the living daylights out of any foe that would dare assault us.

   *"And Jesus came and spoke to them, saying, "**All authority** has been given to Me in heaven and on earth," (NKJV, Matt. 28:18).*

   *"1 Then He called His twelve disciples together and gave them **power** and **authority** over all demons, and to cure diseases.*
   2 He sent them to preach the kingdom of God and to heal the sick," (NKJV, Lk. 9:1-2).

   "17 Then the seventy returned with joy, saying, "Lord, even the demons are subject to us in Your name."
   18 And He said to them, "I saw Satan fall like lightning from heaven.
   *19 Behold, I give you the **authority** to trample on serpents and scorpions, and over **all the power** of the enemy, and nothing shall by any means hurt you.*
   20 Nevertheless do not rejoice in this, that the spirits are subject to you, but rather rejoice because your names are written in heaven," (NKJV, Lk. 10:17-20).

   "You are of God, little children, and have overcome them, because He who is in you is greater than he who is in the world," (NKJV, 1 Jn. 4:4).

DRESSED FOR WARFARE — THE WHOLE ARMOR OF GOD

Spiritual Warfare

All of this armor is not just a passive protection in facing the enemy; it is to be used offensively against these satanic forces. Note Paul's final directive: we are to be *"praying always with all prayer and supplication in the Spirit," (NKJV, Ephesians 6:18).* Prayer is not so much a weapon, or even a part of the armor as it is the means by which we "engage in the battle" itself and the purpose for which we are armed. To put on the armor of God is to prepare for battle. Prayer is the battle itself, with God's Word being our chief weapon employed against Satan during our struggle.

> *"10 Finally, my brethren, be strong in the Lord and in the power of His might.*
> *11 Put on the whole armor of God, that you may be able to stand against the wiles of the devil.*
> *12 For we do not wrestle against flesh and blood, but against principalities, against powers, against the rulers of the darkness of this age, against spiritual hosts of wickedness in the heavenly places.*
> *13 Therefore take up the whole armor of God, that you may be able to withstand in the evil day, and having done all, to stand.*
> *14 Stand therefore, having girded your waist with truth, having put on the breastplate of righteousness,*
> *15 and having shod your feet with the preparation of the gospel of peace;*
> *16 above all, taking the shield of faith with which you will be able to quench all the fiery darts of the wicked one.*
> *17 And take the helmet of salvation, and the sword of the Spirit, which is the word of God;*
> *18 praying always with all prayer and supplication in the Spirit, being watchful to this end with all perseverance and supplication for all the saints," (NKJV, Eph. 6:10-18).*

The armor of God is ours by virtue of our relationship with God! It is freely bestowed upon those who continually draw their life and existence from God. We have resurrection power! Man does not possess this kind of power unless it has been given to him by God!

In the scriptures of Ephesians 6:10-18, we are going to take a deeper look using a Vine's Expository Dictionary of Biblical Words to receive the full meaning, breaking down words and the description of what is being spoken for your benefit. The devil is a genius so we have to know his plan.

Eph 6:10.

"Finally, my brethren, be strong in the Lord and in the power of His might."

In **Eph 6:10, the Key Thought is**: Be strong in the Lord. When that strength comes to you, it will clothe you with spiritual armor! Rebuke the devil!

Eph 6:11

"Put on the whole armor of God, that you may be able to stand against the wiles of the devil."

Let's break this down.

> NOTE: All numbers before the Greek or Hebrew text, are QUICK REFERENCE NUMBERS that are taken from the Strong's Exhaustive Concordance of the Bible. This is for a deeper meaning of the Word. They are also taken from the Vine's Expository Dictionary of Biblical Words. These two books can be used together. [Online: biblehub.com] There is an app for the Vine's. Otherwise they are two different books that you can purchase.

Key Word: Wiles = *methodos*
3180 methodeia (meth-od-i'-ah) meta= with odos= road Means: With a road
From a compound of 3326 and 3593 [compare "method"]; traveling over, i.e. travesty (trickery):
Wiles = methodia, or – 3180 denotes "craft, deceit" "a cunning device, a wile,: and is translated "wiles (of error)" in Eph. 4:14, [KJV paraphrases it, "they lie in wait (to deceive)"] "(with a view to) the craft (singular) of deceit"; in 6:11, "the wiles (plural) (of the devil.)"
[from Vine's Expository Dictionary of Biblical Words copyright 1985, Thomas Nelson Publishers]

***Mental torment. A road to travel, one road and it is headed toward your mind!**
Three Key Words You must know and understand on the subject of spiritual warfare.
1. Wiles. 2. Devices. 3. Deception

"Lest Satan should take advantage of us; for we are not ignorant of his ***devices,"*** *(NKJV, 2 Cor. 2:11).*

Devices [noemata]= a scheming of the mind/a crafty scheme; tick
3540 noema — To fill the human mind with confusion (a deceived mind)
1) a mental perception, a thought (2) an evil purpose. (3) what thinks, the mind, thoughts or purposes.

***Continued mental pressure, mind games**. We are not ignorant of the mind games that Satan tries to pull on us. The devil has a road to travel on to bring "deception" to your mind; "that you cannot go on."

Eph 6:12

"For we do not wrestle against flesh and blood, but against principalities, against powers, against the rulers of the darkness of this age, against spiritual hosts of wickedness in the heavenly places."

In **Eph 6:12, the Key Thought is:** Our fight is not with each other—flesh and blood—but with spiritual forces that influence you at the point of weakness.

Eph 6:13

"Therefore take up the whole armor of God, that you may be able to withstand in the evil day, and having done all, to stand."

In **Eph 6:13 the Key Words are:** Whole Armor of God **and** Evil Day.
In 1 Samuel 17, Goliath and his brothers were of the remnant of giants left to test Israel. Goliath was 13 feet 4 inches tall, weighing in at 700+ pounds. It was the constant threats and mental bombardments that Goliath hit them with every single day for 40 days, day and night, taunting them. This mental harassment crippled them so that they lost sight of the awesome ability of God.

Take A Stand: Stand On The Word!

Dressed For Success – The Armor Of God = Is an Attitude.
A Word in faith—Renewing of your mind.

God has not left you naked before the enemy: He has provided you with spiritual weaponry for a counter attack … "Devil …you are dead meat!"

Eph 6:14 (King James Version)

> *"Stand therefore, having girded your **loins** girt about with truth, and having on the breastplate of righteousness."*

LOINS = osphus is used

(a) in the natural sense in Matthew 3:4; Mark 1:6

(b) as "the seat of generative power," Hebrews 7:5,10; metaphorically in Acts 2:30

(c) metaphorically,

1. of girding the "loins" in readiness for active service for the Lord, Luke 12:35;
2. the same, with truth, Ephesians 6:14, i.e., bracing up oneself so as to maintain perfect sincerity and reality as the counteractive in Christian character against hypocrisy and falsehood;
3. of girding the "loins" of the mind, 1 Peter 1:13, "girding," suggestive of the alertness necessary for sobriety and for setting one's hope perfectly on "the grace to be brought ... at the revelation of Jesus Christ" (the present participle, "girding," is introductory to the rest of the verse).

Truth - 225 aletheia = The truth as taught in the Christian faith, respecting God and the execution of his purposes through Christ, and respecting the duties of man, opposing alike to the superstitions of the Gentiles (non-Jews) and the inventions of the Jews, and the corrupt opinions and precepts of false teachers even among Christians.

Jesus is the ultimate **Truth** (Jn. 14:6).
The Word of God is called **Truth** (2 Cor. 6:7; Eph. 1:13; Col. 1:5; 2 Tim. 2:15; Jn. 17:17).

When you know the **truth**, then you are no longer a P.O.W.

> *"And you shall know the **truth**, and the **truth** shall make you **free**," (New King James Version, Jn. 8:32).*

Free - 1659 eleutheroo = to make free, set at liberty: from the dominion of sin. Done once and for all. "Not to bring us into another form of bondage did Christ liberate us from that in which we were born, but in order to make us free from bondage."

Four Observations Concerning Our Loins Girt With Truth

1. Living by the Truth is living by the Word. Being a Doer of the Word not a Hearer only.

James 1:22-25

"22 But be doers of the word, and not hearers only, deceiving yourselves.
23 For if anyone is a hearer of the word and not a doer, he is like a man observing his natural face in a mirror;
24 for he observes himself, goes away, and immediately forgets what kind of man he was.
25 But he who looks into the perfect law of liberty and continues in it, and is not a forgetful hearer but a doer of the work, this one will be blessed in what he does," (NKJV, James 1:22-25).

Matthew 7:24-27

"24 Therefore whoever hears these sayings of Mine, and does them, I will liken him to a wise man who built his house on the rock:
25 and the rain descended, the floods came, and the winds blew and beat on that house; and it did not fall, for it was founded on the rock.
26 "But everyone who hears these sayings of Mine, and does not do them, will be like a foolish man who built his house on the sand:
27 and the rain descended, the floods came, and the winds blew and beat on that house; and it fell. And great was its fall," (NKJV, Matt. 7:24-27).

***The evil day! You can be victorious if your life is built on the truth!** Planted and rooted in the Word, my house is built on the rock.

John 13:17

"If you know these things, blessed are you if you do them," (NKJV, Jn. 13:17).

2. The loin belt holds everything else up.
3. The loin belt is the center of the armor.
   [the belt of truth— the Word Of God is the center]
4. Every piece of the armor is based on the Word of God.
   Faith and the Word of God are inseparable.

*Right is right even if everyone is against it, and wrong is wrong even if everyone is for it."

*If you continue to do what's right, what's wrong and who's wrong will leave your life.

> *"Therefore submit to God. Resist the devil and he will flee from you," (NKJV, James 4:7).*

Submit to spiritual authority; come under the covering of the local church. Be willing to submit to your spiritual elders, those who have learned the ways of God and know how to fight demons.

* You must be under submission to exercise authority.
* Submission is an attitude more than an action.
* To be strong in resisting the devil, you stay alert and in authority.

> *"For the mystery of lawlessness (that hidden principle of rebellion against constituted authority) is already at work in the world, [but it is] restrained only until he who restrains is taken out of the way," (Amplified Classic Edition, 2 Thess. 2:7).*

> *"26 When angry, do not sin; do not ever let your wrath (your exasperation, your fury or indignation) last until the sun goes down.*
> *27 Leave no [such] room or foothold for the devil [give no opportunity to him]," (AMPC, Eph. 4:26-27).*

Don't go there! Don't let the devil in! Be alert and give **NO** opportunity for the enemy.

> *"12 Blessed (happy, to be envied) is the man who is patient under trial and stands up under temptation, for when he has stood the test and been approved, he will receive [the victor's] crown of life which God has promised to those who love Him.*
> *13 Let no one say when he is tempted, I am tempted from God; for God is incapable of being tempted by [what is] evil and He Himself tempts no one.*
> *14 But every person is tempted when he is drawn away, enticed and baited by his own evil desire (lust, passions).*
> *15 Then the evil desire, when it has conceived, gives birth to sin, and sin, when it is fully matured, brings forth death.*
> *16 Do not be misled, my beloved brethren," (AMPC, James 1:12-16).*

I will not be moved by what I see, what I hear, and what I feel!

I Peter 3:9-12

"9 Not returning evil for evil or reviling for reviling, but on the contrary blessing, knowing that you were called to this, that you may inherit a blessing.
10 For 'He who would love life And see good days, Let him refrain his tongue from evil, And his lips from speaking deceit.
11 Let him turn away from evil and do good; Let him seek peace and pursue it.
12 For the eyes of the LORD are on the righteous, And His ears are open to their prayers; But the face of the LORD is against those who do evil,' " (New King James Version, I Pet. 3:9-12).

Matthew 15:18

"But those things which proceed out of the mouth come from the heart, and they defile a man," (NKJV, Matt. 15:18).

Ephesians 6:14b

*"Having put on the **breastplate of righteousness,**" (NKJV, Eph. 6:14b).*

Breastplate = Strong's #2382 — Noun Masculine — thorax — tho'-rax
primarily, "the breast" denotes "a breastplate or corselet" consisting of two parts and protecting the body on both sides, from the neck to the middle. It is used metaphorically of righteousness, (Eph. 6:14); of faith and love, (1 Thess. 5:8), with perhaps a suggestion of the two parts, front and back, which formed the coat of mail (an alternative term for the word in the New Testament sense); elsewhere in Rev. 9:9,17.

***Righteousness** = right standing with God! [Strong's #1343 dikaiosune] —In a broad sense: state of him who is as he ought to be, righteousness, the condition acceptable to God (a) the doctrine concerning the way in which man may attain a state approved of God (b) integrity, virtue, purity of life, rightness, correctness of thinking, feeling, and acting.

*The ability to stand in the presence of the Father without the sense of guilt or inferiority. Just-as-if (justified) sin never existed.
*Righteousness not only brings forgiveness but also puts you back into the position you had before the wrong was committed. (1 Jn. 1:9).

Five Truths Concerning Righteousness

1. The revelation of **righteousness** is a key to exercising **authority**.

*"For if by the one man's offense (Adam) death reigned through the one, much more those who receive abundance of grace and of the gift of righteousness will **reign** in life through the One, Jesus Christ," (NKJV, Rom. 5:17).*

Reign [strong's #936] basileuo — of believers where "shall **reign** in life" indicates the activity of life in fellowship with Christ in His sovereign power, reaching its fullness, to exercise the highest influence, to control.

Adam:

A) Was given <u>authority.</u> You have <u>authority</u>.
B) Was able to <u>partake</u> of everything given to him. You can <u>partake</u> of everything given.
C) Had the ability to <u>protect</u> what was given to him. You can <u>protect</u> your promises.
D) Enjoyed full <u>fellowship</u> with the Father. You can have full <u>fellowship</u> with the Father.

- Sin consciences will always look at your lack of ability. It looks to the natural to right the wrong and no longer enjoys full fellowship.

2. The revelation of **righteousness** will help you to not **sin**.

"Awake to righteousness, and do not sin; for some do not have the knowledge of God. I speak this to your shame," (NKJV, I Cor. 15:34).

3. The revelation of **righteousness** will establish you, make you **stable**, **fit,** and **unmovable**.

"13 All your children shall be taught by the LORD, And great shall be the peace of your children.
14 In righteousness you shall be established; You shall be far from oppression, for you shall not fear; And from terror, for it shall not come near you.
15 Indeed they shall surely assemble, but not because of Me. Whoever assembles against you shall fall for your sake.
16 'Behold, I have created the blacksmith Who blows the coals in the fire, Who brings forth an instrument for his work; And I have created the spoiler to destroy.

17 No weapon formed against you shall prosper, And every tongue which rises against you in judgment You shall condemn. This is the heritage of the servants of the LORD , And their righteousness is from Me,' Says the LORD," (NKJV, Isa. 54:13-17).

4. The revelation of **righteousness** will bring **peace** into your life.

"The work of righteousness will be peace, And the effect of righteousness, quietness and assurance forever," (NKJV, Isa. 32:17).

The <u>fruit</u> of **righteousness** will bring peace.

- People (believers) live defeated lives because their minds are not renewed by the Word of God to this correct thinking: "I am the righteousness of God in Jesus Christ"

5. The revelation of **righteousness** helps you leave your **past** behind!

"17 Therefore, if anyone is in Christ, he is a new creation; old things have passed away; behold, all things have become new.
18 Now all things are of God, who has reconciled us to Himself through Jesus Christ, and has given us the ministry of reconciliation,
19 that is, that God was in Christ reconciling the world to Himself, not imputing their trespasses to them, and has committed to us the word of reconciliation.
20 Now then, we are ambassadors for Christ, as though God were pleading through us: we implore you on Christ's behalf, be reconciled to God.
21 For He made Him who knew no sin to be sin for us, that we might become the righteousness of God in Him," (NKJV, 2 Cor. 5:17-21).

*You were created for achievement.
*You have the seeds of greatness in you.
*Christians are new creations not rebuilt sinners!

Righteousness is a <u>weapon</u>.
Righteousness is an <u>attitude</u>.
Your mind and attitude have everything to do with how well you perform in life. By developing an attitude of **righteousness** in your life and learning to view yourself through the work of the

cross, your attitude will receive a divine impartation of confidence and boldness that will always put you on the winning side of victory!

Helmet of Salvation

"14 Stand therefore [hold your ground], having tightened the belt of truth around your loins and having put on the breastplate of integrity and of moral rectitude and right standing with God,
15 And having shod your feet in preparation [to face the enemy with the firm-footed stability, the promptness, and the readiness produced by the good news] of the Gospel of peace. [Isa. 52:7.]
16 Lift up over all the [covering] shield of saving faith, upon which you can quench all the flaming missiles of the wicked [one].
*17 And take the **helmet of salvation** and the **sword that the Spirit** wields, which is the Word of God.*
*18 **Pray at all times** (on every occasion, in every season) **in the Spirit**, with all [manner of] prayer and entreaty. To that end keep alert and watch with strong purpose and perseverance, interceding in behalf of all the saints (God's consecrated people)," (Amplified Classic Edition, Eph. 6:14-18).*

Your mind and attitude have everything to do with how well you perform in life.

Helmet [strong's #4030] perikephalaia = salvation is a present experience of the Lord's deliverance of believers as those who are engaged in spiritual conflict.

Salvation [strong's #4991] soteria = (a) deliverance, from danger and apprehension, rescue or safety (physically or morally). (b) of the spiritual and eternal deliverance granted immediately by God to those who accept His conditions of repentance and faith in the Lord Jesus, in whom alone it is to be obtained. Deliver, health, salvation, save, saving.

Save, **Saving** [strong's #4982 and #1295] sozo and diasozo (dia, "through") = to save, to keep safe and sound, to rescue from danger or destruction (a) one (from injury or peril).

1) to save a suffering one (from perishing), that is, one suffering from disease, to make well, heal, restore to health.

2) To bring safely through (a) of the healing of the sick by the Lord (b) of bringing "safe" to a destination (c) of keeping a person "safe"

The knowledge of Salvation and all that it is, puts a Helmet on your head.

When our mind is trained and taught to think correctly in terms of our salvation, that knowledge becomes a helmet in our life!

Five Truths for Effective Spiritual Warfare

Submit to God, Resist the Devil

> *"5 Likewise you younger people, submit yourselves to your elders. Yes, all of you be submissive to one another, and be clothed with humility, for 'God resists the proud, But gives grace to the humble.'*
> *6 Therefore humble yourselves under the mighty hand of God, that He may exalt you in due time,*
> *7 casting all your care upon Him, for He cares for you.*
> *8* ***Be sober****, be vigilant; because your adversary the devil walks about like a roaring lion, seeking whom he may devour.*
> *9 Resist him, steadfast in the faith, knowing that the same sufferings are experienced by your brotherhood in the world.*
> *10 But may the God of all grace, who called us to His eternal glory by Christ Jesus, after you have suffered a while, perfect, establish, strengthen, and settle you," (New King James Version, 1 Pet. 5:5-10).*

1. ***Attitude** — Submit to spiritual authority, come under the covering of the local church. Be willing to submit to your spiritual elders, those that have learned the ways of God and know how to fight demons.

Be Sober —
To be in control of your emotions, be on the lookout.
To be free of any intoxicants.

*You must believe you have authority to exercise authority.
*Submission is an attitude more than an action.
*To be strong in resisting the devil, you must stay in authority.

> *"Now the works of the flesh are manifest … seditions …" (King James Version, Gal. 5:19-20)*

Sedition = conduct or speech inciting people to rebel against the authority, the undermining of the constituted authority.

> *"For the mystery of lawlessness (that hidden principle of rebellion against constituted authority) is already at work in the world," (Amplified Classic Edition, 2 Thess. 2:7).*

2. **Humble Yourself** — Pour your life out and be filled with Jesus, reflect Him not you! You can't whip demons, only Christ IN YOU can!

> *"23 Then He said to them all, 'If anyone desires to come after Me, let him deny himself, and take up his cross daily, and follow Me.*
> *24 For whoever desires to save his life will lose it, but whoever loses his life for My sake will save it,' " (New King James Version, Lk. 9:23-24).*

> *"Then he said to all, 'Anyone who wants to follow me must put aside his own desires and conveniences and carry his cross with him every day and keep close to me!' " (The Living Bible, Lk. 9:23).*

3. **Make a firm decision not to worry** — Give all your cares to God. You have to declare you are not big enough to handle it!

> *"Let Him have all your worries and cares, for He is always thinking about you and watching everything that concerns you," (TLB, 1 Pet. 5:7).*

> *"Cast your burden on the Lord [releasing the weight of it] and He will sustain you; He will never allow the [consistently] righteous to be moved (made to slip, fall, or fail)," (Amplified Classic Edition, Psa. 55:22). [See also 1 Pet. 5:7.]*

> *"But when I am afraid, I will put my confidence in you. Yes, I will trust the promises of God. And since I am trusting Him, what can mere man do to me?" (The Living Bible, Psa. 56:3).*

The Peace of God....
Enables you to successfully fulfill any mission that God will give you in this life.

> *"So don't be anxious about tomorrow. God will take care of your tomorrow too. Live one day at a time," (TLB, Matt. 6:34)*

"6 Don't worry about anything; instead, pray about everything; tell God your needs, and don't forget to thank him for his answers.
7 If you do this, you will experience God's peace, which is far more wonderful than the human mind can understand. His peace will keep your thoughts and your heart quiet and at rest as you trust in Christ Jesus," (TLB, Phil. 4:6-7).

4. **Take control of your emotions**—The Word of God instructs us to take control of our emotions and feelings. When we blow it, it's because we allowed our emotions to take over. The devil is determined to fulfill his purpose to steal, kill, and destroy. He has taken a stand. So we must take our stand! We must determine that we are not going to be subject to demonic spirits and the evil of this world. We must make up our minds to fight!

"Be sober, be vigilant; because your adversary the devil walks about like a roaring lion, seeking whom he may devour," (New King James Version, 1 Pet. 5:8).

"Be alert and of sober mind. Your enemy the devil prowls around like a roaring lion looking for someone to devour," (New International Version, 1 Pet. 5:8).

Feelings are like a sailboat—they go the way the wind blows. Faith is like a steamboat—it goes the way the captain says!

5. **Fight until you win**—In 1 Peter 5:10, it tells us to let the grace of God perfect, establish, strengthen, and settle you. You will fight many things in your life. Some you will win and some you may lose. But through it all, maintain an attitude you are going to fight until God completes what He has begun in your life. You are the only one that can keep that from happening. So, fight until you win!

"Being confident of this very thing, that He who has begun a good work in you will complete it until the day of Jesus Christ," (New King James Version; Phil. 1:6).

The Sword Of The Spirit

"Death and life are in the power of the tongue, And those who love it will eat its fruit," (NKJV, Prov. 18:21).

Important Truths About the Words You Speak

1. **Words release bitterness that defile and hurt many.**

"Looking carefully lest anyone fall short of the grace of God; lest any root of bitterness springing up cause trouble, and by this many become defiled," (NKJV, Heb. 12:15).

"Watch out that no bitterness takes root among you, for as it springs up it causes deep trouble, hurting many in their spiritual lives," (The Living Bible, Heb. 12:15b).

"If you can't say something nice don't say nothing at all"
– Thumper

Bitterness = Poison, extreme wickedness, bitter hatred
Springing = To puff or blow up, to swell up, to germinate or grow
Trouble = To excite; disturbance; annoyance
Defiled = To stain, to dye with another color, to pollute, to contaminate, to befoul. (From untie, loosen, open, incline away)

2. **Let your speech be with grace seasoned with salt.**

"Let your speech at all times be gracious (pleasant and winsome), seasoned [as it were] with salt, [so that you may never be at a loss] to know how you ought to answer anyone [who puts a question to you]," (Amplified Classic Edition, Col. 4:6).

3. **Words have the power of affirmation or destruction.**

Affirm = To declare positively, to strengthen, to support or uphold the validity of; build people's self-esteem; praise them. You cannot affirm them too much.

Your words are powerful. They can bless or curse and bring life or death!

Prov. 12:17-18

"17 He who speaks truth declares righteousness, But a false witness, deceit.
18. There is one who speaks like the piercings of a sword, But the tongue of the wise promotes health," (New King James Version).

Prov. 12:25

"Anxiety in the heart of man causes depression, But a good word makes it glad," (NKJV).

Prov. 16:24

"Pleasant words are like a honeycomb, Sweetness to the soul and health to the bones," (NKJV).

Prov. 18:21

"Death and life are in the power of the tongue, And those who love it will eat its fruit," (NKJV).

Prov. 25:11

"A word fitly spoken is like apples of gold in settings of silver," (NKJV).

Eph. 4:29

"Let no foul or polluting language, nor evil word nor unwholesome or worthless talk [ever] come out of your mouth, but only such [speech] as is good and beneficial to the spiritual progress of others, as is fitting to the need and the occasion, that it may be a blessing and give grace (God's favor) to those who hear it," (Amplified Classic Edition).

4. Don't speak doubt and unbelief, it is an evil report.

"31 But his fellow scouts said, We are not able to go up against the people [of Canaan], for they are stronger than we are.
32 So they brought the Israelites an evil report of the land which they had scouted out, saying, The land through which we went to spy it out is a land that devours its inhabitants. And all the people that we saw in it are men of great stature," (AMPC, Num. 13:31-32).

"So we see that they could not enter in because of unbelief," (New King James Version, Heb. 3:19).

5. Faith words will bring possession of the promises of God.

The Process to Possess

"17 (As it is written, I have made thee a father of many nations,) before him whom he believed, even God, who quickeneth the dead, and calleth those things which be not as though they were.
18 Who against hope believed in hope, that he might become the father of many nations; according to that which was spoken, So shall thy seed be.
19 And being not weak in faith, he considered not his own body now dead, when he was about an hundred years old, neither yet the deadness of Sara's womb:
20 He staggered not at the promise of God through unbelief; but was strong in faith, giving glory to God," (King James Version, Rom. 4:17-20).

1. Confession. Call the promise into your life. (v 17)
2. Believe. In spite of circumstances. (v 18)
3. Consider not. Consider God instead of the circumstance. (v 19)

Consider = To observe fully: To fix one's eyes or mind upon.

4. Stagger not. Strong in faith at the promises of God. (v 20)

Stagger = To separate thoroughly, to discriminate (by implication, decide), or (reflexively) hesitate: discern, doubt, judge, be partial, waver, make (to) differ

5. Be strong in faith by giving glory to God. (v 20)

Strong = In a fixed position, empowered, enabled, to be made strong.

Glory = Honor, praise, worship.

"The entrance and unfolding of Your words give light; their unfolding gives understanding (discernment and comprehension) to the simple," (Amplified Classic Edition, Psa. 119:130).

"To the law and to the testimony! If they do not speak according to this word, it is because there is no light in them," (New King James Version, Isa. 8:20).

The Whole Armor of God —The Metaphor

> *"13 Therefore take up the whole armor of God, that you may be able to withstand in the evil day, and having done all, to stand.*
> *14 Stand therefore, having girded your waist with truth, having put on the breastplate of righteousness, and*
> *15 having shod your feet with the preparation of the gospel of peace;*
> *16 above all, taking the shield of faith with which you will be able to quench all the fiery darts of the wicked one.*
> *17 And take the helmet of salvation, and the sword of the Spirit, which is the word of God," (NKJV, Eph. 6:13-17).*

Let's look at verse 13.

> *"Therefore take up the whole armor of God, that you may be able to* ***withstand*** *in the evil day, and having done all, to stand."*

Withstand *anthistemi* (anth-is-tay-mee); Strong's #436: Compare "antihistamine." From *anti*, "against," and *histemi*, "to cause to stand". The verb suggests vigorously opposing, bravely resisting, standing face-to-face against and adversary, standing your ground. Just as an antihistamine puts a block on histamine, *anthistemi* tells us that with the authority and spiritual weapons granted to us, we can withstand evil forces.

The **metaphor** in Ephesians 6:13-17 is based on the armor and battle dress of the first-century Roman soldier. Clearly, the military metaphor is intended to show the reader that we are engaged in an active battle now. Though some suggest that the viewpoint of a continuous, aggressive struggle minimizes the accomplished victory of the cross, it in fact asserts victory all the more. All spiritual warfare waged today is victorious only on the basis of appropriating the provision of the cross and Christ's blood (Col 2:15).

1) Personal faith that positions itself against evil and
2) aggressive prayer warfare that attacks demonic strongholds are two distinct and complementary facets of spiritual life.

This entire passage lends further support to this perspective: "To stand against" (v 11) means to hold at bay aggressively or to stand in front of and oppose; "wrestle" (v 12) means to engage actively in one-on-one combat; "to stand" (v 13) means to be found standing after an active battle; and "stand" (v 14) means take your stand for the next battle.

The Armor of God (Eph. 6:10-18).

The Armor of God is made up of the following six items. The belt of truth, the breastplate of righteousness, the shoes of the Gospel, the shield of faith, the helmet of salvation and the sword of the spirit. Here is a description of what the "Full Armor of God" is.

1. **Belt of Truth** Ephesians 6:14.
"Stand therefore, having girded your waist with truth," Paul says. Truth is the belt that holds all the other pieces of the armor in place. There are two ways in which truth is a part of the armor of God.

First, it refers to the truths of Scripture as opposed to the lies of Satan. Satan is the father of lies (Jn. 8:44). Jesus said, *"You shall know the truth, and the truth shall make you free" (NKJV, Jn. 8:32).* The great truths of the Bible—the love of God, salvation through faith in Jesus Christ, the second coming, forgiveness of sin, grace and power to live for Jesus—these truths set us free from Satan's lies. Satan would have us believe that we are sinful, lost, and without hope. The truth is that God's love and salvation has set us free from sin and death.

The second way that truth serves as a belt, holding together the full armor of God, is our personal commitment to truth—to living a life that is upright, transparent, and without deceit. Integrity and honesty are vital to your Christian life. People should know that they can depend on you to be a person of truth and principle.

2. **Breastplate of Righteousness** (Ephesians 6:14).
The breastplate covers the heart and shields it and the other vital organs. It has two parts—one to cover the breast and the other covers the back to protect the vital organs of the body. The Bible says, *"Keep your heart with all diligence, for out of it spring the issues of life," (NKJV, Prov. 4:23).* That is what Christ's righteousness does for you. It protects you against all of Satan's accusations and charges. This righteousness is not made up of the good deeds you do. The Bible is clear that none of us are righteous in ourselves (Rom. 3:10).

The breastplate of righteousness is entirely the righteousness of Jesus which He gives us freely when we accept Him as our Savior (2 Cor. 5:21; Eph. 2:8, 9; Phil. 3:9). Righteousness revealed by faith—The Word will furnish you with righteousness.

3. **Shoes of the Gospel** (Ephesians 6:15).

For the soldier, bronze boots for the feet were to cover the front of the leg. A kind of sole was often used to protect the feet from rocks, thorns, etc. Soldiers marching into battle must have comfortable shoes. As soldiers of Christ, we must put on "gospel shoes" that will allow us to march wherever our Lord leads. The apostle John says, *"He who says he abides in Him [Jesus] ought himself also to walk just as He [Jesus] walked," (NKJV, 1 Jn. 2:6).* Jesus said, *"My sheep hear My voice ... and they follow Me," (NKJV, Jn. 10:27).* Satan will try to place obstacles in our path, but in Jesus' strength we can walk forward, following our Lord, obeying Him, and advancing the gospel. Walk in peace by faith: a) standing in faith with the gospel under your feet b) walk in the Gospel of peace.

4. **Shield of Faith** (Ephesians 6:16).

The shield is to protect the body from blows and cuts. In listing the different pieces of the armor of God, Paul says, *"Above all, taking the shield of faith with which you will be able to quench all the* ***fiery darts*** *of the wicked one," (NKJV, Eph. 6:16).* When Satan attacks with doubts, the shield of faith turns aside the blow. When temptations come, faith keeps us steadfast in following Jesus. We are able to withstand all of the devil's fiery darts because we know whom we have believed (2 Tim. 3:12).

What are the fiery darts? It is any missile thrown, as the javelin, spear, arrow, or stone from a sling. The fiery darts perhaps refer to the combustible arrowheads that set fire to the fortifications, ships, houses, and even the shields of the enemy made of wood and leather. They were called *falarica.* To quench these fiery darts, shields were covered with metal. As applied to Christian warfare, they refer to evil thoughts, lusts, passions, and temptations of various kinds. A lot of times, we are our own worst enemy. We need to wake up and realize we are to cast down imaginations (2 Cor. 10:5). This, no doubt, refers to Satan, who is captain of all wicked ones. The term is also used of other wicked persons.

This faith is not something that comes from within us. It is God's gift to us. He gives each of us a measure of faith (Rom. 12:3). Then, as we walk with Him, that faith grows and develops until it becomes a shield, protecting us and allowing us to live a victorious life in Christ. This was Paul's experience. He said, *"I have been crucified with Christ; it is no longer I who live, but Christ lives in me; and the life which I now live in the flesh I live by faith in the Son of God, who loved me and gave Himself for me," (NKJV, Gal. 2:20).* And at the end of that life of faith, he declared, *"I have fought the good fight, I have finished the race, I have kept the faith," (NKJV, 2 Tim. 4:7).* That can be your experience as well, as you use the shield of faith to turn aside everything Satan hurls at you. You build your faith up by praying in the spirit and by reading the Bible.

5. **Helmet of Salvation** (Ephesians 6:17).
The helmet protects the head—perhaps the most vital part of the body since it is the seat of thought and the mind. When we have a sure knowledge of our salvation, we will not be moved by Satan's deceptions. When we are certain that we are in Christ with our sins forgiven, we will have a peace that nothing can disturb. God intends for my mind "to think" like a mind that is controlled by the Holy Spirit.

6. **The Sword of the Spirit** (Ephesians 6:17).
The sword of the Spirit is the only weapon of offense listed in the armor of God. All the other parts are defensive in nature. God's Word—the Bible—is described as *"living and powerful, and sharper than any two-edged sword," (NKJV, Heb. 4:12).* Jesus used this weapon when Satan tempted Him in the wilderness. To each of Satan's efforts to lead Him into sin, Jesus replied, *"it is written ..."* and proceeded to quote Scripture to destroy Satan's temptations. God's Word is truth (Jn. 17:17). That is why it is so powerful. That is why it is so important that we study the Bible and become familiar with its truths and its power. David wrote, *"Your word is a lamp to my feet and a light to my path," (NKJV, Psa. 119:105).* The sword of God's Word both protects us and destroys our enemy—the devil— and his temptations. Speak the Word by faith. In order for the Word of God to have "power", it must come out of your mouth.

7. **Prayer** (Ephesians 6:18).
Although prayer is not one of the pieces of the whole armor of God, Paul closes his list by saying, *"Praying always with all prayer and supplication in the Spirit," (NKJV, Eph. 6:18).* Even when you are clothed with the armor of God, you need to bathe it all in prayer. Prayer is a very important part of the fight against spiritual powers of evil (James 4:7; 1 Pet. 5:8-9). Without this prayer, the Christian armor will be ineffectual, not producing any desired effect (Mk. 13:33; Lk. 21:36; Heb. 13:17). Prayer brings you into communion and fellowship with God so that His armor can protect you. Pray by faith. Prayer is a part of our spiritual equipment. Use it continually and habitually "at every possible moment."

How do I put on the whole armor of God?

Mental preparation removes the element of surprise. This will always give you the upper hand. It isn't as difficult as you might think. All the pieces of the armor are found in a relationship with Jesus. Paul said it like this: *"Put on the Lord Jesus Christ," (NKJV, Rom. 13:14).* When you give yourself to Jesus and "put on" His righteousness, you are clothed in the whole armor of God.

"Mental preparation removes the element of surprise."

We all face these moments and have to advance in spiritual warfare. Be clothed in the whole armor of God. In Jesus, clothed in God's invincible armor, you will *"be strong in the Lord and in the power of His might."* You will *"be able to stand against the wiles of the devil," (NKJV, Eph. 6:10, 11).*

God wants you to use faith as a shield against the attacks of the enemy. For someone to have the attitude of accepting everything in their life as their fate or the will of God is as foolish as a Roman soldier going into battle without his shield. He would be open to every attack of the enemy.

Don't let disappointments and circumstances cause you to put your faith shield down. Keep your faith shield up and the fiery arrows of the devil will not be able to find a lodging place!

Notes:

Chapter 26

Satan – The Devil – Lucifer – Demons

Your real enemy
— the devil —
wants you to ignore
the spiritual reality
behind the physical one.
As long as you are focused
on what you can see with your physical eyes,
he will continue to run rampant
underneath the surface.
The more you disregard him,
the more damage
he is free to do.
The enemy may be invisible,
but he is not fictional.
He is very real, and very persistent,
waging war against us **constantly.**

Chapter 26

Satan—The Devil— Lucifer—Demons

If you call yourself a child of God, but you don't experience peace and rest, and your life is surrounded by a lot of strife and confusion, you can't seem to concentrate or you fall asleep in church, there's something wrong. You need to be made aware of who you are in Christ, the authority He has given you and the arsenal of weapons He has equipped you with to fight and win back your peace. Peace is your right as a child of God. In chapter 25, it talks about the Whole Armor of God for Spiritual Warfare.

As we grow in the Lord and in our discernment, we can begin to understand when we need spiritual victory in certain areas of our lives. We may feel depressed, rejected, separated from God, and so on. This is what the enemy wants. We are also instructed to use our authority against the enemy and **cast him out**, ending his reign in our lives. Do not let the enemy add weight or guilt to something that the Lord is not leading you to deal with. But ask for boldness and courage to deal with what He does show you.

Remember, we have legal authority in the name of Jesus to bind the works of darkness which encompass sin, iniquity, perversion, sickness, disease, infirmity, death, destruction, curses, witchcraft, sorcery, divination, poverty, lack, strife, lust, pride, rebellion, fear, torment, and confusion. We have legal authority to put a stop to these things in our lives.

Don't allow the enemy to put a stronghold in your mind that you don't need to know about Satan and demons. The Word tells us that "through knowledge" the just shall be delivered. Knowledge is the key to deliverance. The more you know about the enemy and his operation, the more you will be able to defeat him and cast him out.

Ignorance of the devil and his demons will rob you of your deliverance, your freedom. The sad fact is, however, all things are not opened to the eyes of most believers. Most believers are blind when it comes to the operation of evil spirits in their own lives or in the lives of others. The Lord desires for every believer to have enough discernment so evil spirts will not be able to hide and rule under the cover of darkness.

Believers are spirit, soul, and body. Demons can occupy a believer's soul (mind, will, and emotions) and physical body but **not a believer's spirit.**

Many believers have not seen the close connection between deliverance and healing. But if we study the ministry of Jesus, we see Him ministering healing to the sick by casting out evil spirits. Jesus always said, "COME OUT!"

Evil spirits have had the time to work themselves into our lives for generations, including the numbers of years most of us walked in sin and ignorance. Don't underestimate the strength and numbers of the enemy. He is hiding and deeply entrenched in the land. He must be exposed and uprooted from his dwelling places, and this will often take much time and warfare. *Know this fact: Deliverance is more progressive than instantaneous.* As we grow in grace and fall out of agreement with evil spirits operating in our lives, the Lord will deliver us from them.

Satan, a Greek form derived from the Aramaic [Heb., *Satan*], an adversary, the great opposer of God and man; the personal name of the devil.

> The devil wants to hurt you! He will tell you that you are of no value, that you are not important. He will insist God will not answer your prayer; you are not good enough.

What he is not

Satan is not evil principle, an error of the mortal mind, a disease germ, an abstract power, or a being with hoofs, horns, tail, and Persian shoes, holding a pitchfork, and presiding over a lake of fire and the realm of the dead. He isn't all red with a mustache and goatee with pointed ears either.

What he is

Satan is a real person. Jesus Christ dealt with him as with a person. Jesus waged war on Satan as on a person. Christ taught that Satan was a real person (Lk. 10:18; Rev. 12:7-12; 13:1-4; 20:1-10). The apostles warned men against a personal devil. Personal conversation is carried on with him (Job 1:6-12; 2:1-7; Isa. 14:12-14; Matt. 4:1-10; Jude 9). Personal descriptions are given of him (Isa. 14:12-14; Ezek 28:11-17). He is an angel with a body, soul, and spirit like all other angels. He is described as a most beautiful creature who fell through personal pride over his own beauty. He has been seen with a body. He will be bound bodily with a chain and cast into a prison. He has a heart, pride, speech, knowledge, power, desires, lusts, and many other bodily parts, soul passions, and spirit faculties. He goes from place to place in a body like anyone else. He has a kingdom. He has access to Heaven. He is a great celestial and terrestrial ruler. He rules the business, social, political, and religious activities of the majority of mankind. His realm is divided into organized principalities and powers in the heavenlies (Dan. 10:12–11:1; Matt. 12:24-30; Eph. 6:10-12). His subjects are fallen angels, fallen men, and demons of various kinds (Matt. 25:41; Jn. 8:44; James 2:19; 1 Jn. 3:8-10; Rev. 12:7-12). He is head of some religions and is a leader in religious affairs (2 Cor. 11:14; 2:9; 3:9).

Personal names and titles are given to him:

1. Lucifer means "day star" or "shining one". (Isa. 14:12-14; Lk. 10:18)
2. Devil means "slanderous". (Matt. 4:1; Eph. 4:25-27)
3. Satan means "the adversary" of God. (Job 1:6)
4. Beelzebub (Matt. 10:25; 12:24)
5. Belial (2 Cor. 6:15)
6. Adversary (1 Pet. 5:8-9)
7. Dragon (Rev. 12:3-12; 13:1-4; 20:1-3)
8. Serpent (2 Cor. 11:3; Rev. 12:9)
9. God of this world (2 Cor. 4:4)
10. The ruler [or prince] of this world means the enemy's approach is not isolated to individuals. (Jn. 12:31; 2 Cor. 4:4)
11. Prince of the power of the air/prince of darkness means the devil does not work alone. (Eph. 2:2; Eph. 6:12)
12. Accuser of our brethren means "one who condemns". (Rev. 12:10)
13. Enemy (Matt. 13:39)
14. Father of Lies means "Liar" and "falsifier." (Jn. 8:44)
15. Tempter means "one who tempts people for the purpose of enticing them to sin". (Matt. 4:3; 1 Thess. 3:5)
16. The wicked one. (Matt. 13:19, 38)
17. That wicked one (1 Jn. 5:18)

The Origin of Satan

Satan was created by Christ along with other beings, principalities, and powers in Heaven and Earth (Job 38:4-7; Ezek. 28:11-17; Col. 1:15-18).

Was Satan here before Adam?

According to Isaiah 14:12-14, Jeremiah 4:23-26, Ezekiel 28:11-17, Luke 10:18, 2 Peter 3:4-8, and other passages, Satan, known as Lucifer, had a kingdom on Earth long before the six days of

Genesis 1:3-2:25 and the creation of Adam. Let's look at each Scripture passage.

Isaiah 14:12-14

*"12 How you are fallen from heaven, O Lucifer, son of the morning! **How** you are cut down to the ground, You who weakened the nations!*
13 For you have said in your heart: 'I will ascend into heaven, I will exalt my throne above the stars of God; I will also sit on the mount of the congregation On the farthest sides of the north;
14 I will ascend above the heights of the clouds, I will be like the Most High," (NKJV).

Jeremiah 4:23-26

*"23 I beheld the earth, and indeed **it was** without form, and void; And the heavens, they **had** no light.*
24 I beheld the mountains, and indeed they trembled, And all the hills moved back and forth.
*25. I beheld, and indeed **there** was no man, And all the birds of the heavens had fled.*
*26 I beheld, and indeed the fruitful land **was** a wilderness, And all its cities were broken down At the presence of the LORD , By His fierce anger," (NKJV).*

Ezekiel 28:11-17

"11 Moreover the word of the LORD came to me, saying,
12 "Son of man, take up a lamentation for the king of Tyre, and say to him, 'Thus says the Lord God: "You were the seal of perfection, Full of wisdom and perfect in beauty.
13 You were in Eden, the garden of God; Every precious stone was your covering: The sardius, topaz, and diamond, Beryl, onyx, and jasper, Sapphire, turquoise, and emerald with gold. The workmanship of your timbrels and pipes was prepared for you on the day you were created.
14 "You were the anointed cherub who covers; I established you; You were on the holy mountain of God; You walked back and forth in the midst of fiery stones.
15 You were perfect in your ways from the day you were created, till iniquity was found in you.
16 "By the abundance of your trading you became filled with violence within, and you sinned; Therefore I cast you as a profane thing out of the mountain of

God; And I destroyed you, O covering cherub, from the midst of the fiery stones.
17 "Your heart was lifted up because of your beauty; You corrupted your wisdom for the sake of your splendor; I cast you to the ground, I laid you before kings, that they might gaze at you," (NKJV).

Luke 10:18

"And He said to them, 'I saw Satan fall like lightning from heaven,' " (NKJV).

2 Peter 3:4-8

*"4 And saying, 'Where is the promise of His coming? For since the fathers fell asleep, all things continue as **they were** from the beginning of creation."*
5 For this they willfully forget: that by the word of God the heavens were of old, and the earth standing out of water and in the water,
*6 by which the world **that** then existed perished, being flooded with water.*
*7 But the heavens and the earth **which** are now preserved by the same word, are reserved for fire until the day of judgment and perdition of ungodly men.*
*8 But, beloved, do not forget this one thing, that with the Lord one day **is** as a thousand years, and a thousand years as one day," (NKJV)*

These passages reveal that he fell, led an invasion into Heaven and was defeated. The serpent (Satan) was an enemy of God before he tempted Adam and Eve. At that time, the earth was cursed and all life was destroyed by the first flood. Satan regained rulership over the earth in Adam's day, usurping (taking over) man's dominion by causing his fall. His relationship to man through the ages has been that of a usurper [*usurper* : a person who takes a position of power or importance illegally or by force], and as long as man tolerates his dictatorship, that long will he remain subject to Satan. Each man can now, by the power of the Gospel, defeat Satan and rid himself of all demon relationships. This is what God demands, and He has provided means whereby it can be attained (Mk. 16:17-18; Lk. 10:19; 24:49; Acts 1:8; Eph. 6:10-18; James 4:7; 1 Pet. 5:8-9). Satan's present position as ruler of this world's system and as the prince of this world will be ended forever when Christ comes (Rev. 19-20), and man will again inherit the earth and live in it forever.

The Fall of Satan

There are several plain scriptures describing this. He fell through pride over his own beauty (Isa. 14:12; Ezek. 28:11-17; 1 Tim. 3:6), and trying to exalt himself above God.

> *"12 How you are fallen from heaven, O Lucifer, son of the morning! How you are cut down to the ground, You who weakened the nations!*
> *13 For you have said in your heart: 'I will ascend into heaven, I will exalt my throne above the stars of God; I will also sit on the mount of the congregation on the farthest sides of the north;*
> *14 I will ascend above the heights of the clouds, I will be like the Most High," (NKJV, Isa. 14:12-14).*

He was cast out of Heaven (Isa. 14:12; Lk. 10:18). If he fell from Heaven, he was cut down to the ground (v 12; Lk. 10:18). This was the reason he did not remain in Heaven. [Hebrew *gada*, to fall a tree; destroy anything; cut down; cut off; cut asunder]. He was forcibly intercepted in his invasion of Heaven and was defeated and cast down as a tree being felled by the woodsman. He was cut down to the ground.

*For more information on Lucifer, do a study from Isaiah 14:12 regarding being cast out of Heaven.

The Work of Satan

In general, his work is to oppose God whenever possible. For this reason, his work varies in some respects with the purposes of God in different ages and dispensations. In Old Testament times, Satan's great work was to cause the fall of man, take over his dominion, and try to prevent the coming of the Messiah into the world in order to avert his own defeat and pending doom.

He talks about giants in Genesis chapter 6.

> *"There were (a) giants on the earth in (b) those days, and (c) also afterward, (d) when the sons of God came in to the (e) daughters of men and they (f) bore children to them. Those were the mighty men who were of old, men of (g) renown," (NKJV, Gen. 6:4).*

(a) [Hebrew *nephilim*, pl. of *nephil*, bully, tyrant, giant]

(b) those days= The days of Noah, after Adam or before the flood.
(c) Also "afterward" means after "those days" before the flood; i.e., after the flood, the sons of God again married the daughters of men and produced a second race of giants on the earth who occupied the land of Canaan in advance of Abraham. The purpose here was the same as before

the flood—to corrupt the race and thereby make it impossible for the pure Seed of the woman to come as predicted.

(d) When the sons of God married the daughters of men, as before the flood, giants were again born to them. This definitely answers the question of where the giants before and after the flood came from (Genesis 6:1-4).

(e) Not from the daughters of Cain as supposed, for no daughter of Cain could be on this side of the flood. They were all killed by the flood (Gen. 6:18; 7:7; 8:18; 9:1; 1 Pet. 3:20).

(f) Women had children by fallen, wicked angels as well as by men. If you will carefully read Genesis 6:4, "*There were giants on the earth in those days, and also afterward, when the sons of God came in to the daughters of men and they bore children to them. Those were the mighty men who were of old, men of renown," (NKJV).* "Came in to" means having sex. *"The sons of God saw the daughters of men, that they were beautiful; and they took wives for themselves of all whom they chose," (NKJV, Gen. 6:2)*

Seth did not have a son until 235 years after creation, and his son did not have a son until 325 years after creation (Gen. 5:3, 6, 9). Where did these sons come from? They could not have been sons of Seth, for these marriages took place when men began to multiply—in the very beginning of the race before Seth had sons of marriageable age. The term "sons of God" proves that they were the product of God, not of Seth. They were the fallen angels of 1 Peter 3:19, 2 Peter 2:4, and Jude 6-7. It was not necessary to emphasize having children by men, but having children by angels was something to make special mention of (Gen. 6:4; Jude 6-7). It was because of this great sin that the Lord was "*sorry that He had made man on the earth" (NKVJ, Gen. 6:6).*

(g) [Hebrew] s*hem*, men of renown, honor, and authority (Num. 16:2; Ezek. 16:14-15; 34:29; 39:13; Dan. 9:15). The giants became the heroes of Greek mythology and primitive truth now corrupted by transmission.

The fact that giants, or beings of abnormal size in body, have lived on Earth is one of the most clearly stated truths in Scripture. [Hebrew]. Nephilim, pl. of nephil, bully, tyrant, giant (Gen. 6:4; Num. 13:33). They were abnormal in bodily size which is clear from the fact that men of Israel were as grasshoppers in size compared to them (Num. 13:33).

A valley of giants is mentioned in Joshua 15:8; 18:16. This is the valley of Rephaim, the name of another branch of the giant races so often mentioned in Scripture (Gen. 14:5; 15:20; 2 Sam. 5:18, 22; 23:13; 1 Chron. 11:15; 14:9; Isa. 17:5). The Rephaim were well-known giants but, unfortunately, instead of retaining their proper name in Scripture, the translators translated it *dead* (Job 26:5; Psa. 88:10; Prov. 2:18; 9:18; 21:16; Isa. 14:9; 26:19) and *deceased* (Isa. 26:14).

The Hebrew root of Rephaim is translated "giant" (2 Sam. 21:16, 18, 20, 22; 1 Chron. 20:4, 6, 8) and giants (Deut. 2:11, 20; 3:11, 13; Jos. 12:4; 13:12). The phrase "remnant of the giants" in Deut. 3:11; Jos. 12:4; 13:12 should be "remnant of the Rephaim," for there were many nations of giants other than the Rephaim who filled the whole country trying to contest God's claim of the Promised Land. They are listed as Kenites, Kenizzites, Kadmonites, Hittites, Perizzites, Rephaim, Amorites, Canaanites, Girgashites, Jebusites, Hivites, Anakim, Emim, Horites, Avim, Zamzummim, Caphtorim, and Nephilim (Gen. 6:4a; 14:5-6; 15:19-21; Exod. 3:8, 17; 23:23; Deut. 2:10-12, 20-23; 3:11-13; 7:1; 20:17; Jos. 12:4-8; 13:3; 15:8; 17:15; 18:16). Og was of the remnant of Rephaim, not the remnant of all other giant nations (Deut. 3:11; Jos. 12:4; 13:12).

The fact that the Rephaim have no resurrection (Isa. 26:14) proves the reality of giants and that they were not ordinary men. All ordinary men are to be resurrected (Jn. 5:28-29); therefore, giants must be a different class from pure Adamites. Isaiah makes it clear that the dead (Hebrew. Rephaim) are now in Hell (Isa 14:9). Solomon confirms this in Prov. 2:18; 9:18; 21:16 where the Hebrew word for dead is Rephaim.

The Purpose of Satan in Producing Giants

It was the purpose of Satan and his fallen angels to corrupt the human race and thereby do away with pure Adamite stock through whom the seed of the woman should come. This would avert their own doom and make it possible for Satan and his kingdom to keep control of the planet Earth indefinitely. It was said to Adam and Eve that the seed of the woman should defeat Satan and restore man's dominion (Gen. 3:15). The only way then for Satan to avoid this predicted defeat was to corrupt the pure Adamite line so that the coming of the Seed of the woman into the world would be made impossible. This he tried to accomplish by sending some of his fallen angels to marry the daughters of men as in Genesis 6:1-4 and producing the giant nations through them.

There are two such eruptions of fallen angels taught in Genesis 6:4. *"There were giants in the earth in those days (before the flood), and also afterward (after the flood), when the sons of God (fallen angels) came in to the daughters of men (any daughters of men—Cain, Seth, and others), and they bore children to them (to the angels)," (NKJV, parentheses mine).*

Satan almost succeeded in his plan during the first eruption, *"for all flesh had corrupted their way on the earth," (NKJV, Gen 6:12b)*; of all the multitudes, Noah and his sons were the only pure Adamites left to be preserved by the ark (Gen. 6:8-13; 1 Pet. 3:19-20). The main object of the flood was to do away with all this satanic corruption, destroy the giants, and preserve the pure Adamite stock so as to make good the guarantee of the coming of the Seed of the woman, as in the plan of God.

Being defeated before the flood did not stop Satan from making a further attempt to prevent the coming of the Redeemer, who should be his final downfall. It was now to his advantage that God had promised never to send another universal flood upon the earth. Satan, therefore, reasoned that he should make a second attempt to do away with Adamite stock. If he came within "eight souls" of doing it before the flood, his opportunities were now even greater with the promise that there would be no such flood. This is the reason for the second group of his fallen angels being sent to marry the daughters of men. Once again, the unions produced giants, and races of them occupied the land of promise, where the seed should be born, in advance of Abraham. Limited by His promise of no flood, God was then faced with the problem of destroying the giant races another way. This explains why He commanded Israel to kill them everyone, even the last man, woman, and child. This again explains why He destroyed all the men, women, and children besides Noah and his family, at the time of the flood. It also answers the skeptics' question regarding why the children were taken away with the adults in the flood. God had to do away with this corruption entirely in order to fulfill His eternal plan and give the world its promised Redeemer. The Redeemer has come now, and so Satan is reserving his forces for a last stand at the second coming of Christ.

So now, it is clear from Scripture that there were giants on the earth both before and after the flood, and that they came from a union of fallen angels and the daughters of men.

Note the following regarding Satan and his activities:

26 Branches of Satan's Work

1. He is the deceiver of all men. (2 Cor. 11:14; Rev. 12:9; 20:1-10)
2. He exercised the power of death until Christ conquered death, Hell, and the grave. (Heb. 2:14; Rev. 1:18)
3. He is the leader of all sinners and backsliders of the human race (1 Jn. 3:8-10; 1 Tim. 5:15) and all spirit rebels. (Matt. 9:34; Eph. 6:10-18)
4. He causes all sickness, disease, and physical and mental maladies in the human race. (Lk. 13:16; Acts 10:38)
5. He takes advantage of all adversities of men to further their rebellion and hold them captive. (2 Cor. 2:11; 1 Tim. 1:20; 5:11-15).
6. He tempts men (Mk. 1:13; 1 Cor. 7:5)
7. Provokes to sin (1 Chron. 21:1)
8. Causes offense (Matt. 16:23)
9. Transforms himself into an angel of light (2 Cor. 11:14)

10. Resists others (Zech. 3:1-2)
11. Enters into union with others against God (Lk. 22:3; Jn. 13:2)
12. Sends messengers to defeat saints (2 Cor. 12:7)
13. Hinders the Gospel (Acts 13:10; 1 Thess. 2:18)
14. Steals the Word of God from men lest they should believe it (Matt. 13:19; Lk. 8:12)
15. Works miracles (2 Thess. 2:9)
16. Contends with messengers of God, endeavoring to hold them captive (Dan. 10:12-21; Jude 9)
17. Hinders answers to prayer (Dan. 10:12-21)
18. Sets snares for men to fall into sin (1 Tim. 3:7; 2 Tim. 2:26)
19. Causes diversion and blinds men to the Gospel (2 Cor. 4:4)
20. Causes double-mindedness (James 1:5-9)
21. Causes doubt and unbelief (Gen. 3:4-5; Rom. 14:23)
22. Causes darkness and oppression (2 Cor. 4:4; 2 Pet. 1:4-9)
23. Causes deadness and weakness (Heb. 6:1; 9:14)
24. Causes delay and compromise (Acts 24:25; 26:28)
25. Causes division and strife (1 Cor. 3:1-3; 1 Pet. 5:8)
26. Makes war on the saints (Eph. 6:10-18)

War on the Saints

The greatest and most important work of Satan among men now is to counterfeit the doctrines and experiences of God as revealed in Scripture in order to deceive saints (2 Cor. 11:14-15; Eph. 6:10-18; 1 Tim. 4:1-7; Rev. 12:9-12). Men are commanded to prove and test all doctrines and experiences in the supernatural realm to see if they are of God or of Satan (1 Cor. 2:12-16; Phil. 1:9-10; 1 Thess. 5:21-22; 1 Jn. 4:1-6). It is certain that every religion, doctrine, and experience among men cannot be of God. We must, therefore, judge them by the plain written Word of God. The knowledge of truth is the first essential in warfare against demons and error. Great is the danger when believers accept anything and everything in the realm of the supernatural as being from the Lord. The fact that the believer is a child of God does not stop the devil from trying in every conceivable way to imitate God to him. Believers are the ones Satan concentrates the wars against.

There are definite ways outlined in Scripture whereby one can detect what kind of spirit is seeking to control him. But if one neglects to study the Word, he may fall prey to one of Satan's demons through ignorance. It must be realized that ignorance is no guarantee against the workings of evil spirits. In fact, one of the chief means by which Satan and his forces try to control men is through ignorance. It accounts for their widespread success in getting men to accept their suggestions, doctrines, ideas, leadings, and guidance. Among the guiding principles useful in detecting good and evil spirits and their operations and doctrines, the outstanding ones are these.

1. Any doctrine that denies or causes doubt and unbelief concerning anything taught in Scripture is from Satan and his demons (1 Tim. 4:1-8). Any religion denying: the inspiration of the Bible; the reality of God as a person; the virgin birth; and divinity of Christ; His miraculous power and supernatural ministry; the death, burial, bodily resurrection, and bodily manifestation of Christ after His resurrection; the bodily ascension to Heaven and coming again of Jesus Christ to set up a kingdom in the world forever; the necessity of the new birth, cleansing from sin and living free from sin; and the numerous other experiences of the Bible—any religion denying these fundamental truths is yielding to "the spirit of error" and not "the spirit of truth" (1 Jn. 4:1-6)
2. Any power, influence, or doctrine that causes one to become passive, inactive, submissive, and unresisting to the workings of supernatural spirits seeking to control his life contrary to the teachings of Scripture is not of God. The Bible says, "Resist the devil" (James 4:7; 1 Pet. 5:8-9). An inclination to approve sin and ignore the necessity of repentance and holy living and a tendency to remove the penalty for sin or doubt that Hell is literal and eternal is promoted by Satan, not God. Just as God requires truth in the mind for the true working of the Holy Spirit in a life, so the devil requires the believing of lies in the minds of men to hold them in bondage. See 1 Cor. 6:9-11; 10:12-13; 2 Cor. 11:3-15; Gal. 5:19-21; 6:7-8; Eph. 6:10-18; 1 Tim. 4:1-9; James 1:22; 2:10.
3. The Holy Spirit can be recognized by the fruit of the Spirit: love, joy, peace, longsuffering, gentleness, goodness, faith, meekness, and temperance (Gal. 5:22-23).

Reminder: Six Earmarks of Holy Spirit Manifestation

(1) A Christ-like spirit of love, patience, and faith in God.

(2) Soberness and keenness of spirit vision.

(3) Deep humility of heart and meekness of spirit, with a lion-like courage against sin, sickness, poverty, disease, discouragement, failure, and everything else causing defeat in the Christian life.

(4) Absolute clearness of the mental faculties and intelligent action in carrying out Bible instructions concerning known duty and personal life as a Christian.

(5) Freedom from faultfinding, surmising [to conjecture or guess without evidence], whispering, and slander, and freedom from all the works of the flesh listed in Mark 7:19-21, Romans 1:24-32, 1 Corinthians 6:9-11, Galatians 5:19-21, and Colossians 3:5-10.

(6) Freedom from any ignorance concerning the divine will. When one is moved upon to act quickly and urgently without knowing whether the act will glorify God or not, it is better to wait and pray until it is clear beyond all doubt that God approves such action. Always remember that 1 John 4:1 commands, *"try the spirits whether they are of God."*

The Character of Satan

The names and various descriptions of Satan reveal his true character as follows. He is: the enemy of all good and the accuser of God and man; the father of lies; a murderer, a sower of discord; an adversary; the first sinner, the first rebel, and first to consecrate himself to self-gratification and to wage war against all society. He is cunning, wicked, malignant, cowardly, a tempter, and a thief. He is without principle in taking advantage of men in their weak moments, in tempting men after great success. He is a genius. He knows how to suggest the use of right things in a wrong way and at a wrong time, in slandering God to man and man to God, in appearing as an angel of light to deceive, and in deluding his followers as to their eternal end. He is presumptuous, proud, deceitful, fierce, and cruel and very aggressive.

Satan has never been known to be merciful, good, loving, kind, gentle, pitiful, patient, or to have any of the graces of God since he became the enemy of God and man. In Scripture, he is compared to a fowler (Psa. 91:3); birds (Matt. 13:4,19); a wolf (Jn. 10:12); a destroyer (Jn. 10:10); a roaring lion (1 Pet. 5:8-9); a serpent (Rev. 12:9; 20:3); and a dragon (Rev. 12:3-12).

Demons

A demon is a fallen angel. When Satan, who was the very highest angel, rebelled against God, he took a large number of the angels with him in rebellion. When their rebellion failed, they were cast out of Heaven. Those angels are now demons. They are very skillful, forceful and fierce. In the same way that angels can reach the very heights of spirituality, demons have the ability to reach down into great depths of hatred, bitterness, and perversion. Demons seem to be interested in tormenting people, possessing them, and leading them away from God and His truth. Just as the angels have archangels and higher powers, the demons have what are called "principalities and powers". Demons can use other people to discourage, distract, and deceive us.

Demon spirits work in groups and seldom alone. There is a leader or "strongman" over each group. Certain spirits will usually link up with one another.

The Doom of Satan

1 Predicted in Genesis 3:15.
2 Accomplished:
  (1) At the First Advent (Jn. 19:30; Col. 2:14-17)
  (2) At the Second Advent (Rev. 20:1-3)
  (3) At the battle of God and Magog (Rev. 20:7-10)

The purpose of the thousand-year reign of Christ after the second advent will be to suppress all rebellion (1 Cor. 15:24-28), and the final defeat of Satan and his hosts at the end of the period (the Millennium) must be accomplished before the earth is entirely rid of rebels. They must be confined to the lake of fire forever before rebellion is finally and eternally overcome. The Earth will be purified by fire and made perfect the 3rd time, and the kingdom of God will be universal over all free moral agents as it was before rebellion was started by Satan and Adam in their respective kingdoms.

Reality

Some people have trouble admitting the existence of such an enemy as Satan. But his presence and activity are necessary to explain the problems of evil and suffering. The Bible makes it plain that Satan exists and that his main work is to oppose the rule of God in the affairs of man.

Mankind did not witness Satan's beginning but, by God's design, shall see his end, one of ceaseless torment and humiliation. [see Isa. 14:12-20; Ezek. 28:16-19; Rev. 20:10]

Reference: The Dake Annotated Reference Bible NKJV page 788-789 Regular Edition Copyright October 2013

Notes:

Chapter 27

Magic – Sorcery – Witchcraft – Divination – Occult

Witchcraft is from the devil, and anyone who practices it will not enter into Heaven.
It is an abomination to God!

When you start dabbling in witchcraft, you open yourself up to demons and demonic influences, which will indeed harm you.

Satan is very crafty, and we must never let him take control of our lives.

If you know anyone who is involved in Wicca, try to help them to save their life, but if they refuse your help, stay away from that person.

Chapter 27

Magic – Sorcery – Witchcraft – Divination – Occult

You are the way you think. The mind has always been a favorite target of the enemy. If the devil can control your mind, he can control your life. Spirits that attack the mind include mind control, confusion, mental breakdown, depression, and mind-binding spirits, insanity, madness, mania, fantasy, evil thinking, migraines, mental pain, and negative thinking. They are all what I call "stinking thinking".

The good news is that you can loose yourself (including your mind) from all evil influences that operate through your mind. Mind control is a common spirit that has been identified by the name "Octopus". Mind-control spirits can resemble an octopus or squid with tentacles that grasp and control the mind. Deliverance from mind control releases a person from mental pressure, mental pain, confusion, and mental torment. Mind-control spirits can enter through listening to ungodly music, reading occult books, pornography, false teaching, false religions, drugs, and passivity.

Christians who dabble in the occult are walking in the flesh according to Galatians 5:19-21 and are in danger of not going to Heaven as a result of such practices. When people become involved and fascinated with familiar spirits and spirits of divination, little by little, they turn their back on God and His Word and look to divination for their daily guidance. The end result is spiritual confusion and, finally, bondage to Satan.

> *"19 Now the works of the flesh are manifest, which are these; Adultery, fornication, uncleanness, lasciviousness,*
> *20 Idolatry, witchcraft, hatred, variance, emulations, wrath, strife, seditions, heresies,*
> *21 Envyings, murders, drunkenness, revellings, and such like: of the which I tell you before, as I have also told you in time past, that they which do such things shall not inherit the kingdom of God," (King James Version, Gal. 5:19-21).*

A willingness to follow after divination for quick answers and power results in long-term problems and in other areas opens a door that allows Satan to harass us and our family to the **third** and **fourth generation**. [See also Exod. 34:7; Num. 14:18; Lev. 26:36; Jer. 32:18.]

> *"3 You shall have no other gods before Me.*
> *4 "You shall not make for yourself a carved image—any likeness of anything that is in heaven above, or that is in the earth beneath, or that is in the water under the earth;*
> *5 you shall not bow down to them nor serve them. For I, the LORD your God, am a jealous God, visiting the iniquity of the fathers upon the children to the **third** and **fourth generations** of those who hate Me," (New King James Version, Exod. 20:3-5).*

Occult practices, such as fortune-telling and witchcraft, were common among the pagan nations of the ancient world. Such attempts to control evil spirits were expressly forbidden to the Hebrew people.

> *"10 There shall not be found among you anyone who makes his son or his daughter pass through the fire, or one who practices witchcraft, or a soothsayer, or one who interprets omens, or a sorcerer,*
> *11 or one who conjures spells, or a medium, or a spiritist, or one who calls up the dead," (NKJV, Deut. 18:10-11).*

"Passing a son or daughter through the fire." This phrase refers to the practice of child sacrifice. This seems incredible to some today, but the very fact that it was outlawed by God indicates it was done in the ancient world. 2 Kings 16:3 records that King Ahaz sacrificed his son in this way. No doubt he thought that such a sacrifice would appease some pagan god. His grandson, Kin Manasseh, sacrificed his sons two generations later (2 Kings 21:6; 2 Chron. 33:6). 2 Kings 23:10 reveals that it was mainly the pagan god Molech who required this awful sacrifice, but other false gods apparently also demanded it (2 Kings 17:31; Jer. 19:5).

Witchcraft — Sorcery — Mediums

There were a number of interchangeable terms for these practitioners: "white", "good", or "unbinding" witches, blessers, wizards, sorcerers. However, "cunning-man" and "wise-man" were the most frequent. There is no such thing as a good witch according to the Bible, period.

The practice of witchcraft, or divination, was a means for extracting information or guidance from a pagan god. The word describes the activity of Balaam, the soothsayer or professional prophet, who was hired to curse Israel (Num. 22:7; 23:23; Jos. 13:22). It also describes the woman at Endor who brought up the spirit of Samuel in 1 Samuel 28:6-12. God would not answer Saul either by dreams and visions, Urim and Thummim, or by prophets, for He had departed from him and had taken the Holy Spirit away from him because of sin. If God had refused to answer him by legitimate means, He certainly would not answer contrary to Scripture (Lk. 16:26). If He would not answer by the Holy Spirit, He certainly would not answer by a demon spirit seeking to imitate Samuel, as is plain here (1 Sam. 28:7-19; 1 Chron. 10:13-14). It is clearly stated that Saul sought information from demons, not from God who refused to answer him. He definitely wanted a witch that had a familiar spirit, to inquire of her spirit *("Seek me a woman that hath a familiar spirit," [King James Version, 1 Sam. 28:7]*). His request was for her to divine by the familiar spirit ("conduct a seance" in 1 Sam. 28:8 is "divine… by familiar spirit" in KJV).

The Bible plainly teaches that communication with the dead can be demon spirits imitating departed loved ones (1 Sam. 28:7-19; Deut. 18:11; 1 Chron. 10:13-14; Isa. 8:19). It is commanded in scores of scriptures not to traffic with demons or seek communication with the dead (see Lk. 12:29; Deut. 18:10-12; 1 Tim. 4:1; Lev. 19:31; Lev. 20:6); God would not allow Samuel to communicate thus through a medium. The seeming appearance of Samuel to the medium was simply the familiar spirit imitating and impersonating him (1 Chron. 10:13-14). When it appeared that Samuel was speaking to Saul, it was the demon speaking; it would know about both Samuel and Saul and their past relationship. Such a demon could also make predictions (Deut. 13:1-3). Isaiah warned later that those who sought the dead were deceived by familiar spirts (Isa. 8:19). The demon spirit practically revealed his identity when he said that Saul and his sons would be with him tomorrow. Saul went to the torment compartment of Sheol or Hades, whereas Samuel went to the comfort side of the underworld of departed spirits.

There is no record of God seeking to intercept the communication of demons and men. Saul inquired of a demon and was answered by one. When God gives answers, His messages come only through the Holy Spirit in different ways, but never through unlawful or unscriptural ways, as here. The case of Balaam is sometimes mentioned as proof that God intercepts messages of Satan and utters His own through the same channel, but this is not true. Balaam was a true prophet as long as he was used of God.

It is stated in 1 Chronicles 10:13-14 that Saul died for his previous sins and also for sinning against the Word of the Lord (which forbade witches and traffic with demons and for asking counsel of one that had a familiar spirit, to inquire of it) and inquired not of the Lord (on this occasion). It was from a familiar spirit, and not Samuel, that he obtained his information.

Jesus taught that it is impossible for the dead to communicate with living persons on Earth, and all scriptures on the subject of the state of the dead, and on Heaven and Hell, completely confirm His teaching. There was an impassible gulf between the compartments so that they could not go from one place to the other, nor go back to the earth (Luke 16:26-31). The only case of any people leaving their place of confinement between death and resurrection is the case of Moses and Elijah whom God brought up for a purpose on the Mount of Transfiguration (Matt. 17:1-8). We must bear in mind though, that this was an act of God and not a demonized witch or wizard. So, we close this finding that 1 Samuel 28:7-19 is the record of a demon impersonation.

All the major prophets condemned divination (Isa. 44:25; Jer. 27:9; 29:8; Ezek. 13:9).

All these forms of superstition, of course, are forbidden, especially because they were seen as more than merely empty ideas, but because their practice invited demonic involvement and workings.

Conjuring Spells

This phrase, also translated as charm, appears in Deuteronomy 18:11, Psalms 58:5, and twice in Isaiah 47:9, 12. Sometimes it is rendered as enchantments. A different Hebrew word lies behind this translation in Isaiah 19:3. Because it is related to a word for bind, it may mean cast a spell — *"spellbinding"*. One scholar suggests it has to do with tying a magic knot.

Probably the most widely known characteristic of a witch was the ability to cast a spell, "spell" being the word used to signify the means employed to carry out a magical action. A spell could consist of a set of words, a formula or verse, or a ritual action, or any combination of these. Spells traditionally were cast by many methods, such as by the inscription on an object to give it magical powers, by a sacrifice or binding of a wax or clay image of a person to affect him or her magically, by the recitation of a series of words or ceremony, by the employment of magical herbs as an ornament or potions, by gazing at mirrors, swords, or a crystal ball for purposes of divination, and by many other means.

Spiritism

The word for spiritist always appears with witch. The root of the word in Hebrew is the verb *"to know"*. In modern English, 'wizard' means "someone very wise or inventive, a very clever or skillful person", but in the Bible, it is always a forbidden thing, a kind of black magic. This is why most modern versions translate the word as spiritist, fortuneteller, or sorcerer.

Wicca — Witchcraft

Also termed Pagan Witchcraft, this is a contemporary pagan, new religious movement. It was developed in England during the first half of the 20th century and was introduced to the public in 1954. Magic and spells depend on what Wiccans call a psychic link. Psychic development can involve training in divination, the attempt to obtain information about the past, present or future by occult means or one's own psychic abilities. The Bible is very clear that divination and any other form of supernatural contact (other than prayer, of course) is forbidden, since it relies on a supernatural power apart from God. In other words, there is no such thing as "white magic".

Many Wiccans say that Wicca is harmless and nature-loving, that it has nothing to do with evil, Satanism, and dark forces. But that is exactly what Satan wants them to believe! Intent on deceit, *"Satan himself masquerades as an angel of light,"* says Paul. *"It is not surprising, then, if his servants masquerade as servants of righteousness."* Paul says that if they don't turn toward God and repent, *"their end will be what their actions deserve," (New International Version, 2 Cor. 11:14-15).*

Unfortunately, they believe it's okay for humans to interact with spirits and spiritual forces any way we choose. To the contrary, the apostle Paul writes that the spiritual realm is potentially dangerous. Therefore, we need to treat it the way God tells us to and be prepared for spiritual battles of good versus evil.

The Bible says in Eph. 6:12-13 (NKJV)

> *"For we do not wrestle against flesh and blood, but against principalities, against powers, against the rulers of the darkness of this age, against spiritual hosts of wickedness in the heavenly places.*
> *13 Therefore take up the whole armor of God, that you may be able to withstand in the evil day, and having done all, to stand."*

Familiar Spirits

Familiar spirits are demons that possess mediums who give their will to them. Familiar spirits imitate dead people, make predictions, promote doctrines, etc. Isaiah said that instead of seeking *"mediums and wizards, who whisper and mutter,"* people should seek the living God (Isa. 8:19). Go to the law and to the testimony, the written Word of God, if you want light. The mediums do not speak according to the written Word of God because there is no light in them.

Occult Bondage

The word '*occult*' means "hidden". Involvement in the occult opens the door for many demons, including spirits of depression, suicide, death, destruction, sickness, mental illness, addiction, lust, etc. Occult practices include: ouija board, horoscopes, palm reading, tea-leaf reading, psychic readers and advisers, drugs, black magic, white magic, ESP.

Curses

Curses provide legal grounds for demons to enter through the bloodline and operate in the family. Strongs #2672 kataraomai verb "to pray against, to wish evil against a person or thing". #332 "to bind by a curse," #2551 "to speak evil" against someone.

Some people have a limited knowledge of what sins may have been practiced by their ancestors.

12 Forbidden Heathen Practices

The rebuke concerns the heathen who superstitiously seek guidance by meteors [also called: shooting star, falling star—the bright streak of light appearing in the sky], planets, signs of the zodiac and all the magic and witchcraft and traffic with demons in the name of astrology, etc. which are condemned by Scripture.

1. Enchantments—practice of magical arts.
   (Exod. 7:11, 22; 8:7, 18; Lev. 19:26; Deut. 18:10; 2 Chron. 33:6; 2 Kings 17:17, 21:6; Isa. 47:9, 12; Jer. 27:9; Dan. 1:20)

2. Witchcraft—practice of dealing with evil spirits.
   (Exod. 22:18; Deut. 18:10; 1 Sam. 15:23; 2 Chron. 33:6; 2 Kings. 9:22; Mic. 5:12; Nah. 3:4; Gal. 5:19-21)

3. Sorcery—same as witchcraft.
   (Exod. 7:11; Isa. 47:9, 12; 57:3; Jer. 27:9; Dan. 2:2; Mal. 3:5; Acts 8:9-11; 13:6-8; Rev. 9:21; 18:23; 21:8; 22:15)

4. Soothsaying—same as witchcraft.
   (Isa. 2:6; Dan. 2:27; 4:7; 5:7, 11; Mic. 5:12)

5. Divination—the art of mystic insight or fortunetelling.
   (Num. 22:7; 23:23; Deut. 18:10-14; 2 Kings 17:17; 1 Sam. 6:2; Jer. 14:14; 27:9; 29:8; Ezek. 12:24; 13:6-7, 23; 21:22-29; 22:28; Mic. 3:7; Zech. 10:2; Acts 16:16)

6. Wizardry—same as witchcraft. A wizard is a male and a witch is a female who practices witchcraft. Both were destroyed in Israel.
   (Exod. 22:18; Lev. 19:31; 20:6, 27; Deut. 18:11; 1 Sam. 28:3, 9; 2 Kings 21:6; 23:24; 2 Chron. 33:6; Isa. 19:3)

7. Necromancy—divination by means of pretended communication with the dead.
   (Deut. 18:11; Isa. 8:19; 1 Sam. 28; 1 Chron. 10:13)

8. Magic—any pretended supernatural art or practice.
   (Gen. 41:8, 24; Exod. 7:11, 22; 8:7, 18-19; 9:11; Dan. 1:20; 2:2, 10, 27; 4:7, 9; 5:11; Acts 19:19)

9. Charm—to put a spell upon (same as enchantment).
   (Deut. 18:11; Isa. 19:3)

10. Prognostication—to foretell by indications, omens, signs, etc.
    (Isa. 47:13)

11. Observing times—same as prognostication.
    (Lev. 19:26; Deut. 18:10; 2 Kings 21:6; 2 Chron. 33:6)

12. Astrology and star gazing—divination by stars the practice of seeking knowledge of the future or the unknown by supernatural means.
    (Isa. 47:13; Jer. 10:2; Dan. 1:20; 2:2, 10; 4:7; 5:7-15)

All the above practices were and still are carried on in connection with demons, called familiar spirits. All who forsook, abandoned God, and sought help from these demons were to be destroyed.

(Lev. 19:31; 20:6; Deut. 18:11; 1 Sam. 28; 2 Kings 21:6; 23:24; 1 Chron. 10:13; 2 Chron. 33:6; Isa. 8:19; 19:3; 29:4; See 1 Tim. 4:1-8; 2 Thess. 2:8-12; Matt. 24:24; Rev. 13; 16:13-16; 19:20)

The good news is that you can deliver yourself!

"Deliver yourself like a gazelle from the hand of the hunter, And like a bird from the hand of the fowler," (NKJV, Prov. 6:5).

"Deliver thyself, O Zion, that dwellest with the daughter of Babylon," (King James Version, Zech. 2:7).

What does it mean to Bind and Loose in Matthew 18:18.

"Assuredly, I say to you, whatever you bind on earth will be bound in heaven, and whatever you loose on earth will be loosed in heaven," (New King James Version, Matt. 18:18).

You have the authority to bind and loose.

Webster's dictionary defines the word '***bind***' as "to make secure by tying; to confine, restrain or restrict as if with bonds ... to constrain with legal authority ... to exert a restraining or compelling effect. (2) It also means to arrest, apprehend, handcuff, lead captive, take charge of, lock up, restrain, check, or put a stop to. Binding is done by legal authority. We have legal authority in the name of Jesus to bind the works of darkness, [the devil, the enemy, Satan] which encompass sin, iniquity, perversion, sickness, disease, infirmity, death, destruction, curses, witchcraft, sorcery, divination, poverty, lack, strife, lust, pride, rebellion, fear, torment, and confusion. We have legal authority to put a stop to these things in our lives and in the lives of those we minister to.

Loose means to untie, to free from restraint, to detach, to disjoin, divorce, separate, unhitch, get free, get loose, escape, break away, unbind, unchain, unfetter, free, release, unlock, liberate, disconnect, and forgive. People need to be loosed from curses, evil inheritance, familiar spirits, sin, guilt, shame, condemnation, control, domination, manipulation, intimidation, mind control, religious control, sickness, disease, deception, false teaching, sin, habits, worldliness, carnality, demons, tradition, ungodly soul ties, ungodly pledges, ungodly vows spoken words, hexes, vexes, jinxes, trauma, and cults. We have legal authority in the name of Jesus to loose ourselves and others to whom we minister from these destroying influences.

---

*For information on "The Extreme Dangers of the Ouija Board" by Michael Bradley www.bibleknowledge.com

If you need help in any of the above items mentioned in this chapter, get ahold of this book: "Deliverance and Spiritual Warfare Manual" by John Eckhardt

---

Notes:

Chapter 28

Forgiveness

When we forgive someone,
it doesn't make them
right or justify
what they have done.
It releases them into

God's hands

so

He

can deal with them.

Chapter 28

Forgiveness

"But one thing I do, forgetting those things which are behind and reaching forward to those things which are ahead," (NKJV, Phil. 3:13).

The past can be a chain that keeps you from enjoying the present and being successful in the future—memory recall that can cause a person to have flashbacks of past experiences. This keeps a person in bondage to traumatic experiences of the past. This spirit causes a person to remember experiences of hurt, pain, and rejection. Although there may be experiences in your life you will never completely forget, you should not be in bondage to the past through your memory.

The enemy should not be able to trigger things in your memory that hinder you in your present or future life. This is why your memory needs to be loosed from bad experiences of hurt and trauma [bind and loosen in Chapters 14 and 27].

Pray the prayer below.

Father God ... I come boldly to Your throne in Jesus' name. I loose myself according to Matthew 18:18, from the effects of all the bad memories, painful memories, and memories of the past that would hinder me in the present or future. I loose myself from all bitterness, unforgiveness, and resentment. I loose to you, Father, those who have offended me or hurt me in any way. I loose myself from all spirits of infirmity as a result of my bitterness. I close that door, right now! In Jesus' name. Amen.

Why should I have to forgive?

Forgiveness is one of the most beautiful and powerful words in our vocabulary. How much pain and unhappy consequences could be avoided if we all learned the meaning of this one word.

King David wrote some of his emotion he personally experienced after he asked God to *"wash me thoroughly from my iniquity and cleanse me from my sin" (NKJV, Psa. 51:2).* King David also said, *"Blessed is he whose transgressions are forgiven, whose sins are covered. Blessed is the man whose sin the LORD does not count against him and in whose spirit is no deceit," (New International Version, Psa.32:1-2)*

Forgiveness:

It is a decision,

not a

Feeling!

With a stroke of His hand, He obliterates the past and permits us to enter the land of new beginnings. What is important to realize is that God's forgiveness is not just a casual statement, it is a complete blotting out of all the filth, dirt, and degradation of our past, present, and future. The only reason our sins are forgiven is that, on the cross, Jesus Christ paid the full penalty.

When we choose not to forgive we end up walking in the dark.

> *"He who says he is in the light, and hates his brother, is in darkness until now. He who loves his brother abides in the light, and there is no cause for stumbling in him. But he who hates his brother is in darkness and walks in darkness, and does not know where he is going, because the darkness has blinded his eyes," (New King James Version, 1 Jn. 2:9-11).*

Because we can't see clearly, we stumble around in confusion. This throws our judgment off and we make mistakes. We become weak, sick, and bitter. Other people notice all this because unforgiveness shows in the face, words, and actions of those who have it.

Just because we confess our unforgiveness toward someone one day doesn't mean we won't have unforgiveness in us the next. That's why forgiveness is a choice we must make every day. We <u>choose</u> to forgive whether we feel like it or not.

When we forgive someone, it doesn't make them right or justify what they have done. It releases them into God's hands so He can deal with them.

To understand forgiveness, what must I do?

1. You must admit to what you have done and own up; that's called repentance (Psa. 51:3-4).

2. Ask for forgiveness (Psa. 51:7,9-10).

What are the results of forgiveness?

1. <u>Reconciliation:</u> When God forgives, there is an immediate and complete change in relationship. Instead of hostility and anger, there is love and acceptance. Instead of an enemy, there is friendship. God is always in the business of reconciliation. (NIV, 2 Cor. 5:19).

2. <u>Purification:</u> The very essence of forgiveness is being restored to our original standing before God. (Psa. 51:7, Rom. 4:7, 1 Jn. 1:9). When God forgives us and purifies us of our sin, **He also forgets it!** (Heb. 8:12 NIV, Psa. 103:12, Isa. 38:17).

3. <u>Remission</u>: Forgiveness results in God dropping the charges against you. He will not enforce judgment because of your sins. (Jn. 8:11, Rom. 8:1).

There are three areas to be realized:

- Forgiveness from God
- Forgiving those who have wronged us
- Forgiving ourselves and putting our past behind us

NOTE: If you have asked for "forgiveness" and <u>*name*</u> what you did to offend someone, and they refuse to receive it, you have done your part for God. Dust your sandals off and **<u>move on</u>**.

What is your attitude?

> *"For as he thinks in his heart, so is he," (NKJV, Prov. 23:7).*

It goes back to what I stated in Chapter 25. You are the way you think. The mind has always been a favorite target of the enemy. If the devil can control your mind, he can control your life.

Are you bitter or resentful? First of all, you need to put your house in order, confessing the bitterness and resentment to God as sin. God knows what is going on, as difficult as it may seem. You have to cough up that hairball. This will be difficult, but God commands it! "*Bear with each other and forgive one another if any of you has a grievance against someone. Forgive as the Lord forgave you," (New International Version, Col. 3:13).* Sometimes those who deserve forgiveness the least, need it the most! Forgiving as the Lord forgave *implies forgetting*. This may be extremely difficult and may require time, but God can change your attitude. Jesus' answer of "seventy times seven" to Peter's question, "*How often shall my brother sin against me, and I forgive him?" (New King James Version, Matt. 18:21) (full passage Matt. 18:21-35).* Sometimes you need to "go the extra mile" (Matt. 5:41) to restore or renew the relationship. The Gospel always cuts across the grain of human reactions in conduct. Until one of the parties involved takes the initiative toward forgiveness and restoration, the broken relationship will continue, as I mentioned above.

There are times when restoration of a relationship is not a healthy action of choice if you have been physically harmed or hurt from that person; common sense is used here. However, forgiveness is always priority number one; you can forgive without contact. Unforgiveness leads to bondage, torment, and you are held hostage, you are a slave to it. If we harbor unforgiveness the door is open to pain and the enemy is allowed into your life.

Unforgiveness and Bitterness

Unforgiveness opens the door for tormenting spirits (Matt. 18). Bitterness opens the door for spirits of infirmity, including arthritis and cancer. It is symbolized by gall and wormwood. Unforgiveness is the result of being hurt, rejected, abandoned, disappointed, abused, raped, molested, taken advantage of, lied to, cheated, talked about, etc.

What if you can't forgive yourself?

If you are truly repentant and have confessed and self-punishment still continues, **you** are guilty of unbelief. Since God has forgiven (1 Jn. 1:9), it is wrong to doubt God. You must take God at His Word. Read David's testimony from Psalms 32. *"Blessed is he whose transgressions are forgiven, whose sins are covered. Blessed is the man whose sin the LORD does not count against them and in whose spirit is no deceit," (New International Version, Psa. 32:1-2).*

And again, false humility could be involved. Self-flagellation (flogging or beating as a religious discipline) makes someone feel better while others take pleasure in reviewing the past over and over and over again. This is like the Scribes and Pharisees *"even so you also appear righteous to men, but inside you are full of hypocrisy and lawlessness" (New King James Version, Matt. 23:28).*

If you are truly repentant, talk about how God sees you as a new creature in Christ Jesus (2 Cor. 5:17). God understands sin and knows how to deal with it. He will forgive sin, if you will repent and confess. We all need to practice what Paul said, *"forgetting those things which are behind and reaching forward to those things which are ahead, I press toward the goal for the prize of the upward call of God in Christ Jesus" (NKJV, Phil. 3:13-14).*

Holy Spirit Conviction or Demonic Condemnation?

Here is something to think about. How can we know if the Holy Spirit is correcting or convicting us? I have learned to call it "*in* and *out*". He is going to correct and discipline you and show you what you did wrong. He is going to get *in* your spirit and get *out*. He is **not** going to badger you or nag at you about the same thing over and over again. He is going to show you the mistake, lay it on your heart to repent and ask for forgiveness, and then He is going to expect us to **move on**. He will keep convicting us until we do something about it.

However, He won't make you feel depressed, guilty, or ashamed like the enemy will. As you grow, in your walk with the Lord, you will be able to (more quickly) identify when it is conviction from the Holy Spirit or condemnation from the enemy.

When you receive condemnation from the enemy, it is different. He wants you to stew on it, on what you did wrong and let it build up inside of you. Oh yes, he is hoping you will take on emotions of guilt, regret, blame, shame, and deep depression. He wants these emotions to plant ugly seeds inside of you, telling you that you are no good, that you will do it again and again and nobody is going to forgive you for your mistakes. These are a few of the lies that the "father of lies", Satan, will plant in your mind.

The key to victory is to remember they are all lies. Don't take the lies in, rebuke them, take your God-given authority over them and refuse to think anything else than what the Word of God says about you.

The enemy is going to attempt to twist and turn your thoughts. He wants to make it hard for you to accept the forgiveness that Christ offers. He wants us to be mad at all people involved. He will always try to plant nasty negative thoughts which are not from God. He wants you to wallow in self-pity.

Does this sound like the Holy Spirit's conviction which only lasts a few minutes or the enemy's condemnation which last three days, three weeks, three months? Our God is a God of second chances. Let's be obedient to act on what direction the Lord gives us. There will be times we make mistakes in our flesh, miss a "God appointment", or allow the enemy to condemn us. Thank God, He gives us a lot of grace to get through those times when we make mistakes.

Let the Past Be the Past

This sweet consequence of not keeping a record of wrongs is that we let go of the past and its effect on the present, knowing that your past does not determine your future. We cast our cares on God and rely on Him to restore the wasted years and to cause everything to turn out good. We find ourselves, almost miraculously, accepting ourselves as we are (just as God does) with all our failures (just as God does) while knowing our potential to make more mistakes. God never becomes disillusioned with us. He loves us and knows us inside and out. How do I know this? I will share a brief part of my life. The testimony I will share with you contains fractured memories of the things I *can* remember. Much of it I have blocked out. I trust the Lord's wisdom and that He is protecting me from the things that would be too hard to face. However, in the things I do remember, for me I strive to be an overcomer.

My Testimony

"Kristina's testimony of her childhood spans from age five to the age of sixteen. This is one of the most precious times in a child's life. But instead of having a safe home of a loving family, enjoying school and playing with her friends, it was a house of horrors, alcoholic chaos, physical abuse and selfishness. Basically forgotten but being told by a friend that God is a God of miracles, she started praying in the woods by her home. She found the answer to her dilemma, God came into her life and she had her first miracle." (Quoted by Jim Bean)

Even though my parents were professional, working-class people, (my father, a draftsman engineer and my mother, a registered nurse) something happened in their young married life, and they became alcoholics and were most all of my childhood days. My father worked during the day and went to the bars after work, and my mother worked nights at the hospital and was home drunk during the day. Sometimes she never made it to work for weeks at a time. However, my dad had no problem working with a hangover. They lost everything they ever owned: beautiful homes, cars, trucks, boats, and travel trailers. We moved a lot in California: from Fremont to Clayton, to South Sacramento, to the small town of El Dorado, then to Placerville, and finally to Sacramento.

During the beginning of their drinking days, I was hit by a car at the age of two in Fremont. You would think that would shock them into NOT drinking, but that was the reverse of things. My older sister was blamed for not watching me which was a terrible burden for her to carry. She had told me years later that they were playing tag with neighborhood kids and, being just two years old, I was laughing and wanting to play chase too. I ran out between two parked cars and was hit. I was rushed to the hospital, unconscious and with terrible facial lacerations. I have a dent on the top of my skull, but I don't really know if that was from the accident. No one has ever mentioned it to me or spoke about it. My parents were told that I probably wouldn't have my permanent teeth grow in properly if any grew in at all. However that didn't happen, all my teeth grew in perfectly straight.

In the early years, my sister was taking tap dancing and my brother was involved in Cub Scouts. My parents were really involved with my older siblings, but as the years passed by, my father became very physically and verbally abusive. I can remember around five years of age climbing up into our bedroom closet. I shared a room with my sister, which had sliding doors for storage above the closet doors. I would climb up into the storage cupboard to hide from the loud arguing. My father grew mean. He wasn't a very tall man—about 5' 8" and stocky. I recall them arguing about me—he didn't want any more kids, calling me an accident and a few more things. It was true. It always seemed that he was angry with me, and I was afraid of him. He had no patience with me. If I left my trike in the driveway, he would run over it. If I left my 2-wheeler in the driveway he would run over that too, on purpose it seemed, to teach me a lesson. I never ever received another trike or bicycle from my parents.

When I was six years old, I became ill suddenly, with an extreme headache, pain all over my body, and a fever. I developed red, painful blisters like a wave across my chest, back, and my right arm. It was traveling up my neck into my jaw. My mother wrapped me up with bandages as the blisters would pop and ooze. It was extremely painful with sharp pains going through my body. This went on for a month before the healing began. She took me to the doctor. He said I had a case of severe shingles. I had to stay at home and stayed in bed most of the time. When I started to heal, I looked terrible so my mom kept me indoors. She told me that people wouldn't understand and she was right, they didn't. When I wanted to play, several parents shut their front door with a horrified look on their faces, as they would grab their child's hand and tell me to go home. Some people back then thought it was contagious; we know today that it is a virus.

Shingles is also referred to as herpes zoster and is a form of infection that affects individual nerves and the skin surrounding them. It is caused by the same virus that causes chickenpox, called the varicella-zoster virus. It is believed that it is more common during times of stress, tiredness or illness when the immune system is likely to be suppressed. I have only a few scars from it. I do remember everything about it. I did receive the shingle vaccine a few years ago. You do not want to go through shingles if you don't have to.

My grandparents came to visit us during my time with the shingles. My grandmother bought me a lunchbox. It was shaped like a red barn with animals in the windows. When I opened it, the thermos was a grain tower, and the lunchbox she filled with farm animals. I was so happy, I truly loved that lunchbox and carried it everywhere. Since I had to stay inside the house, one particular day when I asked if I could go out on the back patio to play since I was feeling better, my mother gave her permission. She let me have some saltine crackers. I loved crackers and filled my lunchbox to the brim with the crackers on the top and my farm animals on the bottom. Crackers make crumbs easily and will make a mess. I went out on the patio with my blanket and lunchbox. There were a lot cracker crumbs on the patio. I had a few little piles of crumbs here and there to feed my farm animals.

My father came out on the patio and saw my mess. I remember how devastated I was when he stomped my lunchbox flat with such heated anger and kicked all my farm animals out into the yard, never to be seen again. I remember crying and sobbing, carefully picking up my lunchbox with both hands, cradling it against my chest with tears streaming down my face.

"Why do you always make a mess?" he asked with his teeth gritted to me as he jerked me up to my feet by my left arm, the one that wasn't bandaged.

I knew that he didn't care about me. Having me come along into his world messed up their plans as my older siblings were in school and now they were going to have to have a nanny for me.

The drinking was mostly from my father but then, as time went on, my mother decided to join him. I remember her saying, "If you can't beat him … join him!"

As it turned out, five years later, they had another accident—a girl. Then again, two years later, another girl. I actually don't ever remember my mother being pregnant. The last child born was born with a congenital hip. She had to have surgery around sixteen months old and wore a brace between her legs for a while. The brace spread her legs wide open above the knees. Her hip did heal properly and she hasn't had any problems with her hip that I know of. I do remember her having a brace but that's all. I don't remember diapers, crawling, walking, or talking toddlers. Nothing comes to my mind. Through the years I don't recall them having a bedroom or playing in the house or yard until I was around twelve years old, I have little moments of memory. I truly can't figure it out. So, I was the child in the middle. My older sister is seven years older, my brother five years older, a sister five years younger, and sister seven years younger than me. I was pretty much alone. My older sister told me that it was like our parents had three separate families.

About the same time the last child was born, we were living in Clayton. My father had an Indian motorcycle along with two of his buddies. They were planning a weekend trip and left me with an old man who lived near Mitchel Canyon Park. This old man was a friend of my parents. He was a gross, smelly man who had a rough, unshaven beard, bad breath, and pale blue eyes. He had a small wine vineyard with wooden barrels of wine in his cellar. I hated going there. This old man would have me sit on his lap and would pull my panties down and touch me. He would threaten me not to tell. This happened two separate times. I tried to tell my mother, but she wasn't willing to listen to me. She was with the other two couples the day they dropped me off there. They were all good friends and would drink wine and play cards.

This particular weekend, they all rode their motorcycles, traveling on a windy road through the hills to the city. One of the couples rode far ahead of the other two. My mother said that they had to pull over off the road for a few minutes. When the other couple realized the other two weren't behind them, they turned around and came back to see what was going on, wondering if someone was broke down. Speeding around the windy road, riding on the white line to find each other, going in opposite directions, two of the couples had a head on collision on the curve and killed each other. It was a terrible pile up. I don't know what happened to the wives but the two best friends of my father were dead at the scene of the accident as my parents narrowly missed them and had their own accident. Though my mother was thrown, neither one of them were terribly injured. That trauma sent my dad over the edge. He was out of control, an evil maniac, violent and dangerous. Our family life went to Hell. It was truly Hell on Earth.

Shortly after the incident, they sent me on a Greyhound bus to Livermore. I was very afraid of all the strangers on the bus. I remember thinking the bus was traveling at a high rate of speed, and I thought we might tip over as the bus leaned from side to side taking the curves. The bus stopped one time at another bus station. I needed to use the restroom but I was afraid that he would leave without me. I couldn't wait to get to my grandma's house.

I spent several weeks, maybe a month, at my grandparents' place during that summer. At the time, they lived in Livermore, California, near a cattle ranch next to the freeway. Their house was very homey, probably built in the 40s with several cement stairs going up to the nice shaded front porch with a porch swing. Grandpa had painted the cement floor a rustic brick color. The cement walkway was beautiful that led to the front porch. It was lined with tree roses that stood about three feet tall and had lots of flowers. The aroma of the flowers was a very pleasant smell. Grandpa was my step Grandpa. He was a tall, stout man with a full head of hair. He always wore khaki pants and a long-sleeved shirt that he would tuck in with a belt. He was a very gentle man, always happy to see me and would cry sometimes. His arms were always open wide to give me a huge hug. We would talk about the farmyard but mostly we had a lot of quiet times together.

Grandpa was a mason and he had built square, brick pillars that stood about 3 ½ feet tall, in the front yard of their property. He used old red bricks that were of different shades of red and white. The top of each pillar was a flat cemented area that he painted white. He placed three white fence boards evenly spaced lengthwise, connecting to the next pillar. The short fence about three feet high, protected the flowers that lined just inside of the yard. The gate to the walkway was a fancy detailed twisted iron that was painted white, with a long, metal rod that you would lift up out of a hole that was in the cement walkway to open the gate. I always thought that was clever. The back yard was huge and was divided with a fairly tall fence so you couldn't see over it. The lawn was lush and green around the front and back yard. There was a huge oak tree in the back yard with a nice swing that he built for me. They also had a huge vegetable garden with no weeds that I could ever see, and the soil was black. I loved going there and would swing for hours. The fence in the back yard had lattice on the top edge that held beautiful vines of flowers. The birds were thick in there and you could hear them sing. Once in a while I would climb up on the lattice and look at the bird nests and sometimes during the winter months, Grandpa would let me have a few nests to take home that were unoccupied. On the other side of the back yard fence was a chicken yard with a hen house and a guest house. Grandpa said it was his dog house. It had a full-size bed and a cedar hope chest, and fancy white wallpaper with tiny flowers. It was very light and clean with two windows. One of the windows was near the front door. It had a nice shady, wooden porch with a wooden screen door. I recall lots of chickens running around with excitement when we were out there. Near one of the trees, Grandma had a large tree stump with a hatchet and two nails hammered into it about two inches apart for the chickens' necks and a garbage can close by.

If you were facing the house standing in the front yard, on the left side of the house, my Grandpa had some very fancy masonry work with lots of colorful ends of glass bottles, pieces of colorful pottery, odds and ends and a fairly large crucifix of Jesus Christ. I knew at a very young age it was Jesus, it was God. I would sit in the grass, cross legged and stare at Him, get up and touch Him, running my finger down His body. I found myself talking to Him and asking Him to "watch this" as I did a somersault and a cartwheel. I actually thought I heard Him laugh and say, "Good job."

Through the next few years, I would always run to see Jesus on His cross who was waiting for me. He knew my pain and my misery. I didn't have to say anything because I didn't know how to say anything. I did know that I wanted to live with my grandparents. I would play for hours outside. I loved playing cowboys and Indians. Most of the time, I was Tonto, the Native American, who was the Lone Ranger's companion. My grandmother made me a headdress from the chicken feathers that I collected from the chicken yard, and she dyed them different colors, sewed them in a headband, and tied it around my head. They were the happy times. When play time was over, she would make apricot fried pies, my favorite, along with fried chicken and mashed potatoes. She was a wonderful cook. There were other times in my life that I found a secret place to go. I would sit next to a creek under an old bridge and pray to God, asking Him to help me. I would listen while watching the water flow over the rocks, I always felt better when I left.

Back home in Clayton, the fighting was ridiculous, and life was starting to change at a rapid rate. My sister was in high school when the horror started in her life as a young lady. She started developing into a big busted young lady in her sophomore year. Dad had told her if any boy or young man tried to take advantage of her, to fight him off to the death! This statement became a mixed message as dad was infatuated with her looks and started molesting her. It started with him touching her breasts and working his way down. My mother walked in on him once when he was fondling her and asked, "What's going on here?" Mom thought that he had stopped but he hadn't. He was constantly pestering her.

Several times she ran away, but most of the time she would go to work with my mother and sleep in the car when she worked the graveyard shift at Pittsburg hospital less than ten miles away. According to my sister, he would take her for rides in his car and say that they would be going to grandma's house but actually, he would turn down an unknown road, pull the car over and do bad things to her. Dad was really hard on my brother too. I am not sure what all he did to him but it definitely was traumatizing to his life.

In the 1960s, a lot of the boys were pegging their pants, taking them in on the sides to make them a little slimmer through the legs and dying them different colors. My mom was helping my brother with his new look when my father came home drunk and saw what was going on. My parents got into a big argument. He went into my brother's bedroom, took all his clothes out of his closet and set them on fire in the back yard. The neighbors all heard the action at our home. Brand new dishes out of the box were thrown out the windows and out the front door. Black eyes on my mother were a monthly occurrence. We lived in a beautiful, nicely landscaped home with hardwood floors and nice furniture. Both of my parents worked. The neighbors stayed away and I wasn't able to play with anyone. At a young age, you do bear the burden of the sins from your parents. You are marked. You are trouble and no one wants you around.

My father loved boats. He built one in our garage and named it after my older siblings. He wasn't happy with it. He had bought a Star Craft. It was pink and white with a windshield. The motor in the boat caused nothing but trouble. On this occasion, we were at Frank's Track Recreation Area. You could see Mount Diablo on a clear day. There was frequent strong winds and fluctuating water levels there. In times of high water, the entire site can be submerged except for portions of the old levees. We were never allowed in the water because it had a lot of debris floating on the surface.

On one particular day, the boat motor suddenly stopped running. Dad, in a heated rage, took the anchor which was tied to a rope and began swinging it over his head to launch it out in the water. It hit my mother in the head. She fell overboard, hitting her head on the side of the boat. He didn't realize that she was knocked out. In his heated rage, he took the cover off the boat motor and sailed it across the water and started working on the motor, not ever giving my mother a second thought. She was knocked out, face up in the water for what seemed like hours. My sister was holding on to her from the side of the boat. He finally got the motor running and retrieved my mother; she was still unconscious. She came to much later when we arrived at the boat dock and was very quiet.

My dad and a couple of his friends were going to look at the motor. They all stepped into the boat and with all three of them standing on the same side of the boat, it flipped over and sunk. I don't know how he got the boat out of there or if they ever did. There was a lot of confusion.

The three of us stayed close to mom on the shoreline. Hours went by with her being quiet. Then he realized that she was in agony and had a broken jaw. He had to take her to the hospital. She had to have her jaw wired shut, along with little hooks that held tiny rubber bands in place. She was in a lot of pain with terrible bruising.

A few months later that summer, we traveled to Lake Berryessa and had our travel trailer already there at Spanish Flat Campground. My father had a new boat; it was a Chris-Craft inboard/outboard. The boat was a beautiful polished mahogany. The motor sounded deep and healthy with lots of power. My father and mother would water ski on one ski, making huge rooster tails as they would lean into the water when they would cut across the wakes. My older siblings were skiing on two skis and learning how to drop one. I don't recall skiing myself. My father made a round board that I would stand on, and I would hold on to a thick ski rope as he pulled me around.

On this trip, my parents were drinking and got into an argument in the boat, out on the middle of the lake. We had our dog, a Boxer named Rebel, with us in the boat. Rebel's leash was around my mother's wrist. She was still recovering with her broken jaw. Dad suddenly punched her, and she fell overboard hitting her head on the side of the boat, and Rebel on the leash was yanked overboard as well. It was shocking! Then he took off in the boat at a high rate of speed and left her and Rebel to drown in the middle of the lake. We were screaming and fearful that they would drown or they would be run over by another boat. My mother wasn't wearing a life preserver.

After 20 minutes or so, he turned the boat around and went looking for them. They were nowhere in sight that I could see as the water was becoming rough and choppy. Finally my sister spotted them. It was a miracle. Rebel was clinging to my mother as she was floating on her back. We got to them. We got Rebel in, then my mother. She was tore up pretty bad from the dog's toenails clawing her as he paddled in a panic. She had a bloody nose, black eye and her jaw still wired together.

We stayed at the campground for a few more days until she got a hair in her mouth. Everything she ate had to be liquid, apparently she must have sucked it up in a straw. She was gagging something terrible so my father had to unwire her jaw carefully, removing all the tiny rubber bands to find what the problem was and removed the hair. He then, rewired her jaw and placed all the tiny rubber bands back on the tiny hooks. It was a frightening situation. I was so concerned for my mom that I asked her if we could live with Grandma. She said no and told me not to mention it again. So I didn't for a couple of years.

For some reason, my father received a new job. We moved to South Sacramento. It was a terrible place to live compared to where we lived before. The house was a lot smaller and dark inside. It was not nicely landscaped but run down. The rooms were very small, but I had my own bedroom. We were moving in and my mother was drunk and fell down and hit her head on the corner of a cabinet. She cut her eyebrow, and it needed stitches. We were new in town and had no idea where anything was. My father was not around so my sister had to find a doctor. She drove there and had to tell the doctor that she was intoxicated and she couldn't get her in the office. The doctor helped get her inside, and he sewed up her eyebrow.

My brother went to a new high school in Elk Grove. My older sister stayed behind in Clayton, which was a couple of hours away. She moved in with some friends so she could finish her last year in high school. Now it was me and my two younger siblings. This is strange to say, but I don't remember my two younger siblings being around at that time, but I'm sure they were.

Now, life at home was downright horrible, and at a young age, I did know the difference. My dad was hardly ever home. We lived in a run-down home with hardly any yard and I didn't like the neighborhood. My mother's drinking was much worse, and she would be drunk for weeks at a time. I don't know if she even worked, but I am guessing probably not since she had to take care of my two younger sisters.

Several times my mother would travel to Clayton to pick up my older sister in our station wagon and would be drunker than a skunk when we arrived to pick up my sister. My sister would just cringe seeing her step out of the vehicle. Many times, my sister would not come home. She told me how wonderful it was to be in a normal family environment and that she would do anything not to have to come home to the alcohol, the fighting, the smelly house with no clean clothes or clean sheets, no washed towels, or a cooked meal. She also didn't want to be around my father. For many years she came home once in a while when she drove her own car and could leave when it got bad. I always thought that she was the lucky one. I had no idea what she was going through at home.

During that time, I was around 10 years old. I hardly went to school. When I did go, I couldn't stand it. I didn't know what was going on and seldom knew that we had homework. I didn't do well at all and was actually flunking. One day, my two little sisters rode their tricycles to my school. I was horrified, wondering how they even got there. It was quite a distance from our house. I knew that moment that something was terribly wrong at home. School was about out for the day. The school called my mother, who was drunk and asleep. She arrived to help me get them home. I don't remember much after that.

I became friends with the girl across the street, which wasn't good. She was a bad influence for me. She would steal my used Barbie dolls from me, and she taught me how to steal. We were caught stealing peanuts to eat one day, from the department store, and I was in serious trouble. I got a whipping with a belt and was grounded for the whole summer to our weed-infested back yard. You know the back yard that I'm talking about. No privacy, no shade tree to climb on, no dirt to play in, but only thistle weeds two feet high and plenty of dog poop. An old swamp cooler up on stilts with stinky water that dripped from the cooler made a muddy swamp in part of the yard. There was an old metal swing set with most of the paint gone; the rust would rub off on your hands and clothes. It was left from the previous renters. The swing set wasn't anchored down so if I was to swing too high, the legs would lift up several feet off the ground. I was concerned that it would turn over and land on me. As crazy as this sounds even to my own mind, I don't recall my younger siblings playing outside. I don't remember them at all during this time.

I don't know where my brother was. I know that he was going to a new high school, but he had dropped out and joined the army. My older sister finished high school. She was now going to a cosmetology school somewhere in Sacramento. She moved in with a couple who had two children—both had muscular dystrophy and were confined to wheelchairs. Once in a while, she would pick me up and I would visit with them. She took care of them and went to school. Around this time, my friend across the street from where we lived in South Sacramento lost her father, who was a fireman, to suicide in their garage. He was a very nice man. I thought it was strange that my friend wasn't upset about it. I realize now that some people grieve differently. Shortly after that, I heard my parents talking about moving again. I told my teacher at school that we were moving. I decided to check myself out of school without a parent there or a note from them. I was out of school for several months before we moved. Nobody at home noticed. We moved to a small town, El Dorado, in the foothills of California. I was going into the sixth grade now.

The house in El Dorado, was a big two-story, pink A-frame. It was an old brick home built in the late 1800s. It sat on the top of a hill. To me, it looked cold and haunted. It had a full basement with a dirt floor. There were no kitchen cupboards, only a small narrow one above each side of the all-in-one unit, a white, enamel metal base with drain boards on each side of the one large farm sink. My mother ended up using an old stand-up freezer to store our dishes and any groceries.

My bedroom was upstairs, down a long, dark, L-shaped hallway in the far back of the house. It was always scary to me. I couldn't stand up straight unless I was standing in the middle of the room because the ceiling came down on each side. My older siblings both had a room closest to the stairway, but they were never home. Their bedrooms didn't have the ceiling problem—their room only had part of a sloped ceiling. The staircase banister was made of beautiful wood, wide enough that you could slide down. The living room was called the parlor. It had two huge doors that you could slide to close at both ends of the room. My parents' room was large, and across from it was the bathroom. The bathroom was long and narrow. The back of the fireplace took up part of the room and the tub sat at the far end along with the toilet and sink. I don't know where my two younger siblings stayed.

I don't ever recall having much food in the house when I was young, let alone a cooked meal. We seldom had store-bought new clothes or new shoes. Once in a while, my grandmother would sew a dress or skirt for me. We didn't have a telephone or a washing machine and dryer. We didn't have a car—it had been repossessed. They borrowed a vehicle from my grandparents. My father drove a company vehicle.

I didn't know when school started after the long, hot days of summer ended. I didn't know where the school was. This year was hard—nobody was around. I went up to the property above us; they had a vegetable garden. I stole a lot of carrots from them. They never said a word to me about it. They owned a bar and tiny restaurant. We had a plum tree, so we lived on carrots and plums that summer. My parents' time and money went to their love of alcohol and cigarettes. It was the Lord that kept watch over us. I truly missed seeing Jesus hanging on the cross on the side of my grandparents' old house in Livermore.

One early morning, I found a dollar in change stuck deep in the couch. This couch had so many deep burnt holes clear down to the wood frame from cigarettes from when my mom would fall asleep with one in her hand. It needed to go to the dump. I decided to head to the small country store downtown El Dorado. As I was walking to the store, I saw a school bus picking up kids to go to school. I had no idea that school had started. I didn't know what to do. My mother had been drunk for weeks, and I had no idea where my father was. I was hiding and watching as the school bus pulled away.

I ran home and searched the house looking for my grandmother's phone number. I called my grandmother collect from a telephone booth. They had moved to a small farming community in Live Oak, California. I told her of the situation, and she took a Greyhound bus to our town. She walked from where the bus let her off to the house on the hill. She had several suitcases that were extremely heavy; you could hardly lift them. They were packed with food, canned and frozen.

For the first time, she saw it all—my mother, sloppy drunk with the same clothes on that she had worn for several weeks and the conditions we were living in with no clean clothes and no food. My mother sobered up pretty fast. A couple of days later, Grandma took my sisters and me to the store and bought us each a dress, under clothes, a light weight jacket, and a new pair of shoes. She stayed for about one week, and my father, her son, finally showed up.

Things were good for a few months. My mother was sober. When the holidays came, I remember my brother had come home from the service in his uniform. He had been in Korea. He stayed a little longer than he should have and was arrested during Christmas vacation. He had gone AWOL.

My mother went downhill. It was my birthday three days before Christmas, which was forgotten. Christmas morning I came downstairs to my father reading the newspaper, sitting in his chair. "Merry Christmas!" No answer. Another messed up Christmas. No Christmas. No Christmas dinner, nothing. I headed back to my room, crying. I hated this life. I wanted to run away but where would I go? This lifestyle can't be right.

In this small town, I met my best friend, Debbie. She lived across the dirt road from us. She was the same age as me, and she had a younger brother. She was gone that whole summer. When I met her, she was my saving grace. I had a girlfriend.

Her mother, Sharon, signed us up for softball to be on the same team. I loved it. I loved the discipline and hard work because I didn't know anything about softball. It was the only thing that was sane to me. It kept me going. I played hard, and I practiced every day with Debbie. We loved it. We played for Eddie's Pizza in Diamond Springs, a short distance from El Dorado. Debbie played catcher and I played first base. We were both very good players and had an excellent batting average. We became very close and I told her only a few things. I was afraid to tell her everything. I was concerned that she wouldn't like me anymore or her mother wouldn't let her play with me. I'm sure her mother must have known what was happening. One day I saw Debbie getting in the freezer in their garage. I couldn't believe the food I saw in there. I occasionally started stealing from their upright freezer. I figured that they wouldn't miss it.

When my brother finally came home, it was a bad deal. My father was so angry with him and very abusive to him. I don't know what started it, but he took my brother in the bathroom of this house. As I mentioned before, the bathroom was long and narrow. It had several windows running along the side of the wall. I could hear my brother crying and my father's loud, drunk voice. I went outside and carefully placed a ladder against the house. I climbed it and peeked through the window. He had my brother strapped to a chair and was cutting chunks of his hair off, clear to his scalp. I was horrified at the sight of it. I was so concerned that something terrible was going to happen to him. He lived through it and left home for good. My father did terrible things to him and was extremely cruel to him. My brother had problems, serious ones, and I believe they all came from my father. My brother was a lost, hurt soul. He started running around with the wrong crowd, getting into trouble and was introduced to drugs.

I hated the thought of ever moving and losing my friend. However, Sharon told me that wouldn't be a problem. We moved to Placerville, California into a house off of Cedar Ravine. I was in the 7th grade. I still played softball. Sharon would pick me up for practice and for the games. It was probably 10 miles to my house from theirs. We were on a different team now.

We still didn't have a vehicle and life was terrible. My father had the company truck. They finally received an old Chevy car. The headliner would sag down and eventually it was ripped out. The car was an embarrassment. It didn't last long and they borrowed another vehicle from my grandparents—a small Ford Falcon truck. We called it the gutless wonder as in we wondered if we were going to make it home.

My parents fought more than ever now. My father joined a club called E. Clampus Vitus. The members called themselves "Clampers". What it was, in my eyes, was an enormous amount of men dressed in red shirts, black pants, black hats, and boots giving themselves permission to be plastered, three sheets to the wind in public and during public gatherings. They were a disgustingly loud, obnoxious group of falling down, drooling men who smelled like an outhouse and brewery who thought they were funny by running into people or making nasty remarks to get a reaction from them and their nasty jokes. Any time there was an outdoor celebration in town, there would be the Clampers.

My mother finally started going to AA, and she had a sponsor. Life was starting to look and feel better. I still had severe trust issues with her. She was sober about 6 months when she planned a week vacation to the Santa Cruz Boardwalk. She rented a room at the Tides Inn Motel; it was a short distance from the beach. She drove an old station wagon with the two girls. I rode with my sister in her little hot pink VW and dad was going to meet us there. They drove separate vehicles because they had to go back to work on Monday.

For the first few days things were nice. We went to the boardwalk and the beach. When Saturday afternoon came, my father and mother went off together in his company truck and said they wouldn't be gone long. They arrived about 4 hours later. As the vehicle pulled up into the parking lot, I could tell from a distance that something was wrong with my mother. Her body language said it all. Mom was drunk—sloppy, falling down drunk. I was sick to my stomach, angry, and I cried. They stumbled up the staircase to the motel room, loud and belligerent. I was so embarrassed I had to run away. I went down to the boardwalk and sat there for hours wondering what was going to happen now. They argued most of the night. Dad was very aggressive. We had the manager come to the door several times with complaints.

The next morning, I was ready to go home. I saw that my father left and my sister too. They left us! I'm twelve with a drunk mother and two small sisters. Trying to keep my mom in the motel room was next to impossible without making a lot of noise. It was a physical struggle trying to keep her indoors. It was exhausting. The manager came several times to tell us to keep it down. Finally, I told him that I didn't know what to do. I had no idea if my dad was coming back for us or even my sister. We were there for the rest of the week, six days of pure Hell. It makes me sick to my stomach just writing this situation out on paper, thinking about how horrible and cruel it was to willfully cause us to suffer with abandonment. It was truly heartbreaking for me. I still can't believe it. I was so angry at my father for getting my mother back on the bottle again and then just leaving us so far away from home with nothing to eat, no money, no one to call. My mother managed to sneak out several times when I was exhausted from lack of sleep. It had to be by the grace of God that she wasn't dead somewhere and that she managed to find her way back to the motel room. It was Friday. We had been there six days when the manager told us to pack up and get out.

There wasn't much to pack up, but I had it together the best way I could. My mother was a little better that morning. She was a mess, a sloppy pig pen as a matter of fact. She was not drunk but had a terrible hangover. She said she was able to drive. My older sister had arrived. She put my younger siblings in the station wagon with my mother at the wheel. She said there wasn't any room in her VW Bug for all of us, so just her and I drove in it. It was a terrible idea and I have felt guilty about that for years. We were headed to an old friend of my mother's, traveling on a two-lane road with the river bordering the road. Suddenly, my mother was all over the road weaving horribly to the left and then to the right, taking up the whole road. At first, I actually thought she was playing around because it was so severe until I saw the girls' faces looking back at us in extreme frightful, appalling screams. I am not sure what happened after that, but she managed to pull off the road, and we got help. I'm so thankful to God for protecting them. It was a terrible decision having them in the vehicle with my mother. It turned out that she managed to hide a bottle of whiskey in the front seat and was extremely intoxicated. We stayed at her friend's place for several days until my mother was truly sober. I don't remember how long we stayed there. I do remember being so torn up about the experience I just went through that I was thankful it was over.

My mother was never sober for very long. Her addiction was way out of control. She would be drunk for months at a time. She had a job working at the hospital on the graveyard shift, which was 11 p.m. to 7 a.m. I have no idea how in the world she managed to keep a job. She must have slept through it. If I wanted to talk to my father about anything, I would have to find him in one of the local bars on Main Street where his company truck would be parked. I couldn't go anywhere without permission from him. How he could find out if I went to a friend's house was beyond me, but he could and he would find me. I couldn't understand what the big deal was about going to visit a friend or having dinner with their family. [It took 50 years for me to figure that one out, with the help of my older sister]. He worked during the day and when it was quitting time, he was in the bar until it closed.

When I turned 13, the house became a nightmare. My father would come home around 2 a.m. He was always heated with an abusive, aggressive anger, staggering down the hallway. My bedroom was the first one on the left. He would fling open my door and yank his belt off, rip the blankets off me, and whip me with his belt as hard as he could, with all his might. His face had the look of extreme hatred. With me screaming and crying, trying to protect myself, he would drag me out of bed and have me wash every dish from the cupboard. He would stack them. I have no idea why this would happen. Why did I have to wash all the mixed-matched dishes that were not even used, that were stacked clean in the cupboard? This went on for a very long time. Each night I would sleep with my eyes half open and my ears tuned in to the sound of a truck on the gravel and cringe when I saw truck lights turning into the driveway as they would shine on the slope I could see from my bedroom window.

I would hope he would walk past my room. Sometimes he would. He did terrible things to me and I hated his guts for it. Sometimes he would get me up and have me sit next to him on our broken-down couch. A few times he tried putting his hands on me but I fought him off. Several times he would pin me down, sit on my chest and put his knees on my arms above my head. I started to buck him off and the fight was on. A few times he burnt my arms with cigarettes. He would lift me up by my jaw until my feet dangled off the ground. He would say, "Don't move." I thought he might break my neck. I knew it was true because I was starting to have severe pain when I threw a softball. The sharp, excruciating pain would radiate from the side of my neck to my jaw which would affect my tongue, and I couldn't speak or move my head for about a minute. I knew what he was capable of doing, and this hurt something terrible. I told my mother about it, but nothing good came out of it. I was getting sick of the physical abuse. There was no one to help me. My sister lived across town. I would spend the night once in a while at her place. I knew that I was going to make it. I knew deep inside. Thank God, my father never touched my two younger sisters.

My mother was having a taxi cab driver deliver the whiskey that she needed so badly. After a dozen or so deliveries, they stopped their delivery service. So she started walking to town to get what she needed. She was finally picked up for shoplifting alcohol several times. She spent some time in jail.

My parents fought continuously. He busted her lip several times, gave her black eyes, etc. He became extremely abusive to her and me. I begged my mother to leave him, but she wouldn't. I decided that I had to do something, I wrote letters to the county judge asking for help for us, my two younger sisters and I, but nothing ever came of it. I was starting to believe we weren't worth the effort. I felt dirty and unloved. The sins of my parents were starting to affect my life, affect my personality. They were in the local newspaper for DUI's and shoplifting. I was starting to hear a few comments from kids at school about my parents. I was in the 8th grade at this time. I did everything I could to get her to stop drinking. I found bottles of whiskey in coat pockets in the closets, under the mattress, in the toilet tank, in old boxes of cereal and in the tool box in the garage. I was at my wits end, and she was very clever. Pouring the whiskey out didn't help.

My teacher was teaching us girls about the "facts of life". We had to watch a film. Our teacher wanted the girls to bring their mothers to sit and watch the film together. My mother had been sober for about 7 months at this time, and I asked her if she thought she would want to come to my school and watch the film with me. She said she would, and she came. We sat next to each other, and I was glad to see her. As the film went on for about 40 minutes, I caught something from the corner of my eye, a movement that I recognized a million times. She was drunk. She was plastered. How did she do it? She never left my side! I figured she must have drunk a huge portion of whiskey as she drove up. But this time was different—I didn't smell it. This time, she switched from Sunny Brook whiskey to Vodka. I had to hurry and try to get her out of the multipurpose room before anyone noticed. I got her in the vehicle along with my things, and she managed to get us home, clear across town. I was so brokenhearted and so tired of hearing the broken promises. *What a liar!* I thought. *What a coward! You can't even deal with a short "facts of life" film; you have to drink to calm your nerves. What nerves?*

It wasn't long after that when I was called into the principal's office for getting into a physical fight with a boy who said some things about my parents and was teasing me about it. We sat there facing his desk when he asked what happened. I told the principal what he said about my parents and that he had called my dad a drunk.

The principal looked at me and said, "He is, isn't he … a drunk?"

With tears filling my eyes I said, "Yes, he is." I just sat there with tears rolling down my cheeks. I was miserable. "So everyone knows? I guess I'm trash because of my parents. Is that it?" Nothing was said. It was a done deal. I sat there by myself as the principal and the boy left the office. I actually thought that I broke my foot from kicking that boy in the shins, but I got myself together and walked out like nothing was wrong.

My escape was school. I tried to do my best. I had to really work hard at homework. I was a slow reader and my spelling wasn't the greatest. I had no one to help me with my studies. I enjoyed math and California History. I loved playing softball and would be excited to see the day come for practice. My friend Debbie wasn't close by. They lived 10 miles away. She truly was my girlfriend. She loved me for me. We seldom talked about my home life. I kept it inside.

It would hurt me deep inside my heart to see the love that school friends would have with their parents. They would come to the games and cheer them on, giving them praises for a base hit. I thought how lucky they all were to have parents or a parent come to their games. Then one day, during our last game for the championship, I was the fourth batter and the bases were loaded. As I walked up to the home plate getting ready for the pitch, I heard, "Come on, slugger!" I couldn't believe it. *I hope not.* I froze and missed the ball. I heard it again. "Come on, slugger, and hit the ball." I stepped away from the plate for a moment and back to it, ready for the pitch. I smacked it so hard. It was a homerun! My teammates were yelling, screaming, and cheering along with their parents. When I ran all the bases, I saw him at the fence. My dad was at the game—the last game of the season and the only game he ever came to. He wasn't drunk, and he actually had a smile on his face. It was a good day. We won the championship, and he spoke a few words of praise to me and left. For a moment I saw something good in him. I really loved my dad and prayed that he would stop drinking. He didn't know me as a person. He knew nothing about me. This gave me some hope.

When things were good at home, it never lasted very long. It would be nice to just have some peace. I couldn't understand why my parents didn't care enough about us to stop drinking. They wasted money and had nothing of any value. I started to have a terrible self-worth. I felt they couldn't care less if we lived or died. I didn't understand why my grandparents didn't take us in. They lived three hours away from us. I thought that maybe they didn't know. I wasn't about to say anything to them. I was afraid they might ask my parents questions.

I went to visit my grandmother one day when I was 14. I met a new friend from my grand-mother's church in Live Oak. He told me that God is a God of miracles, and I told him I truly needed one. He told me to talk to God about it. I didn't have a Bible at the time, but I knew when I was a child that Jesus hung on the cross. I asked the Lord to help me, to come into my life. I told Him that I didn't want to be like my parents. I started spending time in the woods crying out for help and singing to God. What I didn't know was that the Lord was with me. I started singing songs in a different language, my singing was the baptism ***in*** the Holy Spirit without my knowledge of realizing it until 23 years later. In the woods, I started praying for my parents to stop drinking alcohol. Months went by. I went out in the woods every day to talk to God. I would tell Him about my day, what was happening in my life. There came a time that I could step off the school bus and when my foot touched the ground, I knew instantly that my mother was drunk and there were severe problems at home. I still prayed, but God wasn't moving fast enough for me. I was getting desperate.

I wrote more letters to the judge, but never received any reply. I wrote to Social Services asking to be put into foster care but never heard a thing from anyone. My older sister asked me why I would try to split up the family and go into foster care. I told her, "You aren't home. You don't know what I'm going through, what it's like at home. You left. You can always leave. I can't. I need help. I need peace and want something normal. I don't care anymore. If we split up, I can have a normal family life. I would like to sit down at a kitchen table and have a nice meal. How about clean clothes and a bed to sleep in instead of that broken-down couch? Why should it matter to you? If you cared, we would all live with you! That's the truth!" And that was the truth. I was done trying to do this alone and keeping a huge secret. How did she know that I wrote those letters? Who told her? I didn't ask.

She said that she had something very important to tell me about dad and why she had to leave. My mom was in bed and my dad happened to drive up early that day as we were in the garage talking. She had her dog there, an Alaskan Husky Shepherd. His name was Shiloh. He was a beautiful dog with a happy nature and was fun-loving. My dad didn't like the dog and was angry to see it there. He grabbed Shiloh and had him on the floor of the garage trying to strangle the dog with both hands. Shiloh was struggling to get away. We were screaming at him to let Shiloh go. Finally, we were able to get Shiloh away from him by pushing him over, and he lost his grip of him. He told her to get the dog out of there and if he ever saw it here again, he was going to kill him. She left with Shiloh in the car and drove down the dirt driveway as I stood there. He went in the house. I stayed outside for as long as I could. I was surprised that he was home early. Even through all of the screaming, my mom never came out of the bedroom.

I was fifteen, now a freshmen. I had a few friends at school. I was afraid to really get close to anyone. There was one boy, Dennis, who really liked me. His brother was a year older. We did a few things together. I watched him play baseball for our high school, but I really wouldn't give it a chance. Then one day when my mother was passed out in her bed and I was in my room lying on my old couch, which was my bed, listening to music while I worked on my homework, I heard a knock at the front door. *Oh no, who could that be?* I opened the door and it was Dennis's parents and his brother. They had a realtor with them, and they wanted to look at the home my parents were renting. Apparently, it was for sale. *You've got to be kidding me!* That was my first thought. With the door open wide to let them in, I walked out as they came into the house, and I hid myself in the woods until they left. The very next day, filled with shame and guilt, not wanting him to know anything more about me or having to explain anything about my mother and the conditions of this messed up family, I told Dennis I couldn't be his girlfriend. I was so embarrassed that my heart hurt, and I worried myself sick that his brother would say something to cause me further pain. He was sad and hurt. I didn't want to hurt anyone. I just couldn't tell him the truth or even look at him. I just wanted to throw up.

Shortly after that, my father came home again. I had another physical altercation this time along with the belt whipping. He hit me in the face. The force split my nose open, and I had a terrible bloody nose. This time he had me clean their bathroom shower. It was moldy. I worked hours on it. I was tired and walking down the hall when I tripped and fell down. He told me to go to bed. I prayed for help that night. I was wondering if he knew that I wrote the letters. Why would the authorities tell him that I wrote the letters, when I wrote of the abuse I was receiving? I was worried.

The next morning, I was extremely sore, and the belt marks were red and purple and oozing, throbbing, and swollen. They were worse than I have ever had. It was hard to sit down and to walk. Everything in my body felt tight. I made it to my classes, but when it came to PE, I refused to dress down into my gym clothes, which was a jumpsuit that snapped at the top of your shoulders. I told my teacher I wasn't feeling well. She said, "Dress down or you will be getting an F." Most of the girls were already outside with a few of them around as they were dressing down too. I took my clothes off, and for the first time they saw the belt marks across the back of my legs, bottom, and lower back. They were horrified and stared. Miss Rocha cleared out the locker room immediately. Everything started to change that day and it wasn't all good or even in my favor.

A week earlier, my English teacher, Mr. Fairchild, asked the class to write a story about the worst day of their life, so I decided I would, and I did. I wrote every single dirty detail with plenty of adverbs, adjectives, pronouns, and verbs. I had no problem this time writing it all down. It actually felt good, like a good medicine to my soul but also scary wondering what would happen if it got into the wrong hands.

Later that same week, after soaking every day in Epsom salt, I was feeling very good and all the wounds were healed and the bruises were a slightly yellow color. I went to my English class. Mr. Fairchild was a tall man, about six foot three. He was married and was in his mid to late twenties. He was stern about subjects in his class and he didn't like anyone messing around, he was a serious man. Mr. Fairchild made an announcement that there were three students that received an A. He announced their names, and I heard my name. I opened up my folder and saw that he had written a message on the back inside cover. I read it and looked up at him as he watched me read it, and he nodded his head to me. He wrote what seemed like a short story to say he was moved to tears and was beyond words and that he was deeply saddened by what was happening to me and that he had shared my story with his wife. He said that if I ever wanted to talk or needed help after school, he would be there for me. I talked to him once. I just had a hard time trying to say anything. I just couldn't speak the words, I couldn't find them. I continued to pray for my mom and dad. I also would pray for myself, asking God for help, that I didn't want to be like my parents.

My teachers were concerned for me and understood why I couldn't or wouldn't participate and I wouldn't give my opinion on anything. They never pushed me into anything heavy. That was the good part. However, they were very alert to my circumstances. Life at home turned even more horrific for me probably because of the letters that I had sent. There were extreme moments that I thought that someone was going to be killed… that I was going to kill my father for beating me or my dad was going to kill my mother or me.

Near the end of my freshmen year, I was 15. I met a boy leaning against the hallway at school. He was a junior. His name was Sherwood. He was tall, slightly husky, with dark brown hair, and was nice looking. He said, "The next time you see me, say hi." I didn't see him the rest of the school year.

That summer, several weeks after school was out, my older sister and I were in her car, driving through town. We ran into Sherwood, and he asked me several times that afternoon to ride around with him. Finally, I decided I would. We became very good friends and fell in love that summer. He knew my situation at home, and I'm sure his parents knew too. They would ask me questions, but I gave little information. They were nice, loving parents and they were very good to me. Their life was perfect. I was from the wrong side of town.

One hot summer day, I left and ran away. This particular day, my mom had been sober for several months, and things were looking good after she spent some time in jail. She was back working at the hospital. Some days when it was hot, Mom would sleep on the couch in the living room. We had a swamp cooler, and the living room was the coolest place in the house. My dad came home late, angry and intoxicated and was after me. I was able to get loose from his grip. I ran out the front door, and he ran out the garage door. He tried to get ahold of me again, but I was able to break free. I was screaming at him and ran off into the night. I tried to call my boyfriend at a phone booth, but he wasn't home that weekend. A friend from school, Craig, saw me at the phone booth and asked me if I was okay. I told him I needed a place to stay for the night. He said that I could stay at his house with his brother, and I did. *Oh my God! What am I to do?* I got up early to call my mom. She was working at the hospital that night. I told her I was okay. I headed home that morning and my father was waiting for me. He never said a word to me, like nothing ever happened.

A few days later, while my mother was asleep again on the couch, my intoxicated father came home at the midnight hour. He spotted a coffee pot that was plugged in and poured boiling hot coffee over my mom's head while she was asleep on the couch, then causally went to the sink filled the coffee pot with cold water and poured it over her head. I ran into the living room. It was a horrifying sight to witness as she screamed bloody murder from the top of her lungs as her face was forming huge blisters and the skin was falling off in certain areas. She looked like a monster in seconds. I tried to get her shirt off of her but it was so scalding hot as the steam was rising off of it. Her eyes were swelling shut in minutes. Her scalp had blisters, her lips and ears looked like they were melting off. The blisters on her scalp were huge, and she couldn't wash her hair for weeks. The blisters were very sore and tender. It took a long time to heal. Even her neck was blistered and the skin pulled tight. During this horrific attack, he had fallen to the floor. I thought maybe he had had a heart attack and died as I stepped over him. I placed cold washcloths on her face as we both cried.

"Please leave him before he kills one of us!" I begged of her.

"Where would we go?" she said.

"Does it matter, Mom? Anywhere but here."

She wouldn't leave. I didn't bother to check to see if my dad was dead. I figured if he was lying there in the morning, I would check to see if he was breathing. He was gone in the early morning hour.

The new school year had started. Mom was still on the mend with patches of new pink skin along with the older skin. She wasn't working, of course, but keeping sober. My boyfriend gave me an engagement ring for my 16th birthday. My parents never said a word to me about it, when I told them. We were thinking about getting married right after I got out of high school. It sounded like a very good plan. I was excited and happy. Getting pregnant was a distant thought. I was never on time with my cycle and would sometimes skip months, probably because of the stress I was under at home. What I didn't realize at the time was that I was already pregnant.

Several weeks after Christmas, Mom became very depressed. The healing wasn't coming as fast as she had hoped. She started drinking again. I walked in on her as she tried to kill herself with a butcher knife. The struggle with the knife was something I had trouble getting over as she was trying to thrust it into her chest and I was pulling it away. It had penetrated enough to see a lot of blood. Her strength was amazing. I screamed at my younger sister to go to the neighbor's house and call the police. We were still struggling with the butcher knife until they arrived and disarmed her. At that moment, they admitted her to a mental hospital for a 72-hour evaluation. The doctors at that time had the family come together for a "round-table" counseling session. It was there that my father announced that he would not give up drinking alcohol. He said that it was his hobby. It was my turn and the doctors wanted me to talk about it. So I did. *A hobby?* I just cried. I was still praying for both of them. I was about to lose hope. My mother's AA sponsor said to me that they need to get down to the bottom of the barrel. *What? This family has been in a barrel for years. I want to get out of the barrel.* The doctors said, they have a disease—alcoholism is a disease.

"That's bologna!" I cried. "Cancer is a disease. Alcoholism is an addiction!" I cried. "Just like food can be an addiction. It is a selfish addiction! They only care about themselves and to Hell with everything else and everyone else. We can starve and have no clean clothes. But you have your booze and your cigarettes. I know because I have lived with these people all my life! Have you?" They call alcohol spirits. Why would anyone want to drink spirits. They aren't good spirits. It wasn't a good round-table counseling session for me.

During that time, I immediately knew that I had to get out of there. I couldn't stand it any longer. Dad's drinking was still about the same. One night my parents got into another fight and my dad collapsed on the floor again. I ran in the front room and saw him lying there as my mom was wondering if he was dead this time. I kneeled down to hear him breathing. "How long are you going to put up with this?" I was losing respect for my mother for not leaving.

After finally realizing that I was pregnant, I waited before saying anything. Together, Sherwood and I went to find my father to give him the news. He was in the downtown bar.

I remember that he walked around the both of us standing there and said, "You don't have to get married."

I told him, "I want to. We love each other."

I had to go through the court system. I thought that was bizarre to have to go through the system to get married but not when I had been beaten by my intoxicated father and had begged for help. I begged for help, and they turned blind eyes away. They turned their backs and had hoped it would go away.

We got married February 17, 1972. My mother stopped drinking one month after I got married, when I was 16. In March, she was delivered from alcohol while hanging clothes on a clothesline outside their rented home. It was a miracle. As you know, I was praying for a miracle. My mother was addicted to alcohol so in my prayers, I prayed that the love of it and the taste of it would be nasty, that the look of the bottles of whiskey looked nasty and smelled nasty to her. She told me that while she was alone hanging out the clothes, with tears rolling down her face and looking up to heaven crying, she cried out to God that her life was a mess and she wanted help, a miracle for herself … and HE gave it to her. Her desire for it was gone immediately.

Several months later, she quit smoking. I was so grateful for God answering my prayers, even though it took a couple of years. That September, on Labor Day weekend, I gave birth to a seven-pound seven-once baby boy. I didn't know how to have a baby. I actually thought you just pushed the baby out. I had no idea that you pushed like you were having a bowel movement. That was embarrassing. The doctor was very patient with me and told me all about it. My son, Casey, is a beautiful, handsome, warm-hearted caring person. He was a perfect baby—very loving, very kind, and he was mine. I am blessed!

The following year, in the same month, my sister got married on the 2nd of February. She had a heated conversation with my father, and I caught the tail end of it when she said that when it came to sex that he taught her everything she knew. He tried to grab her as she ran to her car and drove away. I just passed it off and didn't ask her about it.

Several years later, my father stopped drinking after getting in a wreck and spending three nights in jail. He read the Bible while locked up and was "delivered" from alcohol. I was around 19 at that time. My dad's life changed. He received a new job and became vice president of a company in Sacramento. They moved to Sacramento and bought a beautiful two-story home and a couple of nice cars. He loved gardening and they had a beautiful yard. He was a changed man. He actually had a fair amount of patience with my two younger siblings. He was going regularly to AA meetings with my mother. We were finally doing family things, weekend family barbecues and a few out-of-town trips to my house.

My husband and I moved to Napa, California. In December of 1975, I was 19, about to turn 20. I was blessed with another healthy baby boy, Christopher. He was born in Placerville too. I stayed the last couple of months of my pregnancy with my in-laws. My son, Christopher, is beautiful, handsome, warm-hearted, and very active. I am blessed to have wonderful good-hearted sons.

This was the total opposite of what I grew up knowing. I wanted them to have a different kind of life. I know in my heart that I didn't do everything correctly, but I truly wanted to learn how to. After my parents were sober, I never worried about it again. Our children never knew what I went through. I didn't think it was necessary to spoil what they had with their grandparents.

I started going to church by myself. Sherwood wouldn't go. The boys went to Vacation Bible School in the summer months, swimming lessons, and Casey started soccer. I was working at a department store in downtown Napa.

On July 4, 1979, I was baptized in water, completely submerged, at Calvary Chapel in Napa Valley. It was a very powerful moment for me. I was washed clean; the old Kristina was lying in that body of water. I was a new person in Christ Jesus. I felt that the Lord gave me the strength and the power to overcome. I started reading the book of Ephesians, the first two chapters. It helped me to realize who I am in Christ.

In July of 1980, my father had cancer and was dying. A few years earlier he had lung cancer. He had surgery, and they removed part of his lung. This time he kept the cancer from us until it was too late. I thought it was a terrible thing to keep from us. Once I knew, it was just a few weeks and he would be gone. I went to see him in the hospital. It was just the two of us. He told me that he was afraid to die, that he had been a horrible father to me for years. I told him that it didn't matter to me anymore, that I had forgiven him years ago when I could really see and feel the change and knew that God blessed me with a father that I could love again so deeply. I shared that God had answered my prayers and even though the time was short, at least I was able to spend some quality time with him.

I didn't know much about the man. There were so many secrets that are unanswered. I know God worked in my heart. He went into a short coma and when he came out of it, he told me that he wasn't afraid anymore, that he saw the light and everything was going to be alright. And I believed him. My grandmother was with my dad when he passed away. He asked for a nice meal. When it arrived, grandma decided she was going to be feeding him, since he was having a difficult time. Dad asked her to hurry, so she was feeding him as fast as she could without making a mess of things. He finished his meal, said it was good, relaxed in his bed, and died. He was gone.

Several years later, I became very unhappy in my 11 year marriage. Sherwood would not go to church with me; he was adamant about it. He became a workaholic. It's not a good reason to end a marriage by any means. I needed something more. Looking back, it was probably from lack of attention due to my childhood and having rejection issues. We were growing apart, and we divorced. At that time, it never occurred to me that my sons would be affected by a divorce. Sherwood never seemed to be home anyway. I was wrong; it did affect them. It took me years down the road to realize that. I'm very sorry in my heart and soul that I had hurt them so much.

I'm truly sorry and have asked for forgiveness and from the Lord as well. Sherwood and I are friends, and we have spent some holidays together and share about our travels, our friends, and children. I'm thankful for that. I pray for my family daily.

I met my husband, Jim, shortly after and we were married in 1983. He was a Christian but not an active Christian. After a couple of years of marriage, I asked him if he wanted to be baptized in our beautiful, clean, Doughboy pool. The water was nice and cool. He agreed, and I had him recite what was told to me during my baptism years ago. I bought him a plaque with the date and gave it to him as a present. The next morning, to our surprise, our pool water was completely black. Not a little dark, we are talking horribly black. I was concerned that maybe something went wrong with the baptism and inquired with a few Christian people, and they had never heard of anything like that before. Jim worked on the pump, we poured pool chemicals in, and nothing seemed to help. We finally had to drain the pool completely. Through the years, we always have a good laugh telling that story. I believe the Lord has a sense of humor.

My son, Christopher, was starting to have heart problems. We were living in Auburn California at the time. His heart would race when he was a small child, but I had always heard from his doctor that it was puberty. The first sign that it was something more serious was when he collapsed on the football field at Placer High. He had surgery to correct a hole in his heart, a birth defect the doctor had said. Shortly after, when he was doing well, Jim decided that we needed to move out of state. His dream was to move to Evanston, Wyoming where he could hunt and fish when he retired in a year.

My brother was in and out of prison. He served time in Vacaville, Tracy State Prison, and finally, Growlersburg Department of Corrections and Rehabilitation. He got into trouble with all kinds of bad company and spent years behind bars. I went to see him a couple of times in Vacaville State Prison. At one point when he was out of prison, he met a woman from Indonesia. Her name was Marilyn. They were married in 1975. They lost a beautiful newborn baby boy on New Year's day and were divorced in 1979. He found the Lord in prison. He was well educated in the Bible, and we would share letters of encouragement to each other. When he got out of prison a second time, he lived in Hilo, Hawaii.

In 1985, Jim's son, Jeff, flew to Hawaii and stayed with my brother for several months. Jeff loved it there, gave his life to the Lord, and they were both active in the church, New Hope Fellowship.

My brother worked in a gym as a trainer and was involved in body building. He won the title of Mr. Hilo at one of the yearly events several times. He had a girlfriend and he fathered a daughter, Tonya. She was a pretty little thing and loved her daddy. He lived there for several years and we flew out to visit him several times throughout the years. He ended his relationship, broke up with his girlfriend, and flew out to California and got a job as a car salesman in Roseville, California.

It didn't last long when he got back into drugs and alcohol. My brother started stealing from everyone he knew which included mostly family and selling it for his habit. Jim wanted me to stay away from him, saying that he was a loose cannon. My mother and I lost track of him for several months and started looking for him every few days in downtown Sacramento. One winter morning, she called me and said that she thought that she might have found him and if I would go with her to check it out. We went together and sure enough, we found him living in a large refrigerator cardboard box hidden in a small, vacant lot. I didn't recognize him at first. He was filthy. His face was twice the normal size, and his lips were cracked with dried blood. His feet were in terrible condition, and he couldn't walk. I don't recall him responding to us. We managed to get him in the car and take him to the hospital. His feet had gangrene, but they were able to treat them. He was hospitalized for a while. He told me that he didn't care about his life anymore and just wanted to die, that the family didn't want him around and no one loved him or cared about him. I told him I did and that I wanted him to live. He asked me why I wanted him to live. "Because I love you," I told him. "And I will prove it to you."

I called my husband, Jim, told him of the situation. He was at work. Jim had a friend who managed to get my brother in a halfway house in Sacramento. He placed him with a man who worked with drug addicts and would be with him twenty four hours, seven days a week. He would keep him for three months. In the late 80s, he was released from the halfway house and asked us if we would fly him back to Hilo, Hawaii. He felt stronger and wanted a different life, and we thought it was the best thing for him to get away from family and bad influences. We arranged for him to catch a flight out of San Francisco airport to Hawaii. Jim was going to work that Monday morning, leaving Auburn to drive to Napa and from there, he had my brother take the Evans airport bus from Napa to San Francisco. He thanked Jim, gave him a big hug, and said that he didn't think he would see him again. Jim said, "Sure you will. Take care of yourself." We sold that place in Auburn, California and moved to Wyoming.

We were now living in Evanston, Wyoming. We were going to a small church outside of town. Christopher's heart problems increased. We found a young heart doctor at the Heart Care Institute in Salt Lake City. He diagnosed Christopher with tachycardia. He had three areas in his heart that needed to be corrected. He had several surgeries in 1991 and 1992. Our pastor was with us every step of the way and traveled to Salt Lake for every surgery and would surprise us, but this time he wasn't there. Christopher had a heart attack on the operating table from the stress of the length of time the doctors were working on him. That surgery was about 10 hours. The surgeon, who was a young India man, came into the waiting room. He said that Christopher's arteries were collapsing and that he had had a heart attack. They placed tubes up into his groin to keep the arteries open and they were going to leave them in place for 24 hours. With the news, Jim started to cry and the doctor too. The doctor had grown very fond of Christopher. At that moment, the Lord spoke to me and told me that everything was going to be all right—to trust Him. I told the doctor that Christopher was going to be okay, and he just sat there shaking his head. I told him again that the Lord told me Christopher was going to be fine. That surgery outcome was not successful as the doctor was not able to correct his tachycardia (cardiac ablation).

My brother called me and said he bought himself a plane ticket to come out to see us in December for my birthday and Christmas but that he could only stay six days. He was excited to come to Wyoming, and we laughed about him coming to snow country and he would probably freeze to death since he didn't own any warm clothing at all. I was so proud of him and couldn't wait to see him in December. But it never happened. I received a phone call right after Thanksgiving. My brother passed away November 30, 1992. He was 42. His death certificate said, "He died from cardiac arrhythmia in minutes from a cocaine overdose. Drug abuse and alcohol, the strongholds and the bondage, he could not overcome. Curses in the bloodline. I know that my brother loved the Lord.

"The Lord is merciful and gracious, slow to anger and plenteous in mercy and loving-kindness." (King James Version, Psalm 103:8) [James 5:11].

After all the surgeries, we needed to sell our home to pay a large amount of the bills. Sherwood's insurance paid a large share, but at that time, Jim felt responsible for taking Christopher out of state, and the burden was his. We sold our home in Wyoming that we owned completely and moved to Stevensville, Montana. We bought a small log home on five acres. It was very run down. Christopher thought he was going to die and wanted to live in Montana, so we decided to move. He still wasn't feeling well and he didn't want any more surgeries. He was tired and was sick of it. We had a lot of work to do on our little place. We were there for a few months when we received a phone call from Christopher's heart doctor in Salt Lake City. He said that a doctor from France, Dr. Gardener, was going to be in Oklahoma City, Oklahoma. He wanted to see Christopher. I told him that we had no money to pay for plane trips, and I wasn't sure that Christopher wanted to do anything and that I would have to call him back. The doctor told me that he wasn't charging us anything; he was going because he wanted Christopher to be healed. He wanted to learn from this doctor from France why he couldn't correct the tachycardia. I was thankful for the call and prayed that Christopher would agree to it. He had been through so much and was looking thin with discoloring under his eyes. We talked about it, and he decided he wanted to go. I called the doctor back and he set everything up and sent us the paperwork.

Jim borrowed money from his boss for our plane tickets to Oklahoma City. We arrived at the airport and called for a taxi. I couldn't find Christopher's paperwork and realized I had actually left all the paperwork on the kitchen table. I prayed that the Lord would help us. I had no idea where to go, only that his check in was at twelve noon. Our cab driver was patient and took us to several hospitals. At 2 p.m., we found it. We checked him into the hospital. Jim and I stayed at the McDonald House next door. His surgery lasted four hours. The two doctors came out and said that it was successful, that Christopher was as good as new and that he wouldn't need any more medication or blood thinners. He was only advised to take penicillin a few days before and after any dental work. That was it. He was healed. Just like God had told me months before in the waiting room at the Holy Cross Hospital in Salt Lake City. Praise the Lord! The just shall live by faith!

My mother stayed sober for 32 years. She died of liver cancer in June 2002. My oldest sister has deep anxiety and severe depression, but is doing well on medication. She is now seeing a psychiatrist. She has carried a terrible secret throughout her life. She loves our father but has bouts of extreme anger. I believe that if she had that moment, that opportunity, like I did with our father, at his bedside when he was dying, her life would have been different. It is a struggle to forgive but you have to. Each day that you are miserable, the devil wins, they win. I was not going to let that happen to me. Take back what belongs to you, your life, your joy.

In writing this testimony she confided in me several different feelings that she felt about me. One was that she was extremely angry and even hated me for having that talk with our father when she wasn't able to. Second, she didn't understand how I was able to make my life full and happy, and she wasn't able to move forward. She knows that our lives are totally different from each other. She wanted our father to validate the things he did to her, but he didn't validate anything specific to me, only that he had been a terrible father. For me I never expected it. I had already forgiven him in my heart. It didn't matter anymore. For over 60 years, she has fought this battlefield in her mind. I'm deeply saddened to know all of the details, all of the raw emotions that are alive in her soul when her perpetrator has been dead since 1980. Forgiveness is a decision you make for yourself to move forward. It doesn't mean that the perpetrator is off the hook. I dedicate the chapter on Forgiveness to my sister.

I believe that alcohol and drug addiction can be passed down through the family bloodline. My mother's father was an alcoholic and my father's father was an alcoholic. My brother had problems with alcohol and drugs. I believe it is a generational curse and it can be broken. The Bible says in Exodus 34:7 that it will go through the third and fourth generations. I truly believe that I broke the curse of alcohol and drug abuse with me and my children. I am blessed with two wonderful sons, (the younger son is now an ordained minister). I have been told from the world's point of view, "professional alcoholic counselors", that my chances of becoming an alcoholic is 600% according to statistics as they have analyzed their scientific data. This might be true if you don't put your trust in the Lord. For myself, I asked the Lord when I was a small child for something different. I am something different. I am free. The fruit of the Spirit increases as we fellowship with Christ, in the Gospel and in the Spirit. Peter said, *"May grace (God's favor) and peace* ***(which is perfect well-being, all necessary good, all spiritual prosperity, and freedom from fears and agitating passions and moral conflicts)*** *be multiplied to you in [****the full, personal, precise, and correct****] knowledge of God and of Jesus our Lord," (Amplified Classic Edition, 2 Pet. 1:2)*

When I met my husband, Jim, he had two children. He became a Christian at a Camp tent meeting in Victor, Montana, about ten years after we were married. He had a God encounter. He was sold out and radically changed. We have been married for 36 years to this date. Jim is also a licensed ordained minister. All of our children know the Lord. My two sons have wonderful marriages. My older son, Casey, and his wife, Kim, have been married for 24 years (to this date) and we have been blessed with two beautiful grandchildren. My youngest son, Christopher, and his wife, Ann, have been married 16 years (to this date) and have blessed us with two beautiful grandchildren who serve the Lord.

Once I removed myself from the situation and dysfunction as a young teenager, I wanted a better life, one without fear. I wanted a sound mind. It was a difficult time but I knew that the Lord had something for me. I think about what the Scripture says in 1 Peter 4:3-6 *"For we have spent enough of our past lifetime in doing the will of the Gentiles—when we walked in lewdness, lusts, drunkenness, revelries, drinking parties, and abominable idolatries. In regard to these, they think it strange that you do not run with them in the same flood of dissipation,* (and they will) *speaking evil of you. They will give an account to Him who is ready to judge the living and the dead. For this reason the gospel was preached also to those who are dead, that they might be judged according to men in the flesh, but live according to God in the spirit," (New King James Version).*

I survived because I have a personal relationship with Jesus Christ. I wanted to do it God's way. He taught me everything I know about love and forgiveness, how to be a better person, how to stop "stinking thinking", how to raise a family, how to be a blessed wife, and how to keep my mouth shut and bridle my tongue (I'm still working on those two). Above all, He taught me how to keep my heart tender, to show love, receive love, and how to forgive others. Yes, I have messed up several times. However, I am not the type of person to lie down for very long. I ask the Lord to help me daily because there is a certain amount of baggage to overcome. My plan in my youth wasn't God's plan, but I can see now that God honored me. I strive to be an overcomer because my past does not define my future. The Lord has shown me that I can do all things through Christ who strengthens me. The heart of the gospel is change and transformation. *"The just shall live by faith," (NKJV, Hab. 2:4).* Christ is the answer to human needs, including cleansing from sin, relationship with God, and hope for the future. When all the circumstances of our lives present a negative picture—in failure and loss or when the natural reaction would be grief or complaint—this is the time to put "faith" in God and in His Word. Living in a manner that honors God and relies on His promises brings success. I know that God knew me before I was created in my mother's womb. I'm made in the image of God. I am created in the image of Christ, in every aspect. My identity is ultimately found in Him rather than any individual identity markers people may have labeled me from my past. So I'm proud of the woman I have become. He didn't make a mistake here. I'm being consistently conformed in the image of Christ, as a daughter of God. I submit all of myself, my personality, and image to His work. He uses all of what I am today for His glory.

Build your house—your life and vocation—on the rock of God's Word. Plan your life by the wisdom of God. Be a success in Him! For I am a believer. "I believe Him!"

I went to Bible school, became an ordained licensed minister. I was a community chaplain for Sacramento Law Enforcement, spent eight years in United in Christ Motorcycle Ministry, my husbands' ministry, working with outlaw gangs and nine years working with my husband in prison ministry. We were asked to be, for a short time, associate pastors for World Inner Cities ministries before we moved to Idaho. Currently, we are very active in our church and have home fellowship group Bible study weekly. I study the Word daily. He is always showing me something new. I always try to be available to meet and pray with people. I want them to succeed and want them to know that there is life after family.

Rev. Kristina Bean
United In Christ Ministries LLC
united.n.christ.outreach@gmail.com

UP DATE:

There was a period of time writing this book that I talked to my older sister about the mind block and lack of memory that I have. I was seeing moments of small pictures, like a puzzle piece. She told me to not open that door, that terrible things happened to me in that timeframe when she and my brother left home and I was there to take the brunt of it. I don't need to know and it would do me no good to know. I am an overcomer. I do have the victory to live a victorious life, through Jesus.

I also found out about ten years ago that my father had a sister. By the time I located her, she had passed away.

Just a few weeks ago, I went to **findagrave.com** trying to remember when my grandfather passed away, when my father's grave popped up. I clicked on it and, to my surprise, there was a newspaper article about him being an army officer and where he was stationed and where his brother was stationed too. He never once talked about having a brother. That tells me, that he must have had a terrible home life when he was child. That generational curse is now broken.

Parents married 1944

My older sister & me

Me at 4 years old

My Grandpa Huff and me

My brother at 7

My brother, Rebel, and me

Eddies Pizza Softball Team. The top row 4th person from the left is me. Debbie is bottom middle.

Me 14, brother 18, sister 21

Parents (active alcoholics) with my brother

Club E. Clampus Vitus

My mother stopped drinking

Me at 21.

My brother's daughter, Celeste

My brother's baptism
Hilo, Hawaii – February 24, 1985

Feb 24th 1985
Kris. my New
Birth in Christ
Jesus our Lord.
In Him you will
find light because
in him there is
No darkness at all.
I love you Sis
your Brother &
friend forever
Stanley

Hilo, Hawaii – January 1986
Brother, friend, Celeste, and Jim

Me, Jim, and Brother
January 1986

At my parents' house. I am 16 years old. My son, Casey, is 3 months old.

At my in-laws' house. I'm 16. Casey is 3 months old.

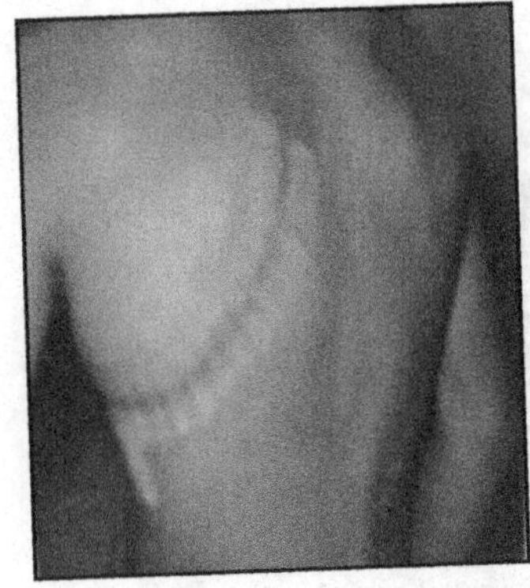

Christopher's heart surgery.
1991

Parents' 30th wedding anniversary
1974

Jim (vest), evangelist Larry Rovack
Camp Tent Meeting – Victor, Montana
August 1994

Evangelist Larry Rovack (Left)
Me (middle)
August 1994

School of Ministry Graduation – June 1999
Jim – top row, second from the right.
I'm right below him in second row.

Jim and I sponsored at our home in Georgetown, California "Kooks For Christ" which was a one-week camp out on our property. Awards (left photo)—every child received an award. Debbie is 3rd top right. Tug a war through the mud pit—the girls won.

United in Christ Motorcycle Ministry
1999

My older sister and her husband

Casey and Kim's wedding
1995

Christopher and Annie's wedding
June 2003

Annie and Christopher

It's difficult to get our whole family together. From left – Conner, Casey, Cameron, Jim, Lexie, Kim, Me, Faith, Annie and Christopher

Sons, Chris and Casey
2017

Christopher, Annie, Jim, Faith, Casey, Kim, Jeff, Cameron, Conner, Me and sitting Rylan.
April 2019

ABOUT THE AUTHOR

Kristina Eby Bean came to the Lord in the 1970s but did not have a solid foundation on which to build. Her husband, Jim, came to the Lord in the 1990s in Victor, Montana at a revival camp tent meeting. Once her husband was "born again", the couple was introduced to a New Believers Study group one week later. That study led them to a very strong, solid foundation, and they went on to bigger and better things for God. They sold out in Montana, traveled to California, and went to Bible college. They are both licensed and ordained ministers out of Abundant Life Fellowship in Roseville, California. They worked the streets and Kristina was a community chaplain for Sacramento Law Enforcement. She also helped her husband with eight years of motorcycle ministry and nine years of prison ministry. They now live in Nampa, Idaho.

REFERENCES

AMPC Amplified Classic Edition Bible. my.bible.com

Armor of God. Pages 256-259. bibleinfo.com (2019).

Bevere, J. (2013). *The Four Type of Tongues & Clarification about Private Tongues.* The Holy Spirit: An Introduction. Palmer Lake, CO. Messenger International

Board, R. A. (1995). *First Things First.* Franklin Springs, GA. LifeSprings Resources (formerly Advocate Press). (Personal permission given from Author Russell Board)

Dake, F. D. (2013). *The Dake Annotated Reference Bible*. NKJV Regular Edition. Lawrenceville, GA. Dake Publishing, Inc.

DeGraw, K. (2017). *Holy Spirit Conviction or Demonic Condemnation.* degrawministries.org
Life in the Spirit Spiritual Warfare Volume lV page 11-12 .www.charismamag.com. permissions@charismamag.com. Lake Mary, FL. Charisma

Eckhardt, J. *Deliverance and Spiritual Warfare Manual.* Lake Mary, FL. Charisma House

Hayford, J. (M.D.) with Hill, K., Harper, L. https://www.renewingworshipnc.org/worship-quotes/

Hayford's Bible Handbook (1995). Nashville, Tennessee. Thomas Nelson Publishers.

Jesus' Family Tree: Seeing God's Faithfulness in the Genealogy of Christ (2014). Torrance, CA. Bristol Works, Inc.

Morris, R. (2016) *Baptism of the Holy Spirit.* gatewaypeople.com Life in the Spirit
Holy Spirit Baptism. Volume lll. page 7-9. www.charismamag.com permissions@charismamag.com. Lake Mary, FL. Charisma

Rose Book of Charts, Maps, and Time Lines (2005). Torrance, CA. Rose Publishing, Inc.

Spirit Filled Life Bible NKJV (1991). Nashville, TN. Thomas Nelson Publishers.

Vine's Expository Dictionary of Biblical Words (1985). Nashville, TN. Thomas Nelson Publishers

Why should I belong to a local church?
https://www.theporch.live/blogs/3-reasons-you-should-join-a-local-church

Wicca-Witchcraft. en.wikipedia.org

Made in United States
Orlando, FL
09 June 2024

47676007R10200